Report On the Attaran Forests

KNIGHT COLONEL SIR ARCHIBALD BOGLE

SELECTIONS

FROM

THE RECORDS

OF

THE GOVERNMENT OF INDIA,

(FOREIGN DEPARTMENT.)

Published by Authority.

No. XXXII.

REPORT

ON

The Attaran Forests,

FOR THE YEAR

1860,

WITH APPENDIX.

CALCUTTA:

PRINTED BY C. B. LEWIS, BAPTIST MISSION PRESS.

1861.

INDEX

TO

REPORT ON THE ATTARAN FORESTS AND THE TEAK PLANTATIONS IN THE TENASSERIM PROVINCES.

[iv]

On the Teak Plantations in the Tenasserim Provinces.

Future Prospects of the Attaran Forests.

STATEMENTS.

APPENDICES.

Page

REPORT

ON THE

ATTARAN FORESTS.

No. 9.

FROM

COLONEL SIR ARCHIBALD BOGLE, KNIGHT,
Commissioner of Tenasserim and Martaban Provinces.

To

CECIL BEADON, ESQUIRE,
Secretary to the Government of India, Foreign Department, Fort William.
Dated Moulmein the 30th November, 1855.

SIR,

In continuation of my letter, No. 6 of 31st ultimo, I have the honor to submit some observations regarding the course which it appears to me desirable to follow with respect to the Teak forests in the Tenasserim Provinces, all the more valuable of which lie on the banks of the rivers Zimmay and Weinyo which flow into the Attaran, and are therefore usually called the Attaran Forests; but before recording my own sentiments, it seems proper that I should give a brief notice of what has been said by others.

1

2. In 1827, Dr. Wallich was directed by Government to visit these Provinces, and to report on the Teak Forests. He did so, and he strongly urged that the whole of the forests should be retained by the Government, and "worked," as the expression is, under the supervision of the public authorities. I beg to quote in the margin* one para. from his report, dated 25th April 1827, which is conclusive, but I might quote many others equally so.

3. The plan recommended by him was partially adopted: for a short time the forests were retained in the hands of the Government; but, in 1829, at the recommendation of the Commissioner, Mr. Maingay, the system was altered, and private parties were allowed to work certain forest tracts on their own account, under the rules noted in the margin.†

4. This system went on for several years; but, about the year 1837, the authorities seem to have become apprehensive that the forests in these parts, which were soon found to be far from inexhaustible, would share the fate of most other forests, and in process of time become wholly exhausted. Mr. Blundell, who had become Commissioner, and whose ideas respecting forest management

---

* No forest exists which can with propriety be called inexhaustible—at least none that is liable to constant and extensive demands for timber. The quantity of teak used for public purposes, both Military and Naval, is so great, and it will go on increasing to so great an extent in proportion as new sources of supplies are opened, that the Martaban Forests, ample as they are, would be soon impoverished, unless they were placed under a vigilant and strict superintendence, their supplies regulated with economy, and their extent gradually augmented. I hope I take a correct view of the case, if I consider all the teak forests which grow in these Provinces as the exclusive property of the state, applicable only to public use, and not to be interfered with by any private individual whatever. Unless this principle be acted upon from the very outset, I will venture to predict that private enterprise will very soon render fruitless all endeavours to perpetuate the supplies for the public service, and one of the principal and most certain sources of revenue will thus be irrecoverably lost. The most important step towards establishing a proper system for the management of the forests, and without which all others can be of no avail, will be a public declaration to the above effect, strictly prohibiting all persons, not duly authorized, from cutting down any of the trees. But this done, the detail of the further management may be accomplished with comparatively trifling expense, and with little trouble.

† Rules of 1829.—1st. All persons applying to fell timber, are directed to point out where they intend employing themselves for that purpose, together with the number of men in their service.

2nd. No timber shall be removed from the banks of any river without the sanction of the Commissioner, his Deputy, or Assistant, having been previously obtained.

3rd. All timber shall be subjected to a duty of 15 per cent. to be levied in kind or in money, at the option of the Commissioner, his Deputy, or Assistant. The timber to be valued by two arbitrators, the one to be selected by the Commissioner, his Deputy, or Assistant, the other to be chosen by the owner of the timber, in the event of a difference of opinion between the arbitrators, the Commissioner, his Deputy, or Assistant shall be at liberty to appoint a third.

4th. It shall be at the option of the Commissioner, his Deputy, or Assistant, to select for the use of Government any portion of the

Teak timber felled in this Province, the value of such timber to be settled by two arbitrators, as above stated.

5th. No Teak trees shall be felled, the girth of which shall not exceed four feet and all such trees felled within that girth will be confiscated by the Commissioner, his Deputy, or Assistant.

seem to have been much in consonance with Dr. Wallich's, therefore proposed that a Conservator should be appointed, with a small establishment, whose duty it should be to decide upon cases of infringement of rules, and all suits relative to boundaries, and to draw up a report on the condition of the forests, "and above all on the eligibility of resuming the permits to cut, and reconstituting a monopoly," a measure which, even before the forests had been much over two years in the hands of private parties, seemed to many to be required.

5. In the correspondence which passed between the Commissioner and the Government, it was explained that the "permits to cut" under which the forests had, since 1829, been worked, were licenses to fell in certain localities, to the exclusion from those particular localities of all other cutters, care having been taken at the time of giving the license, to make it known to the parties, that the permits were revocable at pleasure, and it was stated that although the transfer of these permits had been allowed, yet they had never been recognized as conveying *ought but permission to cut timber in certain localities.*

6. I solicit particular attention to this fact, as having a most important bearing upon the present claims.

7. The chief objects contemplated by Mr. Blundell in the appointment of a Conservator and establishment, were to prevent the cutting of undersized timber or timber of bad quality, to preserve the young trees, and to ensure the planting of others.

8. In March 1838, Mr. Blundell again brought the matter to the notice of Government, stating that every season the forests were becoming more exhausted, without adequate measures being adopted to prevent waste and ensure their renewal in after years ; but it was not till the end of 1840 that the unrestrained working of the forests, which was then seen to be leading to their speedy extermination, induced the Government to take active steps for their conservancy, and to authorize the appointment of a Conservator.—But in the mean time Mr. Blundell had appointed Captain O'Brien to survey and report on the Attaran series of forests, that is on those situated on the Zimmay and Weinyo rivers, and that officer having stated that several of them had been entirely neglected by those who held

licenses to cut in them, that some forests had been completely worked out, without any authority whatever, and that others had been abandoned, apparently from the difficulty of transporting timber from them, Mr. Blundell, in submitting Captain O'Brien's report, requested instructions as to whether these forests should not be resumed, and upon this two questions were raised: first, what should constitute neglect, or in other words failure to work a forest grant? and secondly, what remuneration should be made to parties holding licenses, for trees killed or felled by them, but not removed from the resumed forest?

9. Mr. Blundell, who was certainly extremely well informed on the subject, was of opinion on the first question that if the grantees had not visited their forests or had not brought away any timber from them for two years, that should be held to constitute neglect. On the second question he considered that they were fairly entitled to the value which the trees bore *on the spot;* and where expense had been incurred by them in forming roads or clearing channels in the nullahs, some compensation ought to be made; *but that no compensation whatever should be given for the resumption of the mere right of cutting.*

10. I request attention to this, because the only question which the Government is now called on to decide is the resumption of the right of cutting.

11. No one will, I apprehend, have the hardihood to declare that he has expended any capital in making permanent roads or cutting channels; and if any one should make such assertion, it will not deserve credence; neither will any one be likely to prefer a claim to compensation for trees now killed or felled, but still remaining in the forests; for, from all accounts, the workers of forests have not left a stick remaining; therefore no question can now arise on these points. In my opinion, the only question that can arise is one of compensation for the revocation of the permission to cut timber, and on this point Mr. Blundell's opinion, formed as it was at a time when the nature of the tenure on which the forests were worked was perfectly known and understood, is deserving of much respect.

12. The discussion which had at that time arisen resulted, at Mr. Blundell's suggestion, in his being directed to prepare rules which should define the first point raised, leaving the second to be determined by the circumstances of each case; that they should

provide for the survey and definition of boundaries, impose restriction on the working of all new, or lapsed, or resumed grants, *and secure to Government the right of resumption on failure of the conditions of the grants,* " due notice being first given in the manner which should be most conformable to local circumstances and to the nature of the engagements."

13. In pursuance of the above Mr. Blundell submitted to Government the draft of a set of rules as per margin* upon which, under date the 2nd June, 1841, letter No. 491, the Government of Bengal remarked as follows.

" You will have a separate communication upon the rules which have been published by you for the preservation, the renewal, and the application of the forests immediately under your cognizance and control. You are aware that His Lordship is not favorable to any propositions which may tend to an extensive disturbance even of very unsettled occupations. The primary object of Government is, to mark and define the boundaries of existing forest grants, and to lay down conditions of management. If tho present occupiers will consent to

* Rules dated the 12th April, 1841.

1st. That the farmer keep up such an establishment for the preservation and working of the forests, as may be considered necessary by the Government superintending officer, in order that the trees be felled without injury to those surrounding them, by having proper ropes &c. for lowering them; and that the requisite assistance of men, elephants, trucks, carts, &c. be provided for removing them when felled.

2nd. That no trees shall be killed or felled of a less girth or circumference than six feet, measured round the bark ten feet from the ground.

3rd. That every tree shall bo killed by a broad rim of the bark, say one foot, being taken off round the trunk of the tree near the root, at a height not exceeding two feet from the ground and further by cutting to the spine or through the hard wood to prevent the least portion of sap from rising. This process is only to be done during the months of January, February and March, before the sap commences to rise, and at no other period of the year.

4th. That no tree shall be felled till the expiration of at least two years from the period it has been killed in the manner pointed out in rule 3rd.

5th. That every tree felled be removed from the forest with the least possible delay.

6th. That for every tree felled and removed, five young trees of a proper size shall be planted by the farmer, or by the Government at the expense of the farmer.

7th. That no tree shall be on any account cut up into short lengths (called loozars), but that every tree shall be removed as felled, and be brought in that state (after removing the branches), either down the river to the town, or to sawpits established in the forests.

abide by them, unless in very particular sites required for public objects, they should be confirmed in their holdings. These conditions may be made the subject of a separate correspondence, but measures should without loss of time be taken for the gradual renewal of these forests. Dr. Wallich, the Superintendent of the Hon'ble Company's Botanic Garden will be consulted as to the best means for attaining this object. In the meantime you will be pleased to report whether it will, in your opinion, be preferable to establish nurseries centrally at Moulmain, whence the proprietors of forests might be supplied, or in some spot fenced off from each forest, such nurseries being maintained at the expense of each proprietor. Captain O'Brien in his recent survey scarcely met with a single seedling, which is perhaps owing to the frequent burning of the jungle; it will be necessary therefore to ascertain at what age young trees may, with safety, be transplanted, and your local experience will perhaps enable you to aid His Lordship's judgment on this point."

14. The rules above referred to, together with all the reports and journals, were submitted to the Government of India on the 2nd June, 1841, and a copy of all the documents was forwarded to the Hon'ble the Court of Directors, and on the 8th September, 1841, the rules of 12th April, 1841, were approved of by Government; but Mr. Blundell was again informed of the wish of Government not to disturb the occupancy of the grantees, unless on very strong grounds, and he was desired to report on the practical operation of the rules before he proceeded to enforce the penalty clause, especially with reference to the prohibition against cutting up timber, a matter which was however got over in another way, and the 7th rule eventually cancelled by Government letter, No. 907 of 9th November, 1842.

The letter of the Government sanctioning the rules is quoted in the margin.*

* 2nd Para. His Lordship is averse to disturb the occupancy of the existing petty grantees, and I am desired to request that a report be made as to the practical operation of the present rules before any enforcement of the penalty clause takes place, especially with reference to rule 7, which so far as it is designed to protect the Government duty, may occasionally admit of relaxation, if that duty be previously secured by other arrangements.

15. In 1842 Captain, now Colonel, Tremenheere, who had in 1841 been appointed Conservator of Forests submitted some suggestions for establishing a few centrically situated nurseries, instead of having a nursery at each forest; as it appeared even at this early period that the occupants were either unable or unwilling to plant young trees, and they have certainly adhered to this course ever since.

16. In this year Captain Tremenheere also reported on some forests which he had visited, in all of which the rules framed by Mr. Blundell had been entirely disregarded, and were inoperative; he therefore proposed a series of new rules, which are quoted in the

* Rules dated 11th July, 1842. Leases will be granted to all persons who now possess the right of cutting in the Teak forests of the Tenasserim Provinces assigned to them either by written documents or by the felling and removing of timber carried on therein under the sanction or by permission of the Civil authorities or Superintendent of the Forests at Moulmain. The boundaries wherein the lease-holder is permitted to cut or carry away Teak or any other timber the locality produces, will be defined in each lease, but it will confer no proprietary right in the soil.

The period of lease will not be limited, but will continue so long as the lease-holder shall pay the required observance to the following rules, and shall keep up such establishments for the working of the forests, as may be considered necessary by the superintending officer.

The transfer of a lease from one party to another must be registered in the office of the Superintendent, and no transfer will be valid without such registry.

1st. Every lease-holder shall appoint a responsible agent, to be resident in the forest during the killing, cutting and rafting seasons.

On the first of December of each year, the lease-holders shall make known to the superintending officer the number of gangs they intend to hire for killing trees during the season, and the number and strength of parties of men and elephants they intend to employ in felling, dragging, and rafting in their respective forests, when Government peons in sufficient numbers to prevent any unnecessary delay or obstruction to the work will be deputed with proper instruments to place a mark on each tree to be killed, and on each log to be brought away.

The peons shall make a report to the superintending officer of the number of trees or logs marked, which report, in order to prevent collusion, shall be countersigned by the agent of the lease-holder in the forest.

2nd. The position of the mark will determine the killing and felling point which may be immediately below, but not above it.

3rd. Every tree marked shall be girdled by cutting through the sap wood and penetrating the heart wood, or duramen, to prevent the sap from rising.

"This is only to be done during the months of January, February, March and April."

4th. No tree is to be killed of a less girth than six feet, measured at four feet from the ground.

5th. No tree shall be felled until the lapse of one rainy season after being killed in the manner prescribed by Rule 3rd.

6th. No raft is to enter the Moulmain waters without a pass bearing the signature of the agent employed to inspect them.

7th. For every tree felled, or log brought away, three young trees shall be planted out on their timber sites. This will be effected by persons

margin,* intended to remedy the defects of those of 1841; and these revised rules were, with the concurrence of Mr. Blundell and the approval of the Government of India, duly sanctioned by letter of Bengal Government to Military Board No. 997, of 9th November, 1842, the only alteration made being that *five* young trees should be planted in the place of every tree felled instead of *three*, as proposed by Captain Tremenheere.

17. In this letter there occurs the following passage.

"The leases of the present holders cannot now be renewed for a limited period without a breach of faith, but should it eventually be determined to grant new leases for unoccupied forests, such new leases can be limited to twenty years, renewable on the expiration of that term, provided the lessee be not guilty of any infringement of the forest regulations," but I submit that this must have been penned in perfect forgetfulness, that the tenure on which the forests were held, were mere permits or licenses to cut timber in certain localities, which permits had never been recognized as conveying ought employed by Government, and the expenses are to be defrayed by the lease-holder.

The expense of marking the trees and logs, as directed by the first rule is to be borne by the lease-holder, at the rate of two annas for every tree or log marked, any surplus over the annual outlay on this account will be carried towards defraying the charges for planting provided for by Rule 7th.

Fines and Penalties.—If any lease-holder should neglect the 1st Rule, no timber shall be allowed to enter the Moulmain waters from his forest during the succeeding year.

"For every breach of the 2nd, 3rd, 4th, 5th and 6th Rules, a fine not exceeding 500 Rs. will be levied from the lease-holder."

"The fines are to be levied at the discretion of and by the decision of the superintending officer."

"Information by letter will be given by superintending officer to the Assistant Commissioner's Court, of the amount of fine due to Government by any lease-holder, which letter shall be considered sufficient proof of the validity of the claim and shall be sufficient warrant for levying the amount of fine by distraint on the property of the lease-holder."

but permission to cut, and that they conveyed no proprietary right whatever. It must also have been overlooked when it was proposed to give twenty years leases, renewable on good behaviour, that a Teak tree takes from 80 to 100 years to reach perfection.

18. In November, 1842, the Hon'ble the Court of Directors reviewed the measures of the Government and the local authorities for the management of the forests, from the earliest period down to Captain Tremenheere's appointment, and for convenient perusal, I beg to insert the following paras. from their despatch.

Para. 8th. "Perhaps the most important of the forests in the British possessions in India are those in the Tenasserim Provinces, which being more immediately within your own observation have lately attracted a good deal of your attention, and respecting which you have furnished us with some very interesting information. They appear to be of great extent (according to some accounts, indeed, the whole country is little else than a vast expanse of wood-land, large tracts of which are covered with Teak) and their value is increased by the abundant facilities for water-carriage which they, for the most part, possess. All these forests are the property of the state, and when the Provinces first came into the Company's possession were full of trees of the largest size. For a short time the forests were retained in the hands of Government which exercised a monopoly of the timber trade, but the Government monopoly proving a losing concern, it was determined to throw open the forests to the public, on payment of a duty of 15 per cent. on the timber felled, and, accordingly since the year 1829, it has been usual to grant, upon application, the exclusive right of felling timber, on payment of the above duty, in any locality not previously disposed of. This freedom of trade appears to have given a temporary stimulus to the prosperity of the Province, but to have done so at the expense of its future resources. Both the timber trade and the business of ship-building have flourished exceedingly, but the devastation of the forests has proceeded with equal rapidity; for as the tenure of the grantees is revocable at pleasure, the latter have no interest in the preservation of the forests, and never think of forming fresh plantations, or take any pains to prevent the young trees and saplings from being wantonly destroyed; many of them too, being men without capital, and wanting the means of transport for full grown timber, are in the habit of felling only small trees, or if they do select any of full size, cut them into pieces more easily removable, though by this means they reduced by about two-thirds both the value of the timber and the Government duty upon it. In consequence of the boundaries of the several grants not being accurately defined, mutual encroachments on each other's limits are committed by the grantees, and a wide field is opened to litigation. The local authorities have not failed to point out the necessity of putting a stop to this state of things, and have recommended that the grants made to private persons should be resumed, or at least that a Conservator should be appointed to superintend the management of the forests, and in conformity to the latter suggestion, you have directed Captain Tremenheere of the Engineers, the lately appointed Executive Officer of the Province, to undertake the conservancy of the forests in addition to his other duties. He has been instructed to execute a survey of the forests, examining particularly into their extent and condition; to mark out the limits of existing grants; to select suitable spots for fresh plantations; and to prepare a plan for the future management of the forests. It is also stated to be your intention, so soon as you shall have obtained the necessary information for tracing the boundaries of the several tracts, to allow them to be farmed, on condition that a proper establishment be maintained by the farmer for the preservation of the forests, that only such trees be felled as the superintending officer shall allow, and that young trees be planted in place of those that are cut down.

Para. 9. "We doubt whether these measures will prove efficacious. A survey indeed seems to be an indispensable preliminary to any new system, but it would scarcely be possible for the

Conservator, with the aid of any establishment which it can be proposed to allot him, to exercise so minute and searching a superintendence over such extensive forests as would enable him to prevent the felling of other trees than those selected by himself, or to see that the business of planting is properly attended to; and, even if such interference were practicable, it would still be undesirable to commit to any individual powers so liable to abuse.

Para. 10. " The best and cheapest way to ensure the preservation of the forests held by private persons is, to make it the interest of the latter to take care of them, and to remove every temptation to injure them. With this view, we would recommend that long leases should be granted on condition of payment of a certain percentage on all timber felled, and of an obligation not to clear the land for cultivation or to employ it for any other purpose besides plantation. By another condition the felling of timber below a certain size should be strictly prohibited, and a modification of the duty might be made, to check the wasteful practice of cutting up large timber. The farmer having then an interest in the improvement of his forests, would probably be inclined to plant of his own accord. Even if he neglected to do so, the self-sown plants, which he would no longer have any object in destroying, would in most other situations ensure, to some extent, the perpetuation of the forests. In the Tenasserim forests, however, it appears that owing to the frequent occurrence of fires, or to the overflowing of the streams, by which the newly-fallen seeds are swept away, or to some other unexplained cause, scarcely a single seedling of Teak is now to be found, even in the neighbourhood of large trees which annually shed abundance of seed. It may, on this account, be advisable to make it obligatory on the farmer to supply the places of the trees felled by him by forming new nurseries and protecting them from injury until they attain maturity, and Government might reserve to itself the right of forming nurseries at the farmer's expense in the event of his failing to comply with this condition. The Government Conservator might be allowed to exercise such limited control over private forests as would enable him to see that this condition of the lease was observed, but his attention should be directed chiefly to the forests retained for the supply of the wants of the public service; for it is evidently desirable that here, as in Malabar, Government should reserve to itself a resource independent of the public market ; and we take it for granted that before any further grants are made, some forests, conveniently situated and sufficiently extensive, will be selected and placed under proper management, so as to afford a constant supply of timber, both of Teak and of other useful kinds indigenous to the country, for the wants of the Government of Bengal as well as of the Royal Navy, in case Her Majesty's Government should hereafter wish to have recourse to it."

19. In September, 1844, another despatch was received from the Court, dated 26th June, in which they noticed Captain Tremenheere's revised rules, and generally approved of them, but objected to some parts as likely to prove " exceedingly vexatious, and such as could not be enforced without a number of petty officers invested with powers which ought not to be placed in such hands," and they repeated their suggestions for giving long leases on such conditions as would make it the interest of lease-holders to preserve the forests and maintain a succession of timber trees on their lands.

20. From this time till 1846, when Captain Guthrie, Bengal Engineers, was appointed Conservator of the Tenasserim Teak Forests, nothing of importance appears upon record, but in that year Captain Guthrie, having inspected many of the forest tracts, and deputed others to inspect those he could not visit himself, reported the result in a letter dated 20th June, 1845, from which the following is an extract.

"I may report on the general state of the forests that the General state of forests Zimme and Weinyo. inadequate Government establishment could not enforce the judicious rules made for their working and maintenance. They are worked to produce the greatest and easiest sure profit. Many of the forests on the Zimme and Weinyo (which join and form the Attaran) are worked out ; others are getting gradually cleared of full-sized trees. At the end of five years there will not be 2000 full-sized trees in the forests worked by private persons, and there are but few trees that by their growth will soon attain full size, in consequence of the prevalent practice of felling all trees that approach the full size. There is one very satisfactory point ascertained this season in these forests : viz. the fact of there being very many young trees. Both Captains O'Brien and Tremenheere reported that a young tree was not to be seen. Mr. Salmond saw several. All the most accessible trees have been worked off."

"On the Houndrow, the forest may be considered unworked. In three localities, on the Wein Loung, Authan and Methan, I found trees that have been abandoned, having been killed ten years ago. In the Minnunda there were some fine trees being worked this year, said to have been killed twelve years ago. The present supply of Teak procurable is too small to be of importance ; the size, however, of many of the trees, and the breadth of the annual ring, showing rapid growth, point to this locality as a favorable one for extending the forests by artificial means."

Houndrow.

"The Lhang-booa and Salween, from their approximation to Maulmein and the readiness with which the trees can be brought to market, and from the practice of dragging timbers with buffaloes, are more liable to waste and destruction than other forests. There are a great number of workers on these forests, and from reports received, it appears that fully one-third of the full-sized trees in these forests at present, are either killed or felled."

Lhang-booa.

Captain Guthrie having found that the rules previously enacted had proved inoperative, from the non-enforcement of the penal clause, and that the Attaran series of forests were almost completely worked out, proposed to resume all those in which the rules had not been strictly observed, and gave the following as his reasons.

"Mr. Blundell, in his letter to Government of 28th April, 1837, advocating resumption of the forests, fairly states the argument against the measure, viz., the apparent interference with private rights accompanying the original permits to cut timber, sanctioned by eight years' adherence to that system, and the expense which in justice must be incurred for their outlay towards facilitating their operations in the forests ; this argument is now strengthened by nine years' additional adherence. During all this period, persons receiving permission to cut were continually informed that the permissions were resumable at pleasure ; this notice was useless, as it could be enforced without any breach of faith. That outlay has been incurred towards the facilitating operations in the forests, is undoubted ; it has, however, been solely for the profit of the workers, and not in any way to merit the favorable consideration of Government. They have neither prevented the destruction of under-sized trees, nor the felling of green timber, they have not attended to the past rules ordered by Government, but have, from neglect, annually allowed hundreds of trees to be destroyed by fire, thus depriving the state of revenue and the public of valuable timber.

"The practical result of allowing private individuals to work forests has been shown in their present condition, and the reckless system of working them in the hands of private persons, who argue that the present rules cannot be carried out, being impracticable, that it is impossible to do justice to the forests, and they are therefore to be held excusable for past breaches of forest rules, and wish to carry them on under authority for the future. I advocate their general resumption, and the best mode of doing so for the interests of Government and consideration of the individual may be considered. The question is much simplified from none of the holders having done anything for the prospective benefit of the forests.

1st. "The nature of the tenures being at will, allows of their immediate resumption; there might be apparent hardship, though without reason, as I think has been shown.

Resumption of forests.

2nd. "They might almost all be resumed for breach of forest rules,—the penalty prescribed by the last clause,—but some localities, however, would escape. That the rules have been broken in all the worked forests is, I believe, undoubted; in some, however, proof cannot be brought forward, from their being unworked; in others, breaches that could be proved would be so numerically trifling, that there would be an apparent hardship in enforcing the penalty.

3rd. "The holders might be induced to give up their possessions by payment of money.

"Any system of resumption providing for a variety of cases, would, I think, be complicated and liable to objection, I would suggest a notice to the following effect : it might be either a simple Government order or an explanatory one, thus,—

1st. "The state requires that its forests should be worked to the best advantage.

2nd. "Experience has proved that in the forests entrusted to private individuals, many under-sized and green trees are felled and killed, and at prohibited seasons of the year, when the trees are full of sap; and further that a number of seasoned trees of the full size are annually left on the ground to be destroyed and injured by the periodical fires. This being an improvident, reckless, and wasteful system, and in opposition to the Government rules of 1841 enacted for their preservation and maintenance, the right of resuming the forests at will having been reserved by Government, and further, that resumption being the prescribed penalty for any breach of the forest rules, notice is now given that Government resumes these forests.

3rd. " The occupiers of Government forests have done nothing for the benefit of the forests they hold; yet where capital has been expended in killing, felling and dragging the timber, they shall be allowed a certain period for bringing it away, or a fair value given, under such arrangements as the local authorities shall consider suitable. Unlicensed timber, that is timber cut against rules, to be forfeited and brought down at the expense of the forest-holder."

21. But before receiving instructions on the points referred to in his report, Captain Guthrie resumed several forests, and his proceedings having been upheld by Captain Durand, the Commissioner, the Government of Bengal was appealed to, when the whole question was reviewed in Mr. Secretary Halliday's letter of 7th September, 1846, and the proceedings of the local officers reversed with severe comments.

22. This dispatch is one of much importance; but to quote largely from it would only be to repeat what I have already written, I would beg to refer the Government to it and must, at the same time, remark that whatever reasons for resumption existed in 1846 have gained vast additional strength since then, from the circumstance that the indiscriminate exhaustion of the forests subsequently went on with such rapidity that when Dr. Falconer visited them upwards of six years ago he found little or no Teak timber remaining.

23. In this dispatch, it was observed, para. 9, with reference to the correspondence of 1841, that " the Government desired to preserve and perpetuate the forests without interfering unnecessarily with the operations or speculations of *bonâ fide grantees*, and that the Commissioner had ,on that occasion been reminded that the right of resumption could not fairly be exercised by Government without due notice, and the laying down of fixed rules ;" but I would here remark that there was no such thing as a *bonâ fide grantee*, in what I conceive to be the proper sense of the words: the workers of forests were

merely persons holding permits to cut in certain localities, and according to Mr. Maingy's rules; the said permits being, as admitted by every one, revocable at will, and it seems from the dispatch of the Court of Directors, 30th November, 1840, that the Hon'ble Court at any rate considered they had a perfect right to resume on the rules then in force being infringed : they distinctly say " the tenure of the grantees is revocable at pleasure."

24. In the 12th para. and other places it is argued that the Commissioner's Penalty Clause in the rules of 1841 was never sanctioned by Government; but Captain Tremenheere's rules in which the right of resumption is asserted were sanctioned both by the Government in India and Court of Directors, as is shewn in the 19th para. of Mr. Halliday's letter, and yet in the 25th para. it is stated that no confirmation of the Penalty Clause can be traced. It is not easy to reconcile this with the fact that Captain Tremenheere's rules, sanctioned by the Hon'ble Court on 8th March, 1843, are based on the principle of the duration of leases being dependent on the observance of his rules, and that the permits to cut had always been held to be revocable at will. I beg leave here to quote the 32nd and 33rd paras. and must take the liberty of saying that I have nowhere found that any " *grants* of undefined and disputed tracts for no specified time, but dependent on the pleasure of the authorities for the time being," were ever made; neither can I find that the grantees were ever " obliged by their position to make the most they could in the shortest time out of a very precarious and uncertain tenure." They were *tempted* to make the most of their opportunity, no doubt; but, as far as I can learn, the views expressed above do not appear to be clearly established.

"On the other hand, the measures taken with the grantees have been such as to ensure waste and improvidence. They have been sent at one time with permits to fell timber in given localities, revocable at will; at another, they have received grants of undefined and disputed tracts, for no specified term, but dependent on the pleasure of the authorities for the time being. Even the desire of Government to grant leases for twenty years, as expressed in 1843, seems not to have been carried into effect, but on the contrary, Captain Guthrie as Superintendent, and yourself as Commissioner, have taken pains to impress upon the grantees that their rights may be resumed at any time and they have indeed been practically taught that resumption may occasionally be very suddenly and summarily put in execution against them."

33. " It would be strange indeed if, under such circumstances as these, the grantees were found carefully guarding the Government interests in the forests or establishing nurseries of young trees, or sparing to cut down whatever might soonest suit their purposes. The grantees have been obliged by their position to make the most they could in the shortest time out of a very precarious and uncertain tenure; and their conduct has only been what might have been expected from them."

25. The letter of the Bengal Government of the 7th September, 1846, was replied to by my predecessor, Mr. Colvin, on the 28th October, 1847. He, in some degree, vindicated the conduct of the present occupants of the Attaran Forests, and advocated the cession of the forests to them in perpetuity, on certain conditions calculated to insure the renewal of all felled trees. The following is an extract from his letter.

"In respect to the private occupancy of the Attaran Forests, the fact, I think, has been unduly overlooked in former reports on the forest question that, but for the efforts of the traders who undertook the working of those tracts, the Government would now, in all probability have been very imperfectly informed of the amount or accessibility of the profitable resources of the country in timber. I believe it to be true that a permanent property in extensive forests may often be better managed as a state domain, than when divided into a number of estates held by single persons. There is the peculiarity attaching to forest property, that its returns are extremely distant, and that they are therefore likely to be anticipated and impaired, in the natural desire of individuals for a return by which they may themselves benefit. This is a consideration, which is, of course, of greatly augmented force in reference to the circumstances and calculations of English capitalists in this country. Much outlay or care is scarcely to be expected from them for the renovation of forests, when that object is only to be effected within from 80 to 100 years hence ; but though this be so, and though it be also true that the application of capital has scarcely at all been made, in order to facilitate access to the forests or the use

"On sait que nulle part l' agriculture n'est mieux entendue, mieux conduite, ne surtout mieux protegée que dans les Forêts de l'Etat, l'etendue de ces domaines, qui comprennent un million d'hectares, a permis d'affecter a leur surveillance une administration nombreuse et parfaitement organisée, qui, dans ses rangs superieurs au moins, unit aux avantages de la pratique beaucoup plus de science forestrère que ne peuvent jamais en avoir des gardes particuliers, dont la position personelle n'est susceptible ni de progrès ni d'avenir. D'un autre côté l'Etat propriètaire imperissable, en raison de sa perpètuité même et de la stabilité de possession qui en est la consequence a pu faire ce que ne font guère les particuliers, en adoptant pour une grande partie de ses bois le mode d'exploitation en futaies qui éxige une tres longue attente, mais qui aussi, de l'avis des meilleurs Forestiers, donne incontestablement les produits les plus abondants."

＊ ＊ ＊ ＊ ＊

"Aussi est ce chose remarquable qu'a de rares exceptions près les bois domaniaux qui ont été vendus se deteriorent rapidement, même entre les mains de ceux des acquéreurs qui ont l'intention de les conserver ; les chênes ont presque toujours cessé de s'y réproduire ; ceux que l'exploitation eut ôté ne sont pas remplacés et bientôt cette précieuse espece y aura entierement disparu."

Journal des Économistes, No. 32 Juillet 1844, De la propriète forestière en France.

of them, it is yet certain that large sums have been paid upon private transfers, for the privilege of working particular forest tracts, and that large immediate receipts in revenue to the Government have thence resulted. Where parties are thus situated, there cannot, I think, be a reasonable doubt that they are not to be stigmatized, as if they had merely abused the easy liberality of the Government, and might now, therefore, be, without injustice, summarily ejected from their tenures, because it may be supposed that the Government, with its actual knowledge, can work these forests with greater advantage to itself for the present, and with a better prospect of due conservation and renewal for the future.

"In conclusion, as respects the Attaran tenures, I am prepared to recommend their concession in permanent property to holders, on conditions which I shall specify. The essential difficulty is as to the renewal of the forests. The attempt at nurseries made by Captain Tremenheere have proved, perhaps from want of due care and protection, total failures. If the same result should attend future efforts to propagate the trees, there might be reasonable scruple in making over to private persons such large tracts* of country which it is desirable, I apprehend, that they should possess only as forest holders. If the tree can be successfully propagated by artificial culture, then I have no doubt that the tenure of the forest holder ought to be permanent; or a lease of 99 years, without a certain expectation of a renewal equivalent to perpetuity would, at the expiration of that term, leave the Government with bare forests, and with a further period of nearly a century to wait before Teak could be again reared in them. I can see no way out of this difficulty other than by requiring that, at the end of certain terms of years, say of ten years' terms, the

* The superficial area of the larger forest tracts on the Attaran, and those tracts occupied by Teak.

No.	Forest Holders.	Superficial area of the extent of forest tracts.	Superficial area of forest occupied by Teak trees.	Names of Forests.
		Miles	Miles	
1	Mr. Darwood,	undefined	11	Joon Joonjah.
2	Cockerell & Co.	8	8	Keon Choung.
3	Pascal's Estate,	12	10	Meohoung.
4	Cockerell & Co.	18	13	Megwa.
5	Clarke's Estate,	9	9	Megwa.
6	Mackey & Co.	24	11	Mittigate.
7	Mr. Richardson,	16	8	Ghoon Geo.
8	Clarke's Estate,	18	4	Natchoung.
9	Mrs. Wales,	9	5	Cronkpan.
	Total,	114	79	

grantee should show that he has within his limits teak seedlings growing up, say to the extent of a third or a half of the whole number of trees which have been taken from the forests on an average of the past ten years. A restricted condition of this kind should leave an ample reserve to the grantee for space occupied by more advanced trees already naturally produced, and rising in the forests, (which would of course deprive him pro tanto of space for new plantations) as well as for partial failures in his attempts to raise new plants. I would not mix up the Government officers in plantations within the boundaries of private tenures. The grantee ought to be distinctly responsible for his own failures, and to be allowed to aim at success in the manner which he may think likely to be the least costly and the most effective.

"The grant might include, as suggested in para. 35 of your letter, not only Teak, but all trees and products of the forest, with the reservation to Government of the discretion to impose a duty, should it think fit, not exceeding 10 per cent. upon such trees and produce, in like manner as on the produce of mines.

"The grantees might, either as recommended in the letter of the Hon'ble Court of Directors of 30th November, 1842, be restrained by an express condition from clearing the land for cultivation or employing it otherwise than for plantation, or, if it is thought that the admission of absolute property within the limits above shewn, will be of little consequence in this uncleared Territory of above 25,000 square miles in extent, the property might be made complete and unconditional, subject, as referred to in your letter, to a land rent on the usual terms for any part of the land at any time brought under cultivation. The objection to this last mode of procedure, is that the land might be useless on the hands of the grantee, as he would scarcely find his profit in engaging to pay rent rates for ordinary produce in those comparatively remote districts. On the other hand if the grant be made on the terms stated by the Hon'ble Court, I would allow clearance to the extent of a tenth, or some such proportion of the area, without forfeiture of the grant, so as to allow the grantee to give encouragement to parties to settle near the places where the Teak grows, and to give their useful assistance in Forest conservancy.

"There is a question of some delicacy as to what occupancies of the forests shall be included in the proposed grants, in whatever form these may be made. It would be futile, I think, to give these permanent tenures to many of the Burmese holders of forest licenses who have not the means or the character from which to look for a useful result, were such a concession made to them. I enclose a statement of the working of the Attaran forest during the past four years. It might be well perhaps to make it a condition of a permanent grant that not less than 200 logs shall have been brought down from the tract within some one of the last three years. Parties excluded by this limit might be allowed to hold their tenures as at present, but whenever as many as 50 logs shall not have been brought down from the forests within a consecutive term of three years, the tenure might then be absolutely resumed.

"A similar principle might be applied to the case of the forest holdings on the Lhainboay river. There are now no private occupancies on the Houndrow river.

"Upon a condition such as is suggested above, it might be left to the choice of parties either to apply for grants on the new terms, or to continue in occupation on that condition. Measures were taken last year by two public notifications to obtain a registry of all existing tenures, but no benefit being expected by the occupants from compliance, these remained without effect."

26. The subject of Captains Durand and Guthrie's proceedings having been referred to the Hon'ble the Court of Directors, and a reply, dated 20th October, 1847, having been received, the Government in transmitting a copy to Mr. Colvin intimated to him that the Government sanctioned the lease of the Mittigate Codogway forest to Messrs. Mackey and Co. for ninety-nine years, and with regard to the remainder of the Attaran forest, stated that they might also be leased on the same terms, but the Court having forbidden the grant of any forest in perpetuity, no such grants were to be given.

27. Mr. Colvin's suggestions that only those occupants of forests from whose locations 200 logs had been brought down within the previous three years, should be entitled to leases, and that those forests from which less than 50 logs had been brought down during the same time, should be considered open to resumption, was at the same time approved.

28. In his letter of 21st June, 1848, Mr. Colvin again pressed the reconsideration of the question of the tenure to be granted to the

holders of the Attaran forests, I beg to draw attention to the remarkable argument stated in his 7th para.; in favor of grants in perpetuity that the forests had *already been parted with.* He states, "The question here is not whether it is desirable to part with forest lands to private persons, but whether, having parted with them, it is not better that the transfer to such persons should be on the most secure and acceptable tenure." But upon this I would submit that there is no reason to believe that the Government has ever parted with any portion of the forests: the only thing it ever did, except in the case of one forest the Mittigate Codogway, leased to Messrs. Mackey and Co., was to give permission " to cut timber within certain limits."

29. The Court of Directors in their dispatch of 12th September, 1849, again declined to sanction the transfer of the forests to private persons in perpetuity; the tenures are still precisely what they were in 1829; and the further discussion of forest matters was postponed pending the receipt of Dr. Falconer's report.

30. If any proof were required in addition to that furnished in the reports of Captains O'Brien, Tremenheere, and Guthrie, of the reckless exhaustion of the forests of these Provinces, it is fully supplied in the report of Dr. Falconer from the 44th to the 64th paras. He sums up his observations as follows :

Para. 59. " The general result of my tour of inspection may be summed up thus ; the Teak forests upon the Weinyo and Zimmé rivers are in rapid progress to exhaustion. The forests which were in the hands of native license holders, have been in most instances entirely cleared out both of large timber and of under-sized trees, approaching the regulation standard. The large forests towards the heads of the rivers, held by Europeans of capital, have been actively worked for nearly twenty years, and are also either in the same condition, or will speedily be exhausted. Of the three reserved forests formerly held for Government, the Mittigate Codogway has been leased out, and is now under the full operation of the axe; its resources having been largely drawn upon before it was held in reserve. The only two now reserved, viz., the Thengan-nyee Nyoung, and the upper Mittigate, instead of being intact forests, have been partially worked by trespass, by the adjoining forest holders, the former to a large extent, the latter in a less degree. Both forests contain standing Teak timber of large scantling, the upper Mittigate in particular abounding in the finest trees. So general and indiscriminate have been the fellings upon the Weinyo and Zimmé, that but for the timber in these two reserved forests, it would now be a matter of record only, that Teak of large size has ever been produced on the Attaran.

Para. 60. " Young timber is nowhere rising in adequate quantity either to renew the forests or to keep up the supply. The reason of this having been that the forest regulations, up to 1846, were in-operative, and under-sized trees were felled equally with the large timber, the greater facility of dragging them through the forests, and the ready sale met with at Maulmain, having held out an irresistible inducement for their consumption.

Para 61. " The forests have been worked, even by grantees of capital, entirely with a view to immediate or speedy returns; their maintenance for future supplies, and the creation of prospective pro-perty, have in no case been attended to. The owners have rarely or only at long intervals, visited their grants: they have been in the habit of carrying on their operations by means of native agents, who have conducted them with reckless waste and improvidence. The most destructive agent after the axe, I consider to have been the periodical fires; and these are referable in most instances, in the remote forests on the Attaran, to conflagrations purposely caused by the working parties, so as to clear the grass jungle, and enable them to move with safety about the forests. I believe these fires to have been much more prevalent since the country passed into our hands, than they were when the forests were in the state of nature. Planting young trees, or raising nurseries from seed, has in no instance been attended to by the grantees, or if there has been a solitary exceptional case, the attempt has been made with so little effort to attain success, that there is probably not a young tree in the whole of the forests that owes its origin to the hand of man.

Para. 62. " Although young seedlings of spontaneous growth are occasionally met with, as in the instance mentioned in para. 46, they are, generally speaking, rare in the Attaran forests, and bear no proportion either to the vast quantity of good seed annually produced, or to the trees which have been felled, or are still standing, and con-sequently to the requirements of the forests for renewal.

Para. 63. " In the above summary, I have only added the testi-

mony of a fresh and latter observer, to the statements which have
already been made in the reports of Captains O'Brien, Tremenheere,
and Guthrie, and in the forest records of the Commissioner's office."

31. And in paras. 81 and 82, Dr. Falconer adds. '

Para. 81. " The experience of the last twenty years has shown
that the forests have been worked solely with a view to immediate
returns, and with no regard to the future. The licenses have passed
by transfer from hand to hand, and few of them have remained with
the original holders. The timber trade has been carried on naturally with a view to make the most of a profitable article, while
it lasted. As one source of timber became exhausted, other more
remote tracts were explored, until the traders went beyond the limits
of the Province, and drew their supplies from the Shan states upon
the Thoung Yeen, whence the greater part of the timber is now
derived. Fixed capital never appears to have been invested in any
part of the forests, with a view to operations extending beyond the
duration of the timber then standing, or in prospect of being speedily
available for use. The holders were fully awake to the impending
exhaustion of their grants, but in no one instance was a steady effort
made by them to maintain the value of the property for the future
by planting. Instead of this, the future was anticipated by felling
every tree approaching the regulation standard. It is true that the
tenures, originally held, were simply licenses revocable at will, and
conveyed no permanent right of property, but I do not believe that
this circumstance had much effect practically, in influencing the operations of the holders, for during the period from 1829 to 1846, they
never were disturbed in their possession : the ejectment measures
resorted to by Captain Guthrie were immediately discountenanced
by Government, and large sums were paid for the transfer of
the licenses, showing the feeling of security that was placed
in them. The trade, as has been aptly stated by Mr. Colvin, was
conducted in a spirit of gambling with a hazardous outlay of capital,
and very uncertain returns. The ultimate gains of most of the traffic
would appear to have remained with the prudent capitalists at Maulmain, who purchased their consignments on the spot from adventurers
who had brought the timber to the market.

Para. 82. " If such have been the results of the past, when
the forests were covered with abundance of valuable Teak timber,

what reasonable grounds are there for expecting adequate measures of renewal from the grantees, now that they are bared? If the leases had reference to virgin forests stocked with Teak wood, conditions of renewal might have been enforced, and the Government could have had the full guarantee that the provisions were carried out, by periodical inspections and by forfeiture wherever planting was neglected; but with exhausted forests, where the prospects of return are nearly a century off, how can it be expected that capital will be invested by private parties, with annual outlay in so remote an adventure? Fixed capital in the province of Amherst has still to be created: there is none available at present for such an enterprise; and the only party who can be looked to for undertaking it is the Government itself, for the prospective maintenance of its timber revenue."

32. It cannot I think be questioned that the conclusion here arrived at by Dr. Falconer after a minute study of the question, much inquiry on the spot, and an inspection of the principal forest tracts, viz. that the Government is the only party capable of restoring the forests of Tenasserim, is the only correct one.

33. Throughout the whole correspondence it is painfully manifest that all the difficulties of the question have arisen from the circumstance of the forests having been in the hands of private parties, and from the desire at different times evinced not to eject them, if by any rules or regulations the forests could be preserved in their hands, without injury to the state; rules upon rules have been enacted with this object, but with no other result than to prove the utter impossibility of inducing the permit holders, even by the threat of severe penalties, to abstain from cutting down under-sized timber and unfairly injuring the forests, or to plant new trees. While the authorities have been engaged in framing rules, the holders of permits and many persons without even this restricted authority, have been busily occupied in removing all the marketable timber; it therefore follows that the remedy for this, the first step in fact towards successful measures for the restoration of the forests, is to resume them. Nothing short of this will be efficacious, and this leads to a consideration of the tenure on which they are claimed.

34. I have been at some pains to ascertain this, and I have no hesitation in saying, that from the beginning it has never been anything more than "a permission to cut within certain localities

revocable at will;" and that the "let-mats" or licenses never conveyed any proprietary right whatever.

35. Although a disposition has frequently been shown by different authorities, including the Bengal Government, to regard the fact of lengthened occupancy or use, as conveying a prescriptive right, the Government and the Court of Directors have as frequently shewn that they did not recognize any such claim as of right, and have over and over again, in correspondence as well as in Rules, maintained the right of resumption, which I hold to be incontestible. There certainly does not exist any deed or contract showing that the foresters have any right to be continued in unrestricted occupation.

86. This being the case, I would next consider what the license-holders—they should not I think be called grantees—have done that their let-mats or permits should not be resumed. The only answer to this is, that according to the evidence of every one that has inspected the forest, they have indisputably violated every rule prescribed by the Government,—rules which were for the most part promulgated in a public and authoritative manner, and were well known to all, and have cut down and removed every tree that was worth the removal, until there is now nothing left of the magnificent resources of which these Provinces could boast when annexed to our Indian empire.

37. A favorite excuse urged for not planting, has been that the Teak tree cannot be raised by artificial means; but the fallacy of this has been fully established in various quarters. I have myself without any pains at all raised Teak seedlings. I have conveyed them several days' journey, and planted them with perfect success. I can even point out a Teak tree in Maulmain imported when a seedling from the mountains of Arracan, seven or eight years ago, and now flourishing most admirably; but whatever may have been the difficulties of com-plying with the rules as to planting, there were none in abstaining from cutting under-sized timber, and I think it may be argued that by continuing to occupy forests at will, after the promulgation of the different rules and omitting to procure "sunnuds" or "grants" on more satisfactory terms, the foresters have virtually bound themselves by the provisions of those rules, and have no right whatever to complain of their being enforced against them.

38. The fact is, that if immediate profit could have been derived from it, Teak trees would long ago have been raised by the hundreds

of thousands, but who would plant a tree that takes 100 years to reach ordinary perfection, in a country where money is cheap at 36 per cent. per annum?

39. On the tributaries of the Attaran there are fifty-four forests, of which I beg to submit a list, marked A. Of these eight are unoccupied, and belong to Government. Of the remainder it appears from the records of the Timber Revenue Office at Moulmain very doubtful if there are more than two or three occupants who have brought down more than 200 logs in three years, and would, according to the orders of Government, be entitled to a lease. One of these persons is Mrs. Darwood, the occupant of forest No. 53, she has been working her forest actively—another is the late firm of Cockerell and Co. who hold forests Nos. 50 and 52, and have brought down 431 logs, of which much more than 200 logs were probably from one forest and less than 200 from the other. Mackey and Co. who hold eight forests, including the Mittigate Codogway for which they have a grant, Nos. 20, 21, 24, 26, 44, 46, 47, and 49, from all of which they seem to have only brought down 130 logs, 176 crooks, 400 boat-crooks and 38 stern-pieces during the last three years, and cannot be regarded as being entitled to a lease, the quantity of timber brought down being so small. There is also a Mr. Rushbrook, occupant of Mrs. Wales' three forests, Nos. 8, 11, and 16, who has brought down 200 full sized and five under-sized logs during the last three years; but if all these came from one forest none could have come from the other two.

40. Of the holders of the remaining 32 forests nearly all appear to have abandoned them. None of them have brought down 50 logs, and therefore, in conformity with the orders of 24th April, 1848, they may be considered as already resumed. I request permission to resume them and to make them over to the Conservator of forests for replanting, and solicit orders respecting the forests held by Mrs. Darwood, Mr. Rushbrook, and the firms of Mackey and Cockerell and Co., 14 in all, or 13 excluding the Mittigate settled for ninety-nine years. List B shews the quantity of timber of all kinds brought from the Attaran during the past six years.

41. There are 31 other forest holdings on the Gyne or Hlynebwe and the Salween, as noticed in the reports of Captain Guthrie and others, but they have never been much thought of, the wood being inferior.

4

42. From statements C and D it appears that there are no persons entitled to leases from having brought down from these forests more than 200 logs during three years; and there are only seven persons in the Hlynebwe, and four in the Salween, whose holdings should not be resumed; and I am under the impression that a rigid examination of the tenures in these rivers would show that they were of very imperfect nature.

43. From the foregoing it will be seen that there are only a very few forests of any value, if they may be judged of by what they have of late years yielded; but it might be well before taking a final step to call on all the occupants formally to show cause why their holdings should not be resumed.

44. In the event of the Government being averse to resume the forests from which more than 200 logs have been brought down during a period of three years, I beg to state my opinion that claimants ought not to be allowed to hold them, unless they agree to form immediately in each a nursery of not less than one acre, in such manner as the Conservator may point out, and to fill that nursery with Teak seedlings, from which they will plant out 50 acres of land in the second year at the rate of 100 plants per acre, if required by the Conservator, and as he may direct, and to extend the plantation in the same manner at the rate of 50 acres per annum, until one-half the area taken up and occupied as a forest is planted. They should also be bound to renew all plants which may have died off or been destroyed, so that in each acre there shall, at the end of ten years, be not less than 50 trees; after that, or even in a shorter period, the young trees may be considered as safe; and when the time for cutting down arrives, five new trees should be planted for every one felled.

45. Mr. Colvin proposed that a grantee should at the end of ten years show that he had made a certain degree of progress in planting his grant; but I feel so thoroughly convinced that if such a length of time be allowed, the grantee will do nothing, and that at the end of the ten years the lands will be in no respect improved, that I cannot abstain from recommending that immediate and yearly progressive action be insisted upon.

46. Besides the foregoing, it is of so much importance to the quality of the wood and the credit of the market that killing and felling should be conducted at the proper time and in the proper

manner, that I would recommend that the grantees should be compelled to perform these in the manner which may be pointed out by the Conservator; but it does not occur to me that there are any other points that need be insisted on.

47. The grantees would of course continue liable to pay duty on all timber removed by them from the forests, either at the present or any other rate the Government may see fit to determine, not exceeding a certain maximum, to be fixed at the time of entering into the new agreement, and all under-sized timbers should, as now, be liable to confiscation.

48. If the grantees will not agree to the foregoing terms, the forests should, I think, be resumed. It has been proposed in some of the correspondence, that if the grantee will not plant, the Government should do so at his expense; but quite concurring with Mr. Colvin as to the inexpediency of the Government officers interfering more than can possibly be avoided within private forests, I would not advise this course. If all the forests which are thoroughly exhausted are resumed, the Government will have plenty of space for planting operations, and it is to be hoped that they will be attended with such success as to prove to any private forest-holders which there may then be, that it is entirely for their interest to follow the example set them by the Government, and plant largely.

49. I beg leave to submit a map of the Attaran forests, and I much regret the length of this communication, but I have thought it advisable to extract largely from the previous correspondence, so as to array all the most important facts in one report, and I trust there will not be omitted any thing requisite to your understanding of the case.

A

List of Forest Holders on the Attaran River.

No. as per Map.	Names.	Estimated Area in Square Miles.	
1	Government, ...	½	Not worked.
2	ditto, ...	¾	do.
3	Taracoon, ...	¾	do.
4	Government, ...	¾	do.
5	Shoay Dong, ...	2	do.
6	Doon Can, ...	1½	do.
7	Shoay Yah,...	5	do.
8	Mrs. Wales, ...	¼	Worked.
9	Nga Chuat,...	2	Not worked.
10	Pho Moo, ...	½	do.
11	Mrs. Wales,...	4	Worked.
12	Doon Kan, ...	1¼	Not worked.
13	Khan Taa, ...	1¼	do.
14	Myat Tha, ...	1¼	do.
15	Government, ...	½	do.
16	Mrs. Wales, ...	15	Worked,
17	Government, ...	2¼	Not worked.
18	Shaik Abdullah, ...	1¼	do.
19	Kobitt, ...	¾	do.
20	Mackey and Co., ...	9	Worked.
21	ditto., ...	¾	do.
22	Moung Indah,...	1	Not worked.
23	Ko Jyah, ...	¼	do.
24	Mackey and Co., ...	1	Worked.
25	Ko Byey, ...	¾	Not worked.
26	Mackey and Co., ...	16	Worked.
27	Government, ...	½	Not worked.
28	Moung Waa, ...	1¼	do.
29	Phojah, ...	1¼	do.
30	Shaik Abdullah, ...	¼	Worked.
31	Pothike Kyee, ...	1	Not worked.
32	Pothike Tsoo, ...	1¼	do.
33	Moung Cho, ...	1½	do.
34	Moung Kine, ...	1½	do.
35	Pho-Tsoo, ...	2	do.
36	Taracoon, ...	¾	do.
37	Moung Tan Lai, ...	¼	do.
38	Nga Ban, ...	¾	do.
39	Kobitt, ...	¾	do.

No. as per Map.	Names.						Estimated Area in Square Miles.	
40	Kobitt, ...	...	...	...	...	... ...	½	Not worked.
41	Ko Byo,	...	...	...	...	...	1	do.
42	Ko Long,	...	...	...	...	... ...	1	do.
43	Shoay Po, ...	...	...	...	...	...	½	Worked.
44	Shoay Dong, ...	...	...	...	... ...	1	Not worked.
45	Government,	...	...	...	...	...	1¼	do.
46	Mackey and Co.,	...	...	...	... ...	12	Worked.
47	ditto,	...	...	...	...	...	7	do.
48	Government, ...	...	...	...	... ...	12	Not worked.
49	Mackey and Co., ...	...	...	...	...	8	Worked.
50	Cockerell and Co.,	...	...	...	... ...	11	do.
51	Mr. Pascal,	...	...	...	...	...	2	Not worked.
52	Cockerell and Co.,	...	...	...	... ...	8	Worked.
53	Mrs. Darwood,	...	...	...	...	...	11	do.
54	Nga Kaa,	...	...	...	...	... ...	½	Not worked.

B

Memo. shewing the quantity of Teak Timber brought down from Forests on the Attaran, during the last six Official Years 1849-50, 1850-51, 1851-52, 1852-53, 1853-54, and 1854-55.

Years	Names of Parties.	Description of Teak Timber.							Total.							No. of Forest on Map.
		Full sized logs.	Under sized logs.	Ship Crooks.	Boat Crooks.	Steam Pieces.	Squares.	Slabs.	Full sized logs.	Under sized logs.	Ship Crooks.	Boat Crooks.	Steam Pieces.	Squares.	Slabs.	
1849-50.	Mrs. Wales,	51	0	0	0	0	0	0								No. 8.
	Mrs. Darwood,	15	1	203	24	0	1	64								,, 53.
	Moung Meat Tha,	127	11	0	0	0	0	0								,, 14.
	Moung Kine,	34	1	202	0	0	0	0								,, 34.
	Ko Nai,	0	0	51	0	0	0	0								,, 24.
	Ko Po Way,	1	0	335	0	0	0	0								,, 24.
	Mr. Richardson,	162	2	192	0	0	0	0								,, 24 & 26.
	Mr. Miller, or Creaton and Co.,	92	8	506	0	2	0	0	482	23	1489	24	2	1	64	,, 46 & 47.
1850-51.	Messrs. Creaton & Co.,	398	27	859	0	9	0	0								,, 46 & 47.
	Do. (from Govt. Forest Mittigate,)	156	0	0	0	0	0	0								,, 48.
	Mrs. Darwood,	45	0	1487	0	0	0	0								,, 53.
	D. C. Mackey & Co.,	0	0	693	0	0	0	0	594	27	2489	0	9	0	9	,, 46 & 47.
1851-52	Messrs. Creaton & Co.,	0	0	500	0	0	0	0								,, 20, 21, 44,
	Mrs. Darwood,	258	8	647	0	0	0	85								53.[46,&47.
	Shosy Pho,	8	1	4	0	0	0	0								,, 43.
	Mrs. Wales,	227	0	1	0	0	0	0	488	9	1152	0	0	0	85	,, 16.

[31]

Year	Name								Reference
1852-53	Mrs. Rushbrook (formerly Wales,)	81	8					0	No. 8.
	Nay Doen,	134	0						„ 53.
	Mrs. Darwood,	64	1						
	Creaton and Co. (sold for satisfaction of Government,)	56	51	102			1	8	„ 46 & 47.
		385	55	102	0	1		0	
1853-54	Messrs. Miller & Buchanan,	130	0	176	200	38			„20,21,46,47,
	Shaik Abdoollah,	52	0	5					„ 30. [& 49.
	Mrs. Darwood,	51	0	8					„ 53.
	Ko Shin Gally,	5	0	0					
	Shoay Pho,	93	8						„ 43.
	Umbah,	75	0						
	Mr. Rushbrook,	120	1						„ 16. [& 49.
		526	9	189	200	38		0	
1854-55	Shaik Mahomed for Shaik Abdoollah,	0	0	408	0				„ 30. [46, 47,
	Miller and Buchanan,	0	0	302	200				„20,21,24,26,
	Mr. Rushbrook,	0	0	314					„ 11 & 16.
	Shoay Go,	59	0						„
	Tha Nyo,	1	0						„ 43.
	Shoay Pho,	109	11						„ 53.
	Nga Lan,	0	0	510					
	Mrs. Darwood,	206	0	3					„ 50 & 52.
	Condamine and Morgan,	431	0	0					
		806	11	1537	200	0	0	0	
	Total,	9231	134	6958	424	50	4	158	

NOTE.—These full and under sized logs, &c. were mixed with other Timber belonging to this Firm then lying at their depôt above Nantay Village, and sold by Public Auction by order of Captain Hopkinson late Principal Assistant Commissioner for recovery of Government duty for the year 1847-48, namely, Co.'s Rs. 376-7-9. Regarding the Timber at this place, the exact amount of it cannot be stated, as no report has been made, but at the time of the sale there was a large number which has not even to the present time been brought down to the Ngantay station, and as the wood is kept at a spot which Messrs. Creaton and Co. have occupied as a depôt, above Government duty station, it does not ordinarily appear as part of the stock on hand, and its liability to duty appears to be evaded. The number of these logs can be soon ascertained if requisite.

Timber Revenue Office, Maulmain, 22nd November, 1855.

(Signed) S. R. TICKELL,
Deputy Commissioner A. P.

(Signed) S. R. T.

C

Memo. shewing the quantity of Teak Timber brought down from Forests in Hlynebve during the last six Official years, 1849-50, 1850-51, 1851-52, 1852-53, 1853-54, & 1854-55.

Compiled from the records of the Timber Revenue Office, Maulmain.

Years.	Names of Parties.	Description of Teak Timber.					Total.				
		Full sized logs.	Undersized logs.	Ship Crooks.	Boat Crooks.	Stem Pieces.	Full sized logs.	Undersized logs.	Ship Crooks.	Boat Crooks.	Stem Pieces.
1849-50.	Shoay Moung,	0	0	107	0	0					
	Yeukapah,	0	0	114	0	0					
	Nga Pay,	0	0	196	0	0					
	Yenkapah,	0	0	142	0	0					
	Nga Shoay Yea,	175	0	104	0	0					
	Shoay Moung,	0	0	140	0	0					
	Nga Shoay Yea,	13	0	24	11	31	188	0	827	11	31
1850-51.	Mr. Fowls,	0	0	102	0	0					
	Nga Thee,	0	0	158	0	0					
	Co Shoay Moung,	0	0	152	0	26					
	Ko Yea,	184	0	142	0	0					
	Yenkapah,	2	0	115	0	0					
	Ko Pa Ouke,	99	0	0	0	0					
	Ko Yea,	0	0	177	0	0					
	Yenkapah,	90	0	4	0	0					
	Co Pa Ouke,	0	0	246	0	0					
	Co Ray and Co Moon,	11	1	0	0	0	386	1	1096	0	26
1851-52.	Nga Moo Doung,	0	0	225	500	0					
	Messrs. Buchanan, Paterson and Co.,	0	0	463	0	0					
	Hyder Ally,	0	0	52	0	0					
	Messrs. Buchanan, Paterson and Co.,	0	0	112	0	0					

Year	Name									
1851-52	Shoay Moung,	0	0	100	0					
	Yeukapah,	38	0	180	0					
	Mr. McCalder, Ko Thoo,	0	0	0	1					
	Ko Thoo,	0	0	181	4					
	Tomby Abdoollah,	0	0	196	0					
	Yenkapah,	77	5	219	0					
	Messrs. Buchanan, Paterson and Co.,	0	0							
	Ko Loo,	6	0	58	0					
	Ko Reah,	13	0	137	0	134	51923	500	5	86
	Messrs. Buchanan, Paterson and Co.,	0								
1852-53	Ko Reah,	39	0	54	0					
	Yenkapah,	80	8	1	0	15				
	Tomby Abdoollah,	45	1	0	0					
	Yenkapah (confiscated by Government for Breach of Timber Revenue Rules,),	0	12	0	0	164	21	55	0	15
1853-54	Moung Shoay Doun and Moung Ouke,	0	0	153	0					
	I Oung,	115	0							
	Shoay Moung,	167	15	4	0					
	Tomby Abdoollah,	103	0	0	0					
	Shoay Moung,	121	14	310	0	506	29	467	0	0
1854-55	Do Woo Tsa,	0	0	100	0					
	Ko Byed,	0	0	66	0					
	Ko Shoay Moung,	138	12	594	0					
	Dingaroo,	1	0	152	0					
	Messrs. Buchanan, Paterson and Co.,	0	0	964	9					
	Jyan Shoke (Drift and sold by Public Auction),	40	37	32	0					
	Meat Yea,	58	0	0	0	237	491908	0	0	9
	Total,.....					1615	105 6276	511		86

(Signed)   S. R. TICKELL,
Deputy Commissioner, A. P.

Timber Revenue Office, Maulmain, the 30th November, 1855.

D

Memo. shewing the quantity of Teak Timber brought down from the Forests in the Salween during the last six official years, 1849-50, 1850-51, 1851-52, 1852-53, 1853-54, 1854-55.

Compiled from the records of the Timber Revenue Office, Maulmain.

Years.	Names of Parties.	Locality.	Full sized logs.	Under sized logs.	Ship Crooks.	Boat Crooks.	Stem Crooks.	Full sized logs.	Under sized logs.	Ship Crooks.	Boat Crooks.	Stem Crooks.
			Description of Teak Timber.					Total.				
1849-50.	Co Loon Tha,	Pandon	0	0	135	0	0					
	Co Pan Hue,	ditto	9	0	0	200	0					
	Co Shoay Eik,	ditto	0	0	100	0	0					
	Co Moung,	ditto	0	0	197	0	0					
	Nga Kee,	ditto	1	0	206	0	0					
	Co Pah Hue,	Co Loon	0	0	110	30	0					
	Sayah Gullay,	Pandon	0	0	100	0	0					
	Co Pah Hue,	Co Loon	1	0	50	4	0					
	Nga Poo Thine,	Pandon	0	0	108	0	0					
	China Papoo,	ditto	0	0	113	0	0					
	Nga Yan,	Co Loon	1	0	118	1	1	12	0	1237	235	0
1850-51.	Nga Loon Tha,	Pandon	0	0	85	11	8					
	China Papoo,	ditto	0	0	132	0	0					
	Shoay Moung,	ditto	0	0	112	0	0					
	Shoay Moung,	Meezan	86	0	91	0	8					
	Moung Thike Lay,	Pandon	0	0	122	0	0					
	Shoay Youk,	Co Loon	0	0	205	0	1	86	0	747	11	12

Year	Name	Category					
1851-52.	Moung Hute, ...	Co Loon	26	2	36	0	0
	Co Pay Mee and Shoay Moung, ...	Meezan	206	0	0	0	0
	Shoay Moung, ...	ditto	106	0	0	0	0
	Co Bue, ...	Co Loon	0	0	0	681	0
			338	2	36	681	0
1852-53.	Co Meat Thet, ...	Pandon	0	0	76	0	0
	Mr. Hannay, ...	ditto	0	0	71	0	0
	Meah Neo Bio Meat Yea, ...	ditto	0	0	98	0	0
	Pe Cha, ...	ditto	0	0	82	0	0
	Co Myah Yea, ...	Co Loon	0	0	234	0	0
	Sada Mohamed, ...	Meezan	0	0	67	0	0
		Pandon	0	0	0	0	21
			0	0	628	0	21
1853-54.	Mr. Lemaine, ...	Pandon	8	0	90	3	3
	Way Loo, ...	ditto	0	0	50	0	0
	Meerza Ally, ...	ditto	0	0	64	0	0
	Munser Ally, ...	ditto	0	0	52	0	0
	Kar Tsu, ...	ditto	32	0	263	0	0
	Co Hoot, ...	ditto	152	0	157	0	0
	Co Hoot, ...	ditto	156	16	0	1	0
	Tomby Abdoollah, ...	ditto	0	16	16	0	1
	Ditto (confiscated by Government for Breach of Timber Revenue Rules,)	ditto	0	23	0	0	0
	Co Hoot, ...	ditto	0	0	202	0	0
			348	39	894	0	4
1854-55.	Co Hute, ...	ditto	209	0	198	0	0
	Tomby Abdoollah, ...	ditto	2	17	40	0	0
	Moung Tha and Co Tsat, ...	ditto	2	0	53	0	0
	Co Hute, ...	Co Loon	20	0	98	0	0
	Harzar Saib, ...	Meezan	0	0	97	0	0
	Co Hute, ...	Pandon	0	0	464	0	0
	Carried over,		784	41	3542	927	37

D.—Continued.

Years	Names of Parties	Locality	Description of Teak Timber					Total				
			Full sized logs.	Under sized logs.	Ship Crooks.	Boat Crooks.	Stem Pieces.	Full sized logs.	Under sized logs.	Ship Crooks.	Boat Crooks.	Stem Pieces.
	Brought forward, ...							784	41	3542	927	87
1854-55.	Co Pa Oak, ...	Pandon	0	0	135	0	1					
	Co Hute, ...	Co Loon	89	0	33	0	0					
	Hussun Tsa, ...	Pandon	18	0	12	23	0					
	Co Hute, ...	Co Loon	0	0	0	0	0					
	Co Byew, ...	Pandon	0	0	73	0	0					
	Ditto, ...	Co Loon	0	0	99	0	1					
	Shoay Mein, ...	Pandon	1	0	95	0	5					
	Co Thoon Galay, ...	ditto	0	0	99	0	0					
	Shoay Goon, ...	ditto	0	0	101	0	0					
	Total....							341	17	1597	23	7
	Total......							1125	58	5139	950	44

(Signed) S. R. TICKELL,
Deputy Commissioner, A. P.

Timber Revenue Office, Maulmain.

REPORT ON THE ATTARAN FORESTS.

This Report on the present condition of the Attaran Forests, has

Introductory Remarks.

been prepared in obedience to instructions received from the Commissioner Tenasserim and Martaban Provinces, conveyed in para. 4 of his letter, dated 1st July, 1858. On receipt of this letter, I made arrangements for examining the Attaran Forests myself, left Moulmein accordingly on the 21st July, and returned on the 18th August.

The preparation of this report, however, has been delayed thus long, because I found that without having examined other forests, similarly situated to those of the Attaran, I could not, with sufficient certainty, give an opinion on the present state of the Attaran Forests and their future prospects.

2. Up to 1858, I had principally devoted my attention to the Central Pegu Forests between the Sitang and Irrawaddie rivers, and was not sufficiently acquainted with those east of the Sitang river, which, in many respects, are analogous to those in the Attaran valley.

And even now, although I have had ample opportunities of studying the character of the Teak Forests in all parts of this country, and have spent more than one half of four years in Burmah in these forests, I feel bound to say that many of the opinions set forth in this Report, and the results arrived at, may hereafter prove to be subject to important modifications and corrections.

Hesitation therefore in submitting reports on a subject the very principles of which have yet to be developed, may appear excusable. Their investigation unavoidably involves many questions of a purely scientific nature, and it is not always possible to determine beforehand the extent of time required for a satisfactory completion of researches of that nature.

3. It appears necessary to introduce a few remarks regarding the

Forest surveys how conducted.

method pursued in surveying these forests. These, with observations on the general character of Teak forests in Burmah, constitute the *first* portion of the Report.

6

The method pursued in surveying the Attaran Forests, is the same which I have adopted for the whole of the forests of these provinces. This method is rough and primitive in comparison with the elaborate methods of Forest Surveying in use on the Continent of Europe, but the peculiar character of the Teak forests of this country would render the application of the latter without avail.

The *second* will contain a description of the Attaran Forests in their present state. The *third* will give the history of the Tenasserim Teak plantations, and the *fourth* will treat of the future prospects of the Attaran Forests.

The Teak Forests of these provinces are not, like the Pine and Oak forests of Europe, extensive and well defined tracts covered with one or a few species of trees, all useful and valuable, or nearly so. Teak trees are found scattered in a forest, mainly consisting of trees of. other kinds, all at present valueless, or nearly so, if compared with Teak. Teak trees are either found *singly*, scattered over a wide extent of ground, or they form isolated groups *of a few trees only ;* or, lastly, Teak is one of the *regular constituents* of the forest, bearing a variable, but mostly small, proportion to the trees of other kinds.

Localities where Teak occurs are designated as *Teak-producing tracts*. Between them there are others without any Teak in them, and frequently bearing a forest consisting of a class of trees altogether different. We thus distinguish Teak-producing tracts and localities without Teak. And thus the determination of the value of a forest depends on the following two questions.

First. What is the area of the Teak-producing tracts.

Second. What is the amount of Teak on Teak localities with reference to a given area.

4. The area of Teak localities cannot, in most cases, be determined, The area of Teak localities how in the present state of our forests, in determined. a direct manner by regular survey. For so undefined are the boundaries of most Teak-containing localities in the forests, that to ascertain the outskirts of one of these tracts, and to measure its circumference, would be almost impossible. If the surveyor attempted to circumscribe a tract by regular survey, he would meet with a group of Teak trees, and following up the boundary line of this patch, he would be led to another group, and so on, until at last he would be unable to say of which locality he was surveying the outline.

We must therefore content ourselves with only an approximate determination of the area, such as can be obtained from route surveys taken through the forests in different directions.

In these surveys, Teak is marked wherever it occurs, and the character of the intervening forest which is void of Teak, is noted. The forest maps resulting from these surveys, enable us to form a rough estimate as to how large a proportion of the total area is covered with Teak localities, or any of the other classes of forests. It is clear that this estimate can only be a very uncertain approach to the truth unless the survey is a very detailed one.

With reference to the Attaran, we have no such system of outer surveys to go by, and must therefore take the estimate of the area of the Teak-producing localities from other sources.

The following statements of the area of the different Teak-producing tracts on the Wingco and Zimmay rivers are found among the records of the Moulmein Forest Office.

1. "Estimate of the Teak trees on the Wingco and Zimmay rivers, dated 27th March, 1846, drawn up by Charles Salmond, Assistant Forest Surveyor (Stat. Nos. XV. and XVI.)."

2. "Estimate of Teak trees on the Wingco and Zimmay, dated 29th May, 1851, and prepared by A. Hobday, 2nd Assistant, Forest Department, Tenasserim Provinces, (Stat. Nos. VIII. and IX.)."

The substance of these statements is as follows.

	Stat. of 1846.	Stat. of 1851.
Area of Teak forests on the Wingco,	$48\frac{3}{4}$	$36\frac{1}{2}$
Ditto ditto Zimmay, ...	$118\frac{3}{4}$	$119\frac{1}{2}$
Total, ...	$167\frac{1}{2}$	156

No information can be traced as to how these results have been obtained. It is scarcely possible to imagine that it was done by a regular survey of each forest tract, defining the extent and shape of the same. It appears more correct to assume, that the area here given is the result of a general estimate.

Upon the whole, it is my opinion that these estimates are too high. I have found this verified whenever I had an opportunity of examining a forest sufficiently to form myself an idea of its probable extent. I give a few instances on the margin. Taking these and a few other corrections into account, I believe that we are not far out in estimating the area of

No.	Name of Forests.	Estimated Area.	
		By Mr. Hobday.	By Dr. Brandis.
16	Both banks of Wingco at its source, ...	11 sq. m.	6 sq. m.
26	Goongee,...........	16 ,, ,,	8 ,, ,,
48	Sources of the Mittigate above the Kyouktegu,	12 ,, ,,	0½ ,, ,,
		39 ,, ,,	14½ ,, ,,

the whole of the Teak localities in the valleys of the Wingco and Zimmay at 100 square miles. This nearly agrees with Dr. Falconer's estimate, in para. 86 of his report, viz. 110 square miles.

The total area of that part of the Attaran valleys where Teak is at all to be found, may be estimated at about 500 square miles, so that the Teak localities would appear to occupy one-fifth of the whole area.*

The second question, viz. to determine the amount of Teak standing on a given area of Teak localities is solved in the following manner.

The amount of Teak standing on an area of Teak-producing forest how determined.

The surveying officer proceeds through the locality in question in different directions, measuring the length of the tract pursued by a 100' rope. He and his party count all Teak trees, logs and stumps, visible on both sides from the line of march, each person counting the trees of one or a few classes only and marking the number on bamboos split for the purpose. And in order to prevent the same tree being counted twice in two different classes, the number of trees observed at each turn of the road is called out aloud.

The main classes of trees established in the forests of these provinces are—

First Class.—Trees in girth 6 ft. (or 4 cubits) and above. Estimated age above 62 years.

* Two triangles on both sides of a line 38 miles long, running from the junction of both branches to the mouth of the Peng Choung, beyond which no Teak of any importance is known, the top of the eastern triangle being beyond the Goongee Teak forests, at a distance of 14 miles from the base line, and that of the other at the foot of the western mountain range, near Lloot Shan village, about 12 miles distant from the base line, or $\frac{38}{2}$ (12 + 14) = 494 sq. m.

[41]

Second Class.—Trees from 4 ft. 6 inch (or 3 cubits) to 6′, from 37 to 62 years.

Third Class.—Trees from 1 ft. 6 inch (or 1 cubit) to 4′ 6″, from 10 to 37 years.

Fourth Class.—Small trees in girth below 1′ 6″ (or 1 cubit), below 10 years.

The girth of all trees is measured at 6 feet from the ground.

These classes are the same as those established in my Report on the Pegu Forests for 1856, with an alteration only as regards the third class which, at that time, comprised only the trees in girth from 3 ft. to 4 ft. 6 inches, those in girth from 1 foot 6 inches to 3 feet being included in the fourth class. Further experience has shewn this alteration to be necessary. Teak, as a rule, does not commence to produce seed before it is 10 years old. The first three classes therefore now comprise all seed-bearing trees. The estimated age of trees of the different classes has also received certain modifications from observations made since 1856, which are recorded in Statement XI.

These classes are occasionally subdivided, and the trees of 4, 5, 6 cubits in girth counted separately. Besides green trees, the following are included in the counting : Nathat (trees that have died a natural death) ; girdled (trees killed by girdling) ; fallen (dead trees blown down) ; logs, stumps, trees attacked with epiphytic ficus or creepers.

The average width of the space on which the trees counted are standing is estimated according to the greater or less density of the forest. To facilitate this estimate, the following scale has been established from actual observation.

	Average width of space surveyed,	yds.	miles.
I.—Forest very light, only large trees, without bamboo or underwood,		106	0,06
II.—Similar but less open on both sides of the track,		70	0,04
III.—Here and there underwood and clumps of bamboo,		53	0,03
IV.—Bamboo forest of moderate density,		40	0,023
V.—Dense bamboo forest, or evergreen forest,		26	0,015

It rarely happens in the Teak forests, here and there, only for short distances, that a clear view can be obtained over a greater width than 100 yards, that is over 50 yards on either side of the road.

The length and width of the tract thus surveyed, as well as the trees of the different classes are registered in the forest day-book, a specimen of which is given in the copy of the forest day-book of the tours through the Attaran Forests.

Remarks on the following subjects are added.

1st.—Locality (situation and boundaries).

2nd.—Soil.

3rd.—Other trees occurring with Teak in the forest.

4th.—General remarks on the growth of Teak, the facilities given for the working of the forest and other matters connected with the subject.

6. The forest survey thus gives the proportion of the different classes of trees on a given area, and the general character of the forest.

Corrections to be applied.

But before making use of it for practical purposes, certain corrections must be applied.

First. All classes of trees cannot be seen equally far, and, as a rule, small trees are more likely to be overlooked than large trees. This does not refer so much to the trees of the three first classes, the smallest of which (18 inches in girth) are from 30 to 40 feet in height, but it materially affects the small trees (fourth class) which, if the survey is conducted during the rains or before the jungle fires have cleared the ground, are concealed in the high soft grass or the herbs which cover the ground in most Teak localities during that season.

If the forest is surveyed after the fires of the dry season, the young Teak trees can only with difficulty be distinguished, as they have by that time lost their leaves, and nothing remains of them but sticks blackened by the fires, and frequently even these burnt down; the seedlings not being killed in all cases, but sprouting out again from the root.

It may be assumed that, as a rule, one-half only of the small trees (fourth class) actually standing on the area surveyed are seen and counted. This correction therefore has to be made whenever the statements are required for practical purposes.

Second. Stumps of trees felled are easily distinguished in the dry season, but are frequently concealed by grass during the rains. For forest surveys therefore conducted during that time of the year, the number of stumps actually counted should be doubled.

Neither of these corrections, however, has been introduced in the Statements appended to this Report, as it appears preferable to give the number actually counted and to apply the corrections whenever the results are required for practical purposes.

7. In this manner 42½ square miles of the different forests in

General results obtained.

these provinces have been surveyed, and the results obtained are exhibited in Statements I to V. The following general results, as to the proportion of the trees of different classes and the character of the forest generally are here recorded, as they form the standard by which the present state of the Attaran Forests should be judged.

First. The number of first class trees, in girth above 6 feet, and 62 years old is, in the majority of cases, equal to, or larger than the number of second class trees in the same forest tract.

Second. The number of third class trees exceeds that of the second class, and is, in most instances, more than double its amount. Third class trees are, it will be remembered, from 10 to 37, and second class from 37 to 62 years old.

Third. The fourth class (small trees) is by far the most numerous, it is frequently twice or three times as numerous as the third class, it forms between one-third and one-half of the trees of all classes (without doubling the number actually counted).

Fourth. The average number of Teak trees (large and small) per square mile is generally between 1,000 and 10,000, and the average proportion of the different classes are as follows.

Average number of Teak trees in the Forest.

	On a square mile.	On 10 Acres.	Per Mille	Per Mille, doubling the Fourth Class trees.
Teak First Class, ...	983	15	202	147
,, Second ditto,.........	684	10	139	100
,, Third ditto, ...	1372	21	282	205
,, Fourth ditto, ...	1840	28	377	548
Teak Total,......	4879	74	1000	1000
Trees of other kinds of all sizes, exclusive of Bamboo, ...	48,790	740		

On an average, Teak forms 1-10 of the other trees in the so-called Teak forests, but the proportion of Teak to the trees of other kinds is a very variable one. Sometimes it equals their number, in other instances again it does not form one-hundredth part of the trees in the forest.

8. In the statements from which these results have been obtained, the Forest Surveys of 1856 have not been included. They are recorded in Statement I. of the Report for the Pegu Forest for 1856, and, although conducted on a very limited scale, and in a more imperfect manner than those of later years, they have led to similar results.

Comparison of the results of Forest Surveys, from 1857 to 1859 with those obtained 1856.

An extract of the Statement alluded to, with additional remarks, is here annexed.

Name of Forest.	Estimated Area, the length of Track being known and the width estimated at 0.04 square miles.	Designation of Forest Class.	Number of green trees observed.			
			6 feet in girth and above, first class.	Between 4 ft. 6″ and 6 ft. second class.	Between 3 ft. and 4 ft. 6″ being one-half of the third class.	
Khaboung, ...	1.6	A⁸	1296	480		
North Nawing, ...	1.80	C¹	284	738		
Kyoungzouk, ...	.56	B¹	162	83		
Minhla & Mokha,	2.04	C³	681	1202	1346	
	6 *	C⁴	2423	2503	2793	
After doubling the third class trees, ...			2423	2503	5586	10,512
Per square mile, ...			404	417	931	1752

Per Mille, assuming the fourth class trees to be
377, we obtain first class, ... 144
Second ditto, ... 148
Third ditto, ... 331
Fourth ditto, ... 377
                                                    ────
                                                    1000

The forests met with in 1856 were evidently poor forests, and the surveys were incomplete, yet they generally confirm the results recorded above.

9. These general results, however, must not be understood to

Variations in the general results obtained.

convey the idea, that the forests present throughout the same uniform appearance as regards the amount and proportion of Teak in the same. On the contrary the greatest variety is found to exist. In one locality one class of trees of similar age and size is generally prevailing. We thus find tracts in which the greater portion of Teak trees belong to the first, or second, or third class, or to two of these classes only.

A few instances of four tracts of a peculiar character are given in Appendix No. 1. Tract No. 1, (area one acre) was selected at random from a large extent of forest of entirely similar character. The number of the two last classes forms 30 per cent. only of the whole, whereas the average is 66 per cent. Tract No. 2, contains first and second class trees only. Tract No. 3, measured by Dr. MacClelland in the Bundah Forests, contains only 29 per cent. of the three first classes, whereas it ought to have 62 per cent. But such localities frequently occupy an area of very circumscribed extent only, and the extremes do not therefore appear in the general results of the Forest Surveys, and not even always in the data of one survey alone, yet certain peculiarities have a wider range, and to designate these the forests have been classified as follows.

Those forests where the number of first class trees is more than twice the number of second class trees are designated by the letter A. At the same time the number of first class trees on a square mile is designated by a figure. Thus the general character of the middle Thoungyeen Forests is designated by A^6, that of the Beeling Forests in the Martaban province by A^{89}, which indicates that the number of first class trees on the square mile is respectively between 6 and 700 and 8900 and 9000. As a rule, the forests of class A are what may be called rich forests, having a large number of first class trees on the square mile. Most of them had only been worked very sparingly.

Those forests in which the first class trees are more numerous than those of the second, without exceeding twice their number, are called B forests, and those in which the number of second class trees exceeds that of the first are designated as C. The last named are generally poor forests, and very much worked out. The fourth Division of the Pegu Forests (Southern Forests), the lower Salween, and the Attaran Forests belong to this class. This rule, however, is not without exceptions ;—a portion of the Tyemyouk Forests for instance. In the Tharrawaddie district, Survey No. II. 49, 50, which belongs to this class has 5,908 first class trees on the square mile. This portion of the Tyemyouk Forests is one of the most thriving forests in the country ; the large trees are standing on low hills and around them are belts of rich alluvial soil, on which the trees of the smaller classes are growing up in abundance (see also Survey II. 39 taken on the hills only).

The same latitude obtains with reference to the number of trees on the square mile. Thus if we find that the average number of first class trees on the square mile in the Kannee and Koonoung Forests is 5054, we must not overlook that the number observed in one forest tract was 1526, and that found in another 23,478. In the Beeling Forests the variation is from 1926 to 21,339 trees per square mile, and it is similar in the other forests. Statement No. VI. exhibits these variations in the different forests, and at the same time shows, that of the three forest classes A, B, and C, the two former are of more frequent occurrence than the last, which agrees with the first rule laid down in para. 7.

10. Regarding the trees of other kinds, occurring with Teak in the forests, or constituting the forests void of Teak, the following results have been arrived at.

General character of the forests in which Teak is found.

Teak does not occur in the mangrove forests in the neighbourhood of the tidal channels of the Delta.

A forest of a totally different character commences where the mangrove forest ceases, but this also is void of Teak.

The following trees are most characteristic of this kind of forests, *Pymmah* (Lagerstrœmia reginæ), *Seet* (Albizzia elata), *Baup* (Butea frondosa, Roxb.), *Lepan* (Bombax Malabaricum), *Yindike* (Dalbergia, sp.), *Teinthé* (Nauclea parviflora, Roxb.). In most cases they are scattered over wide extents of elephant grass, or form narrow belts of forest between the paddy-fields. Of bamboos the thorny kind, *Yakatwa* (Bambusa spinosa), is the prevailing species.

The trees mentioned, however, are not always found together : *Seet*, for instance, forms the prevailing tree along the banks of the larger rivers ; *Baup* is characteristic of certain tracts, whether they are covered with elephant grass or paddy-fields; *Teinthé* is the principal tree in wide extents of country which, during two or three months of the rains, are annually several feet under water; and *Pymmah* is the ornament and prevailing tree wherever the forest is more continuous and less interrupted by elephant grass.

Associated with these are a large number of other trees, most of which, however, equally occur in forest of a different description. Some of the more remarkable are. The wood-oil tree *Kanyinben* (Diptero-carpus alata, Roxb.), *Zimbjoon* (Dillenia aurea), *Bambouay* (Careya arborea), *Gyoben* (Schleichera trijuga), *Aukchinza* (Diospyrus, sp.), *Tabookgyee* (Milinsa velutina, Hf. and Th.).

This class of forest may be designated as the *lower mixed forests.*

As we penetrate into the interior of the country and come upon the rising ground which skirts the hills, the forest gradually changes its character. Here three widely different classes of forest fix our attention : these are the *dry,* or *upper mixed* forest, the *Ein* forest, and the *Evergreen* forest.

11. The principal seat of Teak is the dry or upper mixed forest, nearly the whole of the trees of this forest shed their leaves in February, and are not clothed with fresh green till the commencement of the rains. Hence this forest is the principal seat of the jungle fires, which pervade every part of it regularly every year, and often several times a year.

Dry Forest the principal seat of Teak.

The character of this forest is as little uniform as that of the lower dry forest, but two trees, or at least one of them is almost always to be found and frequently is the most prevalent tree in the same.

These are *Pynkado* (Inga xlocarpa) and *Taukyan* (Pentaptera, sp.). Associated with these is a very large variety of others, of which we enumerate the following as having more or less practical interest. *Tabew* (Dillenia speciosa) a small tree of slow growth, magnificent white blossoms and strong wood, and *Myoukmho* (Duabanga grandi-flora, Wall.), a gigantic tree, attaining a girth of fifteen feet, are the characteristic trees of moist valleys in the region of the upper mixed forest. *Didoke Lepan* (Eriodendron anfractuosum ?) with white blossoms is the cotton tree of this region, in the place of the Bombax Malabaricum, with scarlet flowers, which belongs to the lower forests. Abundant are *Nagyiben* (Pterospermum saggitatum) remarkable for its fluted stems, and *Myayah ben* (Grewia microstemma), the leaves of which are used as covering leaves to segars, *Do Ani* (Eriolæna, sp.) and *Pœwoon* (Berrya mollis) are rather scarce, but constant companions of this kind of forest. The wood of both is excellent for oars and spear handles, and might replace ash in this country, if it only were lighter. The never failing denizens of the Teak-producing localities of this forest are the different species of *Shawben* (Sterculia), and indeed without the abundant supply of material for rope which their bark yields, on the spot, the dragging of timber out of the forests would be exceedingly difficult.

Of the class of Leguminosæ a number of trees, most valuable on account of their hard and durable wood, occur in this part of the forests. The following deserve particular notice : *Thitmagyee,* (Albizzia odoratissima) *Boummayzah* (Albizzia stipularis) and *Kokohben* (Dalbergia ?), large trees, and highly prized for cart-wheels. *Thinwin* (Pongamia glabra) does not attain the same size. Its timber is used for the cross bars of Burman harrows. *Yindike* (Dalbergia, sp.) different from that in the lower forest, with heavy black heart wood, makes beautiful handles for dahs and spears, but is heavy and not elastic. *Gwoo Shwoay* (Cathartocarpus fistula), *Madamaben* (Dalbergia, sp.), and several species of Bauhinia, *Soaydan* and *Boaygyin,* are trees of smaller dimensions, but their wood is prized for axles of carts, gun-stocks and axe-handles. But of all, the most valuable are *Pynkadoe* and *Padouk* (Pterocarpus dalbergioides) the former not rarely attains a girth of 10'. When it is used, it is generally felled and sawn up green, and the planks and scantlings thus obtained neither warp nor rend while seasoning. It is one of the most widely spread trees in the province, and is frequently the prevailing tree in the forest.

Padouk is rather scarce in Pegu west of the Sitang river, but abundant in the Teak localities on its eastern feeders as well as in the Salween, Thoungyeen, and Attaran forests. In some parts the prevailing trees in the forest are Padouk and Teak. Thus in the lower portion of the Kaymapjoo forest on the upper Salween, there were found on an area of 0.36 square miles.

Teak trees in girth above 3 cubits, ... 147
Padouk trees, ... 317

A number of Terminalias occur, the wood of which would be valuable if it were more durable. It is, however, used for planking: *Pangah* (Terminalia chebula), *Tessein* (T. bellerica,) and *Leinben* (Terminalia cialata): There are two kinds of *Toukkyan* (Pentaptera macrocarpa, Wall. and glabra ?) belonging to the same family ; and with wood of similar description. *Myoukshaw* (Blackwellia tomentosa) is a constant companion of Teak, the white perfectly smooth bark, which renders the trees inaccessible for monkeys even, distinguishes this tree from all others. Europeans call it the lance-wood, Burmese make of it the teeth of their harrows. Of Lagerstrœmias several species occur in this forest: Duabanga grandiflora has been mentioned above. *Pymnah* also occurs abundantly throughout the lower parts of this region. *Laizah* (Lagerstrœmia pubescens, Wall. ?) is a gigantic tree often attaining a girth of 15'. The wood of this kind deserves to be tested. *Pymmahben* (Lagerstrœmia cuspidata, Wall.) is frequent in the forests east of the Sittang river. It is the tallest of the Lagerstrœmias and some-times attains a large girth (17 feet, Kyoukett Forests, Thoungyeen) ; but the stems are generally fluted like those of Pterospermum semi-sagittatum. Several Naucleas are found in this forest, but they are of little value as timber trees, the largest of them is the *Nhauben* (Nauclea cordifolia) the wood of which is made into combs. Others are *Maou-lettaushi* (N. cadamba), *Bingah, Theinben, Koosan,* etc. Several Bigno-nias likewise occur in this region, particularly in the lower part of it.

Pacthan (Spathodea stipulata) and *Kyoung donk* (Calosanthes indicus) are used for bows and dah handles ; and of *Thakooma* (Spathodea rheedii) the large white flowers are eaten, and the wood is used for yokes and cart-poles.

A species of Cordia (probably new) *Kalametban* is remarkable on account of its beautiful and very fragrant wood, which may one day become an important article of export for furniture. This tree occurs with Teak throughout the country; but unfortunately it is not very abundant, and does not generally attain a larger girth than 4'.

The family of Verbenaceæ to which Teak belongs, has three valuable species in this region : *Kyoonalin* or *Kyoonboe* (Premna pyrami-data, Wall.) with strong durable wood, but of small size (girth about 4') ; *Tansha* (Vitex leucoxylon ; girth 7') and *Yemench* (Gmelina arborea,) girth 12'. The wood of the two latter is used for cart-wheels.

A kind of elm also occurs here, (Ulmus integrifolia) (*Myoukseik*) the wood valuable for house-posts.

12. It remains now to mention those bamboos which most
frequently occur in this part of the
forests.

Bamboos of the dry forests.

They are often so prevalent that the forest might with more propriety be called a bamboo jungle; Teak and other trees occurring only here and there scattered among the bamboos.

The bamboos of Burmah have not yet been sufficiently examined to be identified with the species established by other authors.

There is a great variety of bamboos here (probably from 15 to 20 distinct species) according to their size, they may be brought under four great classes.

Of the first class *Kyathounwah* (Bambusa arundinacea ?) is a characteristic bamboo of the upper mixed forests: it is particularly abundant on the sandstone ridges of the Pegu Yomah, and more scarce in the Tenasserim and Martaban provinces. The stems attain a girth of 12 to 24 inches, with comparatively large cavities and a height of from 60 to 80 feet. It is one of the most elegant bamboos of this country, and very useful for house building, although the stems do not equal in strength those of the thorny bamboos of the plains. In numerous Karen villages, the roofs are made of this bamboo, the stems being split in two halves longitudinally, and laid down so that one always overlaps the edges of two, like tiles.

Of the second class three kinds occur in this region: *Wayah* in the Thoungyeen and Attaran; *Taragoo* in the hills of the Pegu Yomah; *Tabendein Wah*, so-called because it does not form dense clusters like the others, but the stems come up singly. This last kind is abundant in the Attaran: it appears to occur frequently wherever there are limestone rocks near. This kind is prized for fine network, baskets, &c. This kind is called *Karanwah* in some places.

The third class contains five species, which all occur with or without Teak in the upper mixed forest.

Of these *Minwah* (Bambusa stricta, Roxb.) is the most extensively spread. A large portion of the Teak in the southern and Tharrawaddie Forests of Pegu occurs in the *Minwah* jungle. This is one of those which entirely shed their leaves in the dry season, so that, on those wide dry tracts of hills, the traveller is left without any protection from the sun whatever.

Similar in this respect is the *Wapzoogyee*, a different species, which takes the place of *Miuwah* in the Tenasserim provinces : its stems are frequently striped green and white.

Wherever there is low ground between the dry hills near the banks of streams or of water-courses that are dry in the N. E. Monsoon, two other kinds occur, *Tinwa* and *Theiwa* : the former is excellent for mats and both are valuable for house-building.

A bamboo of isolated occurrence in the Teak localities of these provinces is the Royal or umbrella-handle bamboos *(Tiwa)*, said to be abundant east of the Salween, but on the west side occurring on a small district only from the Maytharauk to the Kareenee country. This bamboo is cut and brought down in large quantities for the making of sticks and umbrella handles. Its strength combined with lightness and the regularity of its joints renders it particularly elegant and valuable.

There is a saying, but probably not correct, that under the Burmese rule, only members of the Royal family were permitted to use walking-sticks of this bamboo.

The fourth class contains the climbing and diffusely growing bamboos ; one of them occurs in the upper mixed forests.

Wapzoogelay covers extensive tracts on the dry hills in the Thoungyeen, in Pegu, and in other parts of these provinces. It sheds its leaves, and as its stems do not stand erect, but spread in low arches over the ground, it serves much to increase the violence of the jungle fires. Teak forests therefore, in a jungle of this bamboo are much exposed to severe injury from fires. The number of seedlings is consequently diminished and the destruction of dry seasoned timber very considerable.

13. Teak localities in the upper mixed forests may be divided into the following groups.

First Group.—On even alluvial soil, occasionally under water for a few days in the rains. *Trees and bamboos*, great variety. *Pynkadoe* and *Toukkyan* not prevailing ; *Pymmah* frequent ; bamboos few. *Herbaceous plants*, species of Musa, Curcuma, Zingiber, Globba, *Natcho*, (Baliospermum indicum). More or less shade in the dry season. Jungle fires not regular, and not very dangerous. *Seedlings* abundant. *Stems* of large trees tall and regular. This class of forests is frequent when Teak is found in moist valleys in the neighbourhood of the higher hills : for instance in the Beeling (Martaban), Padah, Moung, Youkthawah forests.

Second Group.—On low undulating hills with good soil. *Trees and bamboos : Pynkadoe, Pymmah, Padouk:* few clusters of *Tinwa* and *Teiwa. Herbaceous plants :* the Teak grass (Pollinia, sp.) covers the ground in the rains with a dense soft mass, often 6′ high. After January this dries up and subsides into a dense mass of dry highly inflammable matter. Some shade in the dry season ; jungle fires regular and destructive. Seedlings less numerous than in first group. Stems of large trees generally tall and regular, unless the locality is otherwise unfavourable, or Toungya cutting has injured the forest. To this class belong the Winyeo forests (Attaran F. D. B. Nos. 1-5), the Mittigate Forest below the Kyouktago (27, 30), a part of the Kyoan Choung Forests, and others.

Third Group.—On arid hills with poor soil, bamboos mostly deciduous. *Trees and bamboos :* Toukkyan, Pynkadoe, Grubin, Sterculias, &c. *Minwa* (on the Salween *Tiwa*) with *Tinwa* and *Tiewa* in moist places, or *Wapzoogyee* (lower Salween), *Yoonzabeen,* or *Wapzoogelay.*

No shade in the dry season. *Jungle fires* regular, but not very destructive. *Seedlings* numerous, but generally burnt down to the ground once or twice before they make a start strong enough to enable them to resist the effects of the fire.

The dry *Minwa* forests on arid hills form a wide belt at the foot of the Pegu Yomah in the Southern Tharrawaddie and Prome divisions.

In some districts *Wapzoogelay* is the prevailing bamboo. Where this occurs, few seedlings only spring up, on account of the density of the jungle and the jungle fires which find ample nourishment in the interwoven masses covering the ground. Of this class are many of the lower Thoungyeen forests, as also some of the Kyoon Choung forests (Nos. 15 and 16), and many others.

Fourth Group.—On higher ridges of the hills with good soil ; bamboos mostly evergreen. *Trees and bamboos : Pynkadoe, Myoukshaw, Kyathaunwa, Tabendein* and *Wayah.* Moderate shade in the dry season. *Jungle fires* not destructive. *Seedlings* numerous. *Stature* of trees excellent.

This class of forest is scarce in the Attaran districts. Nos. 9 and 10, Megwa and Tabew belong to it. It is, however, frequent in the central Pegu Forests. Some of the best of the Tharrawaddie and Southern Forests belong to it.

To this, if we attempt a classification of the Teak forests according to the trees with which Teak is associated, the following must be added :—

Fifth Group.—Teak in Ein forest.

Sixth Group.—Teak in evergreen forest, and a *further group* might be added, comprising Teak when it occurs in deserted Toungyas. Toungya cultivation certainly changes most remarkably the character of the forest, but this change is, in most instances, only a temporary one, the forest gradually returning to its original description.

14. The Ein or Dipterocarpus forest is a forest of very peculiar character composed of the same trees whenever it occurs.

Ein Forests.

Its principal constituent is Dipterocarpus grandiflora, Wall. the *Ein ben.* With this occur, but in smaller number, other species of the same family : *Theizah* (Shorea obtusa, Wall.) and *Eingyin* (Hopea suava, Wall.) The Bengal saul (Shorea robusta), hitherto supposed to occur abundantly in these provinces, has not yet been identified.

The wood of Ein is good for planks, if sheltered from the rains, but if exposed, decays rapidly. The two others, however, although belonging to the same natural family, yield hard and durable timber. Of other families the forest contains several Dillenia (*Byooben*), several Eugenias (*Tabjahben*), a small species of Lagerstroemia with large flowers (*Koonpymmah*), a number of Gardenias, the wood of which is used for carving, Holarrhena pubescens (*Lettankben*), with soft wood used for the soles of sandals, *Ananben* (Fagraea, sp.) valued on account of the durability of its timber ; also a species of Oak (Quercus semiserrata), (*Thitcha*), and a valuable fruit tree (Pierardia sapida), or *Kanazoeben*. Strychnus Nux Vomica, *Khaboungben*, occurs both in this and in the last named forest.

Two of the most valuable trees of the province are frequently found in the Ein forest, the Varnish tree (Melanorrhoea usitatissima) (*Thetsee*), and the Catechu tree, *Sha*, (Acacia catechu). A species of pine also is found in the Ein forest of the Thoungyeen valley (Pinus massoniana, Lawb. or P. Lattevi, Masson).

Ein forest occurs exclusively on dry gravelly soil, and although the ground is covered with an abundance of seedlings, yet the trees stand far apart and the forest remains open. This is a remarkable fact indicating a barren soil, in which a small proportion of the seedlings only come to perfection, and a remarkable light-seeking tendency in the tree, which does not permit trees to grow up except very far apart.

8

In Europe a scale has been established of the different forest trees with reference to the amount of light required for their healthy development. In Burmah the trees of the evergreen forest stand lowest on this scale, as their seedlings spring up in the densest shade, the Teak tree maintains a kind of medium position, and the Dipterocarpus grandiflora stands at the top of the scale.

As a rule, Teak does not occur in the Ein forest, and when it does, isolated trees are scattered here and there, or it is on the outskirts of the forest only, in the neighbourhood of Teak-containing localities. Very frequently Ein forests alternate with Teak localities, the former occupying gravelly hills and the latter covering the alluvial soil around them. One of the numerous instances of this kind is well described by the late Captain Latter in his report on the Thoungyeen forests.* But it is worthy of record, that to the north in the Prome district, Teak is found more frequently associated with Ein, than in the southern part of the country.

Dense Evergreen Forests.   15. The last class is the *dense evergeeen forests.*

The principal characteristic of this forest is : that jungle fires do not enter it, it is in most cases the original forest of the country, in which all trees attain their greatest size. In many places, for instance in the Thoungyeen, the average height of the tops of trees is between 150′ and 200′ from the ground, so that the ground is clothed with an unbroken stratum of vegetation of that depth.

There is a great variety of trees in this forest and many of them are not sufficiently known. Even Burmans have names only for a few of them. Anonaceæ are numerous ; a species of Cyathocalyx (*Boukthoe*, Burman, *Zacquatto*, Karen) bears an eatable fruit, the orange-coloured rind encloses a gelatinous pulp between the large seeds. Another is Guatteria nitida with elegant bunches of orange-coloured fruit. Several species of Myristica, a Sterculia, fruit with wings bent like the keel of a boat, Scaphium Wallicha, occur, together with a number of species of the Dipterocarpus family, mostly attaining a gigantic height, Hopea odorata or *Thingan*, the tree most used for canoes, *Thinkadoe, Kaumhoo*, used for the same purpose, and probably belonging to the same family. Several Garcinias occur here, and a Nephelium with a fruit not unlike the Letchee.

* Printed Report on the Forests of the Tenasserim Provinces, page 155.

Albizzia odoratissima (*Thitmagzyee*) and Cassia Roxburghii are some of the Leguminous trees found in this forest.

Several species of oak and chestnut are also among these evergreens: Quercus Amherstiana, Wall. (*Thitcha*), Quercus lappacea, Wall., Castanea feros, *Kyantza*, also a species of Antiaris (*Myahseik ben*), the juice of which is used by the Karens to poison arrows, but the poison does not seem to be equal in its pernicious effects to that of the Javanese, Antiaris toxicaria. This is one of the largest trees in these provinces. One which I measured in the Thoungyeen, had a girth of 38 feet and a height of 250 feet.

Another large tree is the Artocarpus mollis (*Tounbein*), the timber used for canoes. Most of the rattans are found in this forest, of which Calamus latifolius, Roxb. (*Yaematta Kyein,*) is the most valuable kind for the rafting of timbers. The long flexible stems of this palm, often 200 feet long are as strong as the best rope, and an indispensable article for timber rafts. Other palms also form a part of the evergreen forest, the (*Mimboben*), Caryota urens, *Theinben*, (Calamus erectus), *Zanoongben* (Wallichia caryotoides) and *Zalooben*, Licuala peltata and spinosa. Here also is found the wild betel palm, a species of areca with small oblong-shaped seeds, which, however, are applied to the same use as the cultivated betel nut.

A great ornament of this forest is an arborescent fern (Alsophila), the stem of which attains a height of 20 feet.

Of bamboos the most common is *Wanöe*, a creeping species with very large leaves. Wherever the slopes of the hills are too steep to admit of large trees, this bamboo covers the rock and forms an impenetrable jungle. Of the largest kind there are two, *Wanet* and *Kyellowah*, with stems often exceeding 120' in heighth and 2' in girth. It is very likely that one of them is the mother plant of the cultivated large bamboo (*Wahlo*) (Bambusa gigantea). These bamboos, however, do not generally occur intermixed with the trees of the evergreen forest, but separate on rocks, or steep slopes.

Teak has been found only in a few instances in this kind of forest, and wherever this is the case, there is every reason to believe that the locality was originally covered with forest of a different character. The Teak trees in the evergreen forest attain a gigantic heighth, being obliged to draw themselves up towards the light between their fast growing companions. But seedlings are wanting, the dense shade does not favour the springing up of young Teak, although it does not impede the growth of the trees properly at home in the dense shady forest.

16. The different classes of forests here described rise to an

Climate of Forest found at an elevation of beyond 3000'.

elevation of 3000', which is the upper limit of Teak, beyond this the vegetation assumes a different character. On dry soil a belt of pine forest (Pinus khassyana, Royle), with Gordonia and Vaccinium, takes the place of the Ein forest of the plains and on rich soil, an evergreen forest clothes the mountain sides with trees altogether different from those of the evergreen forest of the plains.

Lower Winyeo Forests.

17. I now proceed to detail the results of my own examination of the forests on the Attaran.

I left Maulmain by boat on the morning of the 21st July, reached the junction of the rivers Zimmay and Winyeo on the 23rd, and the landing-place of Croonkamoon village on the Winyeo on the evening of the 24th.

No. of trees on the square mile,	
First Class, ...	528
Second ditto, ...	1142
Third ditto, ...	1667
Fourth ditto, ...	1159
Nathat, ...	112
Girdled, ...	122
Logs, ...	42
Stumps, ...	219

From this place I commenced the examination of the forests. On the 26th explored those marked Nos. 5 and 6 on Mr. Hobday's map and known as Dooncan's and Shoedoung's forests.

The 25th was devoted to the survey of Shore Yalis forest (No. 7,) and in the evening I reached the village of Llootshan, situated on one of the feeders of the Pabyah Choung, at the foot of the great mountain range which separates the Attaran valley from the sea shore. Ceaseless torrents of rain, which, with few interruptions, during the whole of our tour rendered every path a stream and every small mountain brook a torrent, and which put the possibility of gaining a view from any elevated point out of the question, frustrated my plan of ascending this mountain range, so as to see with my own eyes what the Karens told me could be seen ; viz. the Teak forests of the Winyeo to the east and the sea to the west of the mountain range.

On the 27th explored a forest on a south tributary of the Pabyah Choung, which is not enumerated in Mr. Hobday's list of forests, and which the Karens say is known only to themselves and a few foresters.

Night overtook us, and we encamped in pelting rain under an over-hanging limestome rock of the Kyouktaga hills.

The forests below this (Nos. 1 to 15,) may be classed as a separate group (the lower Winyeo forests). According to Mr. Hobday's statement, the area of these forests amounts to 18.25 square miles.

The lower part of the valley of the Winyeo is a wide plain with slight undulations, but with numerous isolated masses of grey limestone rock, often several miles long and rising abruptly to a height of several hundred feet.

The ground in the neighbourhood of these rocks is generally covered with dense evergreen forest.

The same kind of forest is also found near the foot of the great mountain ranges to the west between the limestone rocks, wide tracts of undulating ground with dry gravelly soil extend, covered with *Ein* (Dipterocarpus grandiflora, Wall.).

The Burmese saul (*Eingyin*) invariably a companion of the *Einben* in other parts, is scarce in the Attaran valley, but the *Ananben* (Fagræa, sp.) occurs in its stead.

Teak is here neither in the Ein nor in the evergreen forest, it is only found in the mixed forest which principally consists of *Pymmah* (Lagerstrœmia reginæ and cuspidata, Wall.), *Kyoonboe* (Premna pyra-midata, Wall.), *Zimbjoon* (Dillenia aurea), *Bambouay* (Careya arborea) and *Pynkadoe* (Inga xylocarpa).

Padouk trees of large size, up to 15′ in girth, occur occasionally in this forest. I met with a number of logs of large girth cut, but which had been left lying in the forest, as after cutting they were found too heavy for removal.

In the heart of this forest and frequently near the Teak localities, huge old jack trees are found, up to 12′ in girth, some still bearing fruit; these are thought to be the remains of the old Taline villages which studded this country, before their inhabitants were driven away during the Siamese wars.

This mixed forest which changes its character according to soil and locality, occupies the greater portion of the area of the lower part of the Winyeo valley, interrupted only here and there by clearings for Toungya cultivation or by paddy-fields in the country below Croon-kamoon Choung.

It is here that the Teak-producing localities occur, always in the plains, and in most cases skirting the banks of the Winyeo or its tributaries, but always on high ground not exposed to the annual floods of the river. This must, however, not be understood to mean that Teak never occurs on ground exposed to inundation : there are excellent Teak forests in different parts of the provinces where the water stands almost annually several feet deep, and similar localities may not be wanting on the Attaran, although I have not met with them.

On the western range of mountains, Teak is not found, not even on the spurs and hills running out from the same.

The natives took particular care to assure me, that the Teak localities were not near the hills, but near the river, and indeed our march from the Croonkamoon Choung to Majitto viâ Llootshan, on which we were obliged to keep close to the hills, as the different streams were too swollen with the rain to allow of our crossing them, lower down, tended to confirm their statement, for we met with only one Teak forest on the whole way.

The proportion of trees observed here shews that the forests, as a whole, belong to class C, and are remarkable for the small number of first and fourth class trees. The soil does not appear very favorable for the springing up of small trees, and the large proportion of stumps sufficiently explains the fewness of large trees.

The growth of the trees in these tracts is very inferior. Out of the whole of the two first classes (1229 trees above 3 cubits in girth), only 28 trees were found of fine and straight growth, the remainder were all either forked, or branched, or crooked.

Many of the large trees remaining are attacked with creepers or epiphytic ficus, but this is not sufficient to account for their inferior value, there is something in the situation or soil of the forests in the lower part of the Winyeo valley which prevents their attaining the tall regular and clean stems found in the other Attaran forests. Teak does not as a rule produce fine and long timber in the neighbourhood of the sea, and it is not impossible that it is this circumstance which shews its effect in this way. The soil is the same, to all appearance, as that in other localities producing excellent timber. These forests therefore are not likely to be important for the supply of fine and straight timber fit to be converted into squares for export, but rather as yielding crooked pieces for ship building.

The size which the trees have attained, though deformed in

stature, is very considerable. Four trees in the Pabyah forest had girths of 10′, 15′, 19′, 21′ and three other trees, forming one single stem, had a joint girth of 24′.

Few of the lower Winyeo forests are at present actively worked, indeed I could not ascertain that timber was brought away from any of them. The original Lethmats of six out of the fifteen are said to have been cancelled about six years ago.

18. On the 29th, went on to the lower Majitto village, and after crossing the Winyeo on the 30th, examined the forests which extend along the upper course of that river, reached the Thinganneennoung Teak plantation on the same day, and remained there till the 4th August; engaged in examining the country about.

Upper Winyeo Forests.

Number of trees on the square mile.

First Class, ...	621
Second ditto, ...	564
Third ditto,..............	640
Fourth ditto, ...	463
Nathat,..................	42
Girdled, ...	112
Logs, ...	121
Stumps, ...	647

The Teak localities above the mouth of the Majitto Choung, form what are here designated the Upper Winyeo Forests. The country is more hilly, the hills dividing the Zimmay and Winyeo valleys, approaching the river on the east and the outrunners of the coast range on the west. Dense evergreen forest in the plains, and dense bamboo jungle on the hills, with occasional tracts of open mixed forest form the main features of the forest in this region. Teak is found alike in these three classes of forests on both sides of the Winyeo and its main tributary the Thinganneennoung to a considerable distance towards their source.

It is abundant on the groups of hills on the left side of the Winyeo near the junction, and large numbers of second and third class trees of very fine growth occur in the evergreen forest, which clothes the slopes of the laterite hills between both streams about five miles above the junction. In this locality, the trees of the evergreen forest itself, are not larger than the Teak associated with them : they are apparently of the same age.

The number of trees observed is noted on the margin. As a whole, the forests belong to class B., with a deficiency in small trees and a very large proportion of stumps. On examining the data of the forest day-book, it will be found, that in those localities where Teak occurs in the dense evergreen forest, and where consequently there is not sufficient light for young Teak to spring up, seedlings are almost entirely wanting (see No. 8 *a.* and *b.*).

The growth of Teak in this part of the forest is very good, almost the whole of the large trees having straight tall stems, free from branches to a considerable heighth. But it does not follow that all large trees remaining are valuable, for the greater number are hollow or attacked with epiphytic ficus, or injured in their growth by a load of creepers, or from other causes unfit for the market.

It may be said that with few exceptions all good trees above five cubits in girth, and most of those above four cubits have been removed, numerous stumps indicating their former existence, and the numerous logs once good, but now half-destroyed by fire, remaining as a proof of the wasteful mode of working.

The greater part of the upper Winyeo forests belong to those which in the list are shewn as Mrs. Wales' forests, and which are now in the hands of Mr. Rushbrook. They are designated as No. 16.

Besides these there is No. 17, the reserved Government forest of Thinganneennoung.

This forest was reserved in 1841, by the then Commissioner, Mr. Blundell, on the report of Captain O'Brien.

It does not appear that the boundaries of this reserved tract were ever determined; but it is quite apparent, that the tract has never been reserved at all, except on paper. For the same traces of the same wasteful working are found within the boundaries of the surveyed forest as well as beyond them. Captain O'Brien (in 1841) found many of the finest possible trees in this tract, out of which about 500 had lately been killed (see extract from Captain O'Brien's journal, Appendix No. 4.) But Dr. Falconer and before him Mr. O'Riley in 1848, found little timber left worth felling or removing, and my observations entirely confirm their statements.

It is here that, on Dr. Falconer's suggestion, an extensive Teak nursery was established by the late Mr. Smith under the direction of the late Conservator of Forests, Mr. E. Gemmer, and by the orders of the then Commissioner, Sir A. Bogle.

As the question whether the Attaran Forests may advantageously be renewed by planting, has been named as one of the points to be discussed in this report, the history of the different plantations of the Tenasserim Provinces, with remarks on their success, has been given in a separate Chapter of this Report.

19. On the 5th August, I left Thinganneenoung and crossed over to the head waters of the Megwa.

Megwa and neighbouring Forests.

Number of trees on the square mile.

First Class, ...	642
Second ditto, ...	962
Third ditto,..	1047
Fourth ditto, ...	2256
Nathat,...........................	132
Girdled, ...	497
Logs,.............................	460
Stumps, ...	1582
Attacked with Ficus, ...	55

The line of hills which here forms the watershed between Zimmay and Winyeo is low, but higher ranges are to the east of it, the drainage from which runs into the numerous tributaries of the Megwa, which river winds through a narrow gorge between two of these ranges. This circumstance has given rise to a remarkable dispute between the holders of the forests on both sides. The holder of forest No. 16, on the Winyeo, assumed the right of felling timber on the head waters of the Megwa, and attempted to establish his right by dragging a number of logs across to the Winyeo. Some of these are still in situ, where they had been abandoned half way between the two rivers. Near our path we counted seven, five doogies, and a number of other logs.

The case was brought before the Civil Courts of Maulmain, who took the correct view of the matter, determining that the hills which form the watershed between both rivers, should also be considered as forming the boundary line between the Zimmay and Winyeo forests.

Teak on the Megwa is found in the mixed forest. Both on the slopes of the hills and in the valleys, its growth is very fine. The trees are tall with straight stems without branches. The number of large trees left standing is remarkably great, 1840 first class trees on the square mile.

In their general appearance, these forests are not unlike those on the spurs of the Yomah in the Tharrawaddie or Southern Forest division, with this difference only, that here Teak is found on a few only of the numerous mountain ridges, whereas in Pegu, nearly every ridge or spur is covered with Teak. (A description of the Megwa Forest in 1841, by Captain O'Brion, see in extract from Journal, No. 2).

The next day, 6th August, was devoted to the exploration of the forests on the east side of the same ranges, the west side of which we had examined the day before. This side of the hills is drained by the Tabew and Tseikgyee Choungs, the one a feeder of the Megwa, the other falling into the Zimmay river. Teak is found both along the banks of the Zimmay and higher up on the hills. The two localities are separated by a belt of Ein forest, which covers the first terrace of the hills.

9

The character of the higher forests is similar to that of the Megwa ; the lower portion, which stretches along the river, belongs to the second group on low undulated ground.

This has evidently been one of the finest Teak localities any where. We observed 500 first class trees on the square mile. But the forest is at present more remarkable on account of the large number of old Teak stumps and an abundance of young Teak trees. The stumps from four to ten feet high, stand close to each other, and are of immense girth. Many of them are very old. A Karen chief who accompanied me, stated that he had himself assisted in felling the first trees in this forest more than twenty years ago, and he pointed out some of the largest stumps as cut by his people at that time.

The upper surface of these stumps is not smooth, but indented by deep furrows, evidently formed by the rain, but no other signs of decay could be observed.

Indeed pieces of seasoned Teak in the forests, if they escape destruction by fire, appear to be almost imperishable, whereas stumps or logs of nearly all other kinds of trees leave no trace behind after a few years. No more striking proof could be given of the superiority of Teak over most other woods of the country, than the fact that the forests abound in Teak trees, dead or fallen, branches, stumps, &c. whereas the remains of other trees dead or blown down are very scarce, yet the average proportion of other trees to Teak in Teak-producing tracts is as 10 to 1, and all kinds are equally exposed to being blown down by the wind, or to death from natural causes.

Another peculiarity of this forest is the large number of young Teak trees forming 5-8ths of the total number of green trees observed, 493 were counted, and 1000 were probably standing on an area of only about 80 acres. This is explained by the open nature of the forest, there being little bamboo and not many large trees of other kinds. The natural reproduction of Teak is going on here as well as in any part of the forests of these provinces.

The average girth of most of the seedlings observed was 12″ and their height 30′, so that their age may be estimated at about seven years.

Perhaps there was, about 1851, a season with more dew and rain than usual, which checked the violence of the jungle fires and thus favoured the springing up of seedlings, or the timber-cutters did not set fire to the jungle as usual. There are numerous trees here of the third class, with a girth of from 18″ to 4′ 6″ and consequently from 10 to 37 years old. Many of them must have been seedlings when the forests were explored by former observers, from Captain O'Brien in 1841, to Dr. Falconer in 1848, so that the general impression, that young Teak was scarce in the Attaran Forests, can only have been produced by the circumstance, that all these surveys were made in the dry season, and that Teak seedlings without leaves and scorched by the jungle fires were overlooked.

In the Megwa, Tabew and Tseikgyee Forests, we met with parties engaged in cutting and dragging timber. The parties in the Megwa were employed by the holder of the upper Zimmay forests, No. 53, (Mrs. Darwood).

Those in the Tabew and Tseikgyee forest stated that they were working for the owners of the Natmo estate who hold possession of the Megwa, Tseikgyee, Kyoukpyah and Kyoon Choung forests.

At Tseikgyee 53 doogies had been dragged to the river's bank, ready to put into the water.

After crossing Zimmay, we examined the Kyoukpyah forest, which stretches along the river, to the neighbourhood of the Kyoon Choung. Teak is very scattered here. It is found both in the dry and evergreen forests on low hills, which cover the whole space between the mountain range east of the Zimmay and that river. Our survey gave only 266 first class trees on the square mile. From the hills on the left side of the river beyond the Tseikgyee forest, we had had a good view of a large part of this forest, and the Teak trees being just in blossom, we could distinguish them by their greyish colour. We counted 150 large trees on a space which could not be much less than one square mile. Such inspections of a forest from an elevated point in the neighbourhood are very instructive, as Teak may be known by an experienced eye almost at all times of the year. During the dry season it may be recognized by the large panicles of fruit which terminate the branches, giving them a peculiarly elegant appearance. When in flower, Teak, if seen from a distance, may be confounded with several other trees which blossom at the same time, Terminalia, sp. Pentaptera, sp.; but after some practice Teak is easily distinguished.

The forests of this group (Megwa, Tabew, Tseikgyee and Kyoukpyah) are like those in the Winyeo valley, deficient in the number of first class trees ; only the Megwa forest belongs to class B. ; the others are C. forests, the number of first class trees being smaller than that of the second.

The number of fourth class (small) trees is in a fair proportion, but the number of stumps is unusually large.

20. On Monday the 9th August, I proceeded towards the Kyoon Choung and upper Zimmay forests, while my assistant, Mr. James Barker, went to the Mittigate Codogway. The 9th, 10th and 11th August were devoted to the examination of these several tracts.

Kyoon Choung Forests.

Number of trees per square mile.
First Class, ... 936
Second ditto, ... 751
Third ditto,......... 1263
Fourth ditto, ... 809
Nathat,................ 133
Girdled, ... 479
Logs,.......................... 361
Stumps, ... 2017
Attacked with ficus, ... 378

The Kyoon Choung forests, have long been considered as the most valuable portion of the Attaran Forests;

and, certainly even in their present exhausted condition they afforded ample proof, that their value has not been overrated.

The Teak localities stretch along the Kyoon Choung and its tributaries from the banks of the Zimmay river up to the hills, and some patches of Teak have been found on the hills themselves.

Mr. Hobday in his statement, exhibiting the state of the Attaran Forests in 1851, estimated the area of the Kyoon Choung forests at eight square miles, and this estimate is probably correct.

The greater part of the forest is on slightly undulated almost level ground. It is very open, brushwood being scattered, and bamboos scarce there as well as in the Winyeo and Tseikgyee forests, the ground is covered with the high soft Teak grass (Pollinia, sp.), which drying up soon after the end of the rains, forms a dense mass of dry inflammable matter, and considerably increases the vehemence of the annual jungle fires. Only on the elevated ground between the Kyoon Choung and the Mittigate, Teak is found in a dense bamboo jungle.

The small proportion of fourth class trees (seedlings) is a remarkable feature in this forest. Their number (280) does not equal one-fourth of the whole number of green trees observed.

This is remarkable, as the Tseikgyee forest, similar in many respects to this, abounds in seedlings. Probably the jungle fires have been more destructive here. Dr. Falconer (page 21 of printed report) states that he did not observe any young seedlings in the Kyoon Choung, and continues as follows :—

"Their absence here was readily explicable from the great force of the annual conflagrations, of which we saw striking marks every where, in burnt strewn logs and charred stumps."

The very large number of stumps (2017,) on the square mile, is another characteristic of this forest, proving that its resources have not been worked sparingly. A large number of these stumps have brought forth offshoots, and many of these have attained a considerable size from 3´ to 5″ 9″ in girth. The existence of these offshoots proves that the trees were felled green, without having previously been killed. Teak is very prone to bringing forth these side-shoots, whenever the main stem is cut away, and on deserted Toungyas, trees are often observed with numerous side stems forming a circle round the old stumps.

But if the tree is left standing to season on the stock after girdling, no offshoots are produced. They thus afford in this instance an unmistakeable proof of a most improvident system of working, which although repeatedly reported upon by the officers deputed to examine the forests, has never effectively been checked, although it has brought a great deal of badly seasoned timber into Moulmain.

The proportion of first class trees is a fair one. On the elevated ground, in the less accessible parts of the forest, these trees are remarkable for the beauty and regularity of their

Concerning the practice of felling green Teak, see extracts from Captain O'Brien's journal, Nos. 3, 5, 6, 8 and 10.

growth. But in the main portion of the forest near the streams very few trees in girth above 6 feet are left standing. Those left are mostly deformed or hollow, loaded with creepers or attacked with epiphytic ficus, and contain no timber of any value. Out of 424 first class trees remaining, no less than 131 were found to be attacked with epiphytic ficus, which is at the rate of 378 per square mile.

Assuming that the Kyoon Choung Forests cover an area of 8 square miles and that the surveys made, give an adequate idea of its general character, they would at present contain—

First class trees, ...	7488	Or correcting the number
Second ditto,..............	5808	of small trees and
Third ditto, ...	10,104	stumps.
Fourth ditto,..............	6472	12,944
Stumps, ...	16,136	32,272

Captain O'Brien in 1841, estimates the number of trees fit to cut at from 10 to 12,000 (see extract from Journal No. 4,) and Mr. O'Riley in 1851, states, that he considers the number of trees in girth between 3 and 12 cubits to be between 9 and 10,000. These estimates agree well with the results of my observations, if it be borne in mind that between 1841 and 1851, a considerable portion of the trees fit to be felled were cut down faster than the young trees could come up to the size of those removed, and that since 1851 the forest has been worked but little. Mr. Hobday's statement (1851,) estimates the number of full-sized standing trees at 1400 only, which certainly is very far out.

The Kyoon Choung forests, with a part of those on the Megwa, Tseikgyee and Kyoukpya, belong to the Natmo estate. These forests were first in the hands of Captain Warwick, then of Messrs. Cockerell and Co. and afterwards of Lady Eglinton.

During the dry season of 1851, Mr. O'Riley undertook their examination, on behalf of the administrators of Lady Eglinton's estate, and it is very much to be regretted that his report, dated 5th May, 1851, which contains many excellent observations, has never been published. I have only once had an opportunity of perusing it, and have extracted from it the estimate mentioned above.

In Mr. Hobday's statement, dated 29th May, 1851, Messrs. Mackey and Company appear as the holders: at present the forest is in the hands of Mr. W. Wallace.

21. The upper Zimmay Forests are much poorer than those along the Kyoon Choung. Teak occurs only in scattered patches here and there, over large extents of evergreen and other forests. I only examined that portion which is situated on the east side of the Zimmay river. That on the west side is known as the Mayzelee Forest, but both portions are said to have very much the same character. Towards the south, I went as far as the Methabuee Choung. There are a few Teak localities beyond (near the Megathat) but they are said to be of very limited extent. Teak thus decreases and at last disappears here, as it does on the Winyeo, as we approach the head waters of these streams.

Upper Zimmay Forests.

Number of trees on the square mile.

First Class,	389
Second ditto,	751
Third ditto,	973
Fourth ditto,	292
Nathat,	88
Girdled,	70
Logs,	35
Stumps,	522
Attacked with ficus,	35

It is very different in the central Pegu Forests, on the hills between the Irrawaddie and Sitang rivers. Here Teak increases as you approach the sources of the streams. But then we have in that part of Pegu to deal with hills of a widely different character. They do not on an average exceed an elevation of 2000 feet, and are consequently dry and well adapted for Teak. In the whole of the country east of the Sitang river, all larger streams take their rise from mountain ranges considerably exceeding 3000 feet. Here the vegetation is a different one, the dense shady evergreen forest which in Pegu only here and there crowns the crests of the higher ridges, or clothes the slopes facing the north, or thrives in deep and moist valleys, occupies in the Tenasserim and Martaban provinces, a vast area covering nearly the whole of the mountains, and extending far into the plains, limiting the occurrence of Teak to isolated localities of no considerable extent.

As a rule it may be assumed, that in those regions, where the greater part of the streams and streamlets have running water throughout the year, Teak will only be found near the lower portion of the course of these streams and not higher up near their sources.

The upper Zimmay Forests are very poor in fourth class or small trees, they only form 121 per mile, or not quite one-eighth of the green trees observed.

The number of first class trees is also small. The most numerous are the trees of the second and third class of from 10 to 62 years of age. There are many tracts in these forests containing almost exclusively trees apparently from 30 to 40 years old, which would indicate that the years preceding 1828, when the working of the forests commenced, were particularly favorable for the springing up of Teak seedlings.

The Upper Zimmay Forests are at present in the hands of Mrs. Darwood. In Captain O'Brien's Journal (1841), they appear as Mr. Darwood's forests (see extract from Journal No. 3).

22. The forests along the Mittigate Codogway and its tributaries are most remarkable. Either because the trees stand at some distance from the stream, or for other reasons, comparatively little timber appears to have

Mittigate Codogway Forests.
Number of trees on the square mile.
First Class,..................... 989
Second ditto,................ 1887

Third ditto, ...	1295
Fourth ditto, ...	235
Nathat, ...	487
Girdled, ...	4825
Logs, ...	923
Stumps, ...	148
Attacked with ficus, ...	256

been removed from this tract. But the trees remaining are not green. They have been killed in a wholesale manner, about 15 years ago and many of them have since fallen, or been destroyed by fire. The traveller does not here, as in the other Attaran forests, wander through a field of stumps, but he finds himself in the midst of a forest of dead fallen trees.

The number of living trees observed of the different classes was 860, and that of stumps only 29, but there were counted on the tract 1121 dead trees standing or fallen, not including the 95 Nathat trees, that had died from natural causes.

These tracts were visited by Captain O'Brien in 1841. He describes a locality near the upper course of the Codogway about two miles long with several thousand trees from 3 feet 6 inches to 6 feet in circumference and states that this locality had never been visited or worked (extract from journal No. 7).

It would appear that in 1849, the Mitigate Codogway Forests together with the Mitigate proper were made over as a grant to Mr. Donald Campbell Mackey for the period of 99 years, on the condition, that all timber from the Mitigate Codogway should pay in the proportion of 25 to 15 upon the general rate of duty levied on Attaran timber. A memo. of grant dated 22nd January, 1849, is attached hereto (Appendix No. 6,), but I must add that I have not been able to obtain any information as to whether the grant was actually made in this form or not. However, from para. 126, of the Selections from the Records of the Bengal Government, No. IX. on the Teak forests of the Tenasserim Provinces, it is clear that the firm of Messrs. Mackey and Company were allowed to hold the Mitigate Codogway under a temporary license.

It is evident that at the time the trees described above were killed, it was intended to remove them, and it is difficult to say why the grantees or holders should so entirely have neglected them. One object of the license or grant, viz. to ensure an effectual working of the forest, has certainly not been attained, and the grantees appear to have placed a very low value upon their right.

The remaining forest groups that were examined are the Mitigate proper or lower Mitigate, the Mitigate Kyouktaga, and the Zimmay Forests below the mouth of the Mitigate. They were surveyed from the 12th to 16th August. The forests of the Mitigate proper cover a considerable extent of country : their area is estimated by Mr. Hobday at twelve square miles. They extend from the mouth

Lower Mitigate Forests.

Number of trees on the square mile.

First Class,	282
Second ditto,	101
Third ditto,	92
Fourth ditto,	803
Nathat,	52
Girdled,	288
Logs,	249
Stumps,	1096
Attacked with ficus,	215

of the Mitigate to within 4 or 5 miles from a range of hills running from N. N. W. to S. S. E.

The space between the Teak localities and the foot of these hills is covered with dense shady evergreen forest. The hills themselves are clothed with forest of the same character, but where the rock is near the surface, and the slopes are consequently arid, the dry and open Ein forest composed of Dipterocarpus, Quercus, Castanea and Gordonia takes its place. Teak is wanting on these hills. Here is one of the habitats of what the natives call the wild toddy palm, an elegant palm with fan-shaped leaves, which here and there occurs on the hills, both in Pegu and in the Tenasserim Provinces.

From the summit of this range a fine view of the whole valley of the Zimmay river is obtained, reaching to the south as far as the Kyoon Choung, and as far as the Maou Choung to the north.

The general appearance of this valley, which here has a width of from ten to twelve miles, is that of an immense unbroken forest with isolated patches of Teak, principally along the streams, and here and there extensive tracts of Toungya clearings.

On the west side it is bounded by a range of low hills, dividing the Zimmay and Winyeo rivers, and gradually merging into the plains to the north. Beyond this range are seen the dark and rugged masses of limestone rocks which dot the valley of the Winyeo from near its junction with the Zimmay to the mouth of the Thinganneenoung Choung. Behind these rise the outlines of the coast range, which intervenes between the valley of the Winyeo and the sea-shore. To the east of the line of hills from which the view just described is obtained, stretches another valley running parallel to that of the Zimmay, but only about three miles wide.

10

This valley is drained by the sources of the Mitigate stream, which finds its way through a deep gorge called the Kyouktaga, or gate of rock.

In the bottom of this valley some Teak occurs, generally known as the Mitigate Kyouktaga forests.

The lower Mitigate forests are remarkably poor in first class trees, only 282 on the square mile. The number of stumps found (1096 per square mile) shews that although rich, they were never equal in intrinsic value to the Kyoon Choung or Mitigate Codogway forests. The ravages of the Toungya cultivators have added much to the injury done by the wood-cutters. The road from Meekouk village to the mouth of the Mitigate, leads almost without interruption through Toungyas, some of them under cultivation at the time of our visit, some had been deserted lately and others long ago. On these, numerous trees are more or less injured by fire, and whatever seasoned timber was observed, either lying on the ground or standing (girdled or Nathat) was all half burnt.

24. The upper Mitigate or Kyouktaga forest, is one of those remarkable localities where Teak occurs in the dense shade of an evergreen forest, similar to several localities near the mouth of the Thinganneenoung stream (designated as the sixth group). Such company has a two-fold effect on the Teak in the forest. First the trees attain an immense height and a straight growth; being drawn up by being hedged in by numerous fast growing companions, and at the same time being fed abundantly by the constantly increasing fertility of the soil. For there is a vast difference between the moist and loose black soil of the shady evergreen forest, which is enriched year after year by the products of the gradual decomposition of leaves, branches and other debris of the forest, and the barren soil of the dry forests, where the whole of the leaves and branches falling from the trees are annually consumed by the jungle fires, and the ashes instead of affording nourishment to the trees are washed away by the first rush of the rain.

Mitigate Kyouktaga Forests.

Number of trees on the square mile.

First Class,	318
Second ditto,	14
Third ditto,	0
Fourth ditto,	0
Nathat,	1562
Girdled,	88
Logs,	562
Stumps,	155
Attacked with ficus,	318

Absence of seedlings is another characteristic mark of this class of forests. Light, and free circulation of air, two conditions indispensable for the development of Teak seedlings, are wanting. It is clear that, under these circumstances, forests of this description, although they may contain valuable timber, can have no permanent value, the facility of reproduction being altogether excluded. These forests are, so to say, in the last stages of their existence, the remains of a forest of different character, which, at one time, afforded facilities for their growing up, but which has since been replaced by trees of a different character.

It is interesting to compare the description which different observers at different times have given of this forest. Both Captain O'Brien in 1841, and Dr. Falconer in 1849, agree in considering this as the finest Teak forest on the Attaran river, both as regards number and size of the trees, and the abundance of fine timber on the ground (see extract from Journal No. 9, and Dr. Falconer's report, para. 55.)

It is evident that since Dr. Falconer visited it many of the green trees must have died and fallen, for although every locality containing Teak above the Kyouktaga was carefully examined, and probably more than one-fifth of the whole of the Teak trees met with, the number counted amount only to 43 and every one of these was attacked with the epiphytic ficus. Like the Thinganneenoung, this has nominally been a reserved forest, but has not been spared from the ravages of the axe.

At present its value consists only in the seasoned timber it contains, which may be estimated at 1500 trees at the outside.

25. It remains now to describe those of the lower Zimmay forests which I had an opportunity of examining. Below the mouth of the Mitigate, wide extents of dry Ein Forests commence, and it is between these that most of the Teak localities are found. On these tracts the trees stand very isolated, so that a vast extent of ground has to be gone over before any considerable number of large trees is met with.

Lower Zimmay Forests.

Number of trees on the square mile.

First Class,	425
Second ditto,	1213
Third ditto,	1666
Fourth ditto,	1303
Nathat,	45
Girdled,	118
Logs,	43
Stumps,	584
Attacked with ficus,	15

The growth of the Teak trees, however, is good, the stems being straight and regular.

In most of the places visited, the number of undersized stumps, in girth below 5', was very considerable, a sure sign that these forests had at one time been in the hands of natives. Of large trees few only are left, but the proportion of trees of the other class is a fair one, and the number of trees of the second and third class is very considerable; indeed many parts of the forests consist exclusively of trees from 3' to 4' 6" girth, apparently from 20 to 40 years old. This circumstance was noted by Captain O'Brien: see extract No. 10.

The upper Goongee Forest is situated in a valley similar to that of the Mitigate Kyouktaga Forest, and the Goongee stream makes its way in a like manner through a gorge of the hills. But the forest has altogether a different appearance. Teak does not here grow in the shade of the dense evergreen forest, but it is associated with the trees of the upper mixed forest. It has a fair proportion of seedlings.

The upper Goongee forests were found to be actively worked by parties from Maulmain.

Elephants were employed to push the timber down the stream, as the water was not sufficient to float them.

The logs we saw were doogies, 30 feet long, and in girth from 5 to 7 feet. Their shape was irregular, not cylindrical, but more or less fluted, like the old timber remaining in the Pegu forests and left as not worth removing by the former workers of the same. Neither here nor in the Tseikgyee or Megwa Forests, did we observe any fine large pieces similar to those which at one time are said to have formed the standard of the Attaran timber.

26. After having thus given a sketch of the present condition of the Attaran Forests, it remains to discuss their past history and their future prospects.

Attaran Forests, first worked on Government account. Dr. Wallich's recommendation.

Whatever information regarding the management of the Attaran Forests previous to 1850, is available from public documents is found collected in the summary of papers relating to the Tenasserim forests (pages 61 to 177 of the Selections from the Records of the Bengal Government, No. IX., Calcutta, 1852), and in Dr. Falconer's Report on the Tenasserim Teak Forests (pages 5 to 10 of the same publication).

It will thus be necessary to refer only in a summary manner to a few of the more important points.

The existence of Teak-producing localities in the Attaran district became known soon after the occupation of the Tenasserim Provinces in 1826. It appears that they yielded some timber before that time, but that they were never worked to any considerable extent. Dr. Wallich visited a portion of the Zimmay Forests as high as the Mittigate, in April and May, 1827. The practical result of his researches is contained in the following remarkable passages of his report to the Supreme Government.

" No forest exists which can, with propriety, be called inexhaustible ; at least none that is liable to constant and extensive demands for timber.

Page 77 of Summary.

The quantity of Teak used for public purposes, both Military and Naval, is so great, and it will go on increasing to so great an extent, in proportion as new sources of supplies are opened, that the Martaban forests, ample as they are, would be soon impoverished, unless they were placed under a vigilant and strict superintendence, their supplies regulated with economy, and their extent gradually augmented. I hope I take a correct view of the case, if I consider all the Teak forests which grow in these provinces as the exclusive property of the state, applicable only to public use and not to be interfered with by any private individual whatever. Unless this principle be acted upon from the very outset, I will venture to predict that private enterprize will very soon render fruitless all endeavours to perpetuate the supplies for the public service, and one of the principal and most certain sources of revenue will thus be irrecoverably lost."

Dr. Wallich's recommendations were followed out for a short time only, during which the forests were worked on Government account, and the timber mostly employed for public purposes. In May, 1829, "The failure of the experiment of cutting and exporting timber for the Calcutta market induced the Government to adopt Mr. Maingay's

Page 81.

repeated suggestions to throw open the forests to private individuals." This failure, as far as can be gathered from the documents, consisted in the following occurrence.

" It was proposed to ship some of the timber as an experiment to the Calcutta market. Accordingly, in May, 1828, a cargo of 511 logs of

Page 81.

Teak, valued at Rupees 6,000 nearly, was conveyed in the Hon'ble Company's Ship *Ernaad* from Tavoy to Calcutta, where shortly after its arrival it was sold by public auction at a loss of Rupees 250 nearly. This unfavorable result put a stop to further shipments of timber for the market."

If instead of sending the timber to Calcutta, a stock had been formed at Maulmain, and the timber regularly been disposed of by public auction on the spot, the result of the operations might have developed itself in a more favorable manner.

27. However the desire to raise the timber trade of Maulmain

Change of system, licenses granted to private parties.

more rapidly overruled all considerations for the future, and the measure was carried out to give lethmats or licenses, to cut timber in particular localities in the forests to a number of speculators both Europeans and Natives. The result of this measure has been the destruction of the Attaran Forests, but it certainly has given a great start to the timber trade of Maulmain, and although the quantity of timber brought down from the Attaran Forests has not apparently been very considerable, it was sufficient to attract a certain amount of capital and to induce a number of parties to establish timber depôts and ship-building yards at Maulmain. The maintenance of these establishments afterwards compelled the owners to open out other sources of timber more distant and more difficult of access, as the supply from the Attaran Forests began to flag. Statement VII. gives an account of the quantity of timber brought down from the Attaran, from which it will be seen that up to 1847-48, it amounted to 6,753 tons per annum, corresponding to an equal number of trees removed ; whereas after that time it dwindled down to 963 tons per annum.

The lethmats for working the Attaran Forests were granted under the following rules framed by Mr. Maingay, at that time Commissioner of the Tenasserim Provinces.

" *Rule of* 1829.—All persons applying to fell timber are directed

Page 81.

to point out where they intend employing themselves for that purpose, together with the number of men in their service.

" 2nd. No timber shall be removed from the banks of any river without the sanction of the Commissioner, his Deputy, or Assistant having been previously obtained.

" 3rd. All timber shall be subjected to a duty of 15 per cent. to be levied in kind or in money at the option of the Commissioner, his

Deputy, or Assistant. The timber to be valued by two arbitrators, the one to be selected by the Commissioner, his Deputy, or Assistant, the other to be chosen by the owner of the timber: in the event of a difference of opinion between the arbitrators, the Commissioner, his Deputy, or Assistant shall be at liberty to appoint a third.

"4th. It shall be at the option of the Commissioner, his Deputy, or Assistant to select for the use of Government any portion of the Teak timber felled in this province, the value of such timber to be settled by two arbitrators as above stated.

"5th. No Teak trees shall be felled, the girth of which shall not exceed four feet, and all such trees felled within that girth, will be confiscated by the Commissioner, his Deputy, or Assistant."

The only reference in these rules to the perpetuation of the forests was the clause that only Teak trees of a girth exceeding four feet shall be felled. It does not appear, however, that this clause was ever enforced, and had its observance been secured, it would have contributed but little towards protecting the forests.

28. It is necessary here to expose the fallacy that forests constituted as the Teak-producing tracts of these provinces are; will suffer no material injury provided large trees only are felled,

The Rule prohibiting the felling of trees under 4 feet, does not secure the protection of the forests.

All Teak localities that have not been worked to a great extent or injured by Toungya cultivation are found to consist mainly of large trees with a comparatively small proportion of the smaller classes. We observe this in most of the Moong and Padah, some of the Youk-thawah and Thoukyaghat, Kannee and Koonoong, and in the whole nearly of the Martaban, Beeling, Upper Doomdamee and the Shwoaey-lay and Northern Tharrawaddie Forests.

If the Beeling Forests, for instance, were to be worked on the principle of allowing the whole of the trees above 4 feet in girth to be cut down, more than one-half of the seed-bearing trees would be removed, viz.

First Class trees, ... 8902 per sq. mile.
Second ditto ditto, ... 3571   ditto.
                                                       ————
Total of trees to be removed ,..................... 12473
Third Class trees below 4' 6" left standing, .. 8568
                                                       ————
Total of seed-bearing trees, ... 21041

And as the third class trees produce a very small amount of seed only, and many of them no seed at all, the quantity of seed to be expected would be reduced to a very small proportion of what was available before the working commenced. The damage done thereby would thus be sufficient to injure any forest consisting of Teak alone. But Teak only forms a certain proportion, on an average one-tenth, of the trees in the forest. Many of the other trees germinate more easily and grow up more rapidly. Bamboos certainly do.

Now the first effect of cutting away large Teak trees is to open out the forest, and to afford more light for the springing up of seedlings. But it is not Teak alone that will benefit by this change, other trees being more numerous, will be enabled thereby to take possession of more ground than they occupied before, and the locality from having been a rich Teak forest will, in most instances, deteriorate into a forest of other trees with a sprinkling of Teak only.

If the effect upon localities of a limited extent is considered, the injury is seen to be much more serious. Take for instance (out of many others similarly situated) the surveys Nos. 31 to 33, of the Boben Forests, under Section II. Tharrawaddie: they give an aggregate result of

First Class trees above 9 feet in girth   116 on 6.368 sq. miles.

Ditto	7' 6"	ditto	163
Ditto	6'	ditto	813
			——1092
Second Ditto	4' 6"	ditto	106
Third Ditto	1' 5"	ditto	180
Fourth Ditto	small	ditto	89
			—— 375

These forests require opening out, so as to enable seedlings to spring up, but if the whole of the trees above 6' in girth were cut down, very few would remain to shed seed and to keep down the growth of trees of other kinds.

But it might be urged that, provided the standard of the trees allowed to be felled were only raised sufficiently high, the protection would be complete.

If, for instance in the Boben Forests, all trees above 9 feet in girth were cut down, no material injury would accrue to the forest, as this would remove one-eleventh only of the seed-bearing trees. But in other forest tracts, this proportion would be found to be a different one.

Thus in No. 6, of the Moong and Padah surveys (Pochek Toung) the number of 9' trees is 124, or more than one-third that of the three first classes (356), and a similar proportion is found to prevail in many of the Youkthawah, Thoukyaghat and other forests. But we must take Teak as it actually occurs in groups of from 3 to 10 trees of the same size and age, in order fully to appreciate the danger of regulating the selection of trees to be felled by their size only. For, if such groups are conveniently situated for the removal of the timber, the wood-cutter will, without transgressing the rules, cut down the whole, and thus altogether make over the locality to other kinds of trees. To exclude therefore the smaller sizes is in itself not a sufficient protection of the forests : a judicious selection of the trees to be felled from among the larger classes is the only measure that effectually secures them against devastation.

29. The permits were considered to be revocable at pleasure, and no boundaries between the localities assigned to the different permit holders were fixed. With reference to this, Mr. Blundell, Mr. Maingy's successor, wrote as follows in April, 1837.

Character of the permits.

"Under the rules of 1829, parties who desired to cut timber were allowed 'permits' or licenses, to do so in certain localities, to the exclusion of all other cutters from those particular localities ; care being taken to make it known to them that the permit was revocable at pleasure, and though the transfer of these permits had been allowed, yet they had never been recognized as conveying aught but permission to cut timber in certain situations. So long as the timber was procured near the banks of the river, and while the market for it was in its infancy, this system answered very well ; but as competition and the number of cutters increased, it created great confusion regarding boundaries, as no survey was made when licenses were granted, and it was impossible to have defined correctly any other boundary than the banks of the river. As parties went further inland, they trenched on each others' imaginary boundaries ; this caused disputes and led eventually to suits in the courts, which (Mr. Blundell stated) we have not the means of deciding with any satisfaction to ourselves or to the litigant parties."

Page 86.

At the same time, Mr. Blundell alluded to the possibility of its

11

becoming advisable to resume the permits to cut, and to reconstitute a monopoly, but states that this would involve the interference with apparent private rights accompanying the original permits to cut timber, sanctioned by eight years' adherence to the present system, and would lead to expense, which in justice must be incurred in compensating the holders of the original permits for their outlay towards facilitating their operations in the forests.

30. The necessity for adopting measures for securing the preservation of the forests from further destruction was, it appears, at that time keenly felt by the authorities at

The necessity of adopting measures for preserving the forests felt at Maulmain. Mr. Blundell's rules.

Maulmain. Mr. Blundell repeatedly proposed the appointment of a conservator of forests, with the necessary establishment, and this proposal not meeting with the sanction of Government, he deputed in 1840, Captain O'Brien of H. M.'s 63rd Regiment to survey and report on the forests of the Attaran. Captain O'Brien's report and journal throw much light on the condition of the forests at the time. Extracts of the journal are given in appendix No. 4. The substance of the report is,

That the extent and value of the forests had been greatly overrated and that they had been worked in a destructive manner without any regard to their permanence.

That a large proportion of the timber felled had been cut green, without having previously been killed.

That the trees were felled in a wasteful manner, the stumps left being often 10 feet high, and a large portion of the upper part of the stem with branches remaining on the ground, to be consumed by the fires.

That large numbers of undersized trees had been felled.

That several forests had been entirely neglected by those who held licenses to cut in them, and, lastly, that

Some forests had been completely worked out without any authority whatever.

On the ground of this report, Mr. Blundell proposed the resumption of all permits and the leasing or farming out of the forests under new rules as follows.

" Notice is hereby given, that from and after the 1st proximo, the permits under which individuals are now allowed to fell Teak trees within certain localities will be cancelled and resumed, and such localities will

Page 100.

be leased or farmed out to the same individual for a period of twenty years under the following rules.

"*Rules dated the* 12*th April,* 1841.—1st, that the farmer keep up such an establishment for the preservation and working of the forest as may be considered necessary by the Government Superintending Officer, in order that the trees be felled without injury to those surrounding them, by having proper ropes, &c. for lowering them, and that the requisite assistance of men, elephants, trucks, carts, &c. be provided for removing them when felled.

"2. That no trees shall be killed or felled of a less girth or circumference than 6 feet, measured round the bark 10 feet from the ground.

"3. That every tree shall be killed by a broad rim of the bark, say 1 foot, being taken off round the trunk of the tree near the root, at a height not exceeding 2 feet from the ground, and further by cutting to the spine or through the hard wood to prevent the least portion of sap from rising.

"This process is only to be done during the months of January, February and March, before the sap commences to rise, and at no other period of the year.

"4. That no tree shall be felled till the expiration of at least two years from the period it has been killed in the manner pointed out in rule 3.

"5. That every tree felled be removed from the forest with the least possible delay.

"6. That for every tree felled and removed, five young trees of a proper size shall be planted by the farmer, or by the Government at the expense of the farmer.

"7. That no tree shall be on any account cut up into short lengths called loozars, but that every tree shall be removed as felled, and be brought in that state, after removing the branches, either down the river to the town or to sawpits established in the forests.

" On proof of breach of any of the above rules, the locality wherein such breach may have been effected will be at once resumed by Government.

" The transfer of a lease of any forest from one party to another must be registered in the office from which the leases are issued, and no transfer will be valid without such registry.

" The duty on timber will be continued to be levied as usual."

These rules are more comprehensive than those of 1829. They provide for an efficient working of the forests, and by demanding the speedy removal of the timber from where it is exposed to destruction by jungle fires, they aim at greater economy ; they also insure an improved quality by prohibiting the cutting in pieces of the logs and insisting upon the trees being well-seasoned before felling. And to a certain degree they are intended to secure the permanence of the forests, by protecting all trees below 6 feet in girth or 62 years of age, and by demanding the planting of 5 young trees for one tree felled.

But rules like these, full of detail, may, to a certain degree, be carried out in forests worked by a Government establishment, or by Government contractors who have no dealings with any one but with Government Officers ; but it is difficult to see how parties independent of Government and working with a view to obtain the greatest immediate returns can be made to observe them, without constantly obstructing their operations. Government certainly does not appear to have contemplated a strict enforcement of these rules.

31. For although they were approved by Government, on the 8th

Mr. Blundell's rules sanctioned, rendering the licenses liable to resumption for breach of the same, on the understanding, however, that the occupancy of the grantees should not be disturbed unless on very strong grounds.

Page 111.

September following, " Mr. Blundell was informed of the wish of Government not to disturb the occupancy of the grantees unless on very strong grounds; he was therefore desired to report on the practical operation of the rules before he proceeded to enforce, especially with reference to the prohibition against cutting up the timber which, so far as it was designed to protect the Government duty, it was thought would admit of relaxation, if that duty could be previously secured by any other arrangement."

The leases were thus made formally subject to resumption by Government for any breach of the rules, but at the same time the express wish of Government was recorded, that the occupancy of the grantees should not be disturbed except on very strong grounds.

Before Captain O'Brien had completed his survey, Captain Tremenhere, Executive Engineer at Maulmain, was appointed Superintendent of Forests. He examined a portion of the forests in company with that Officer and visited them a second time in March, 1842. In his second report, he states that in all grants visited by him, the forest rules, framed by Mr. Blundell, had been entirely disregarded.

"Many undersized and young trees had been killed and felled;
many trees had been felled before
having been killed, or before the expir-
ation of the prescribed interval between killing and felling; many trees
had been killed for several years, but had not been felled; and a great
many trees had been killed and felled above the killing mark."

Page 113.

32. Captain Tremenhere considered that the rules were rendered
ineffective through the circumstance
that only the extreme penalty of immediate resumption of the grant was
provided for any breach of them, as it was generally believed by the
natives that the Government could not desire to have all the forests
thrown on their own hands. He therefore proposed fines and penalties
instead of immediate resumption, and suggested that the planting of
young trees in the place of those felled or brought away, should be done
by persons employed by Government at the expense of the leaseholder.

Captain Tremenhere introduces fines instead of resumption, as the penalty for breach of the rules.

"*Rules, dated 11th July,* 1842.—Leases will be granted to all persons who now possess the right of cutting
in the Teak forests of the Tenasserim
Provinces, assigned to them either by written document or by the felling
and removing of timber carried on therein under the sanction or by the
permission of the Civil authorities or Superintendent of Forests at
Maulmain. The boundaries wherein the leaseholder is permitted to cut
or carry away Teak or any other timber the locality produces, will be
defined in each lease, which will confer no proprietary right in the soil.

Page 114.

"The period of lease will not be limited, but will continue so long as
the leaseholder shall pay the required observance to the following rules
and shall keep up such an establishment for the working of the forests
as may be considered necessary by the superintending officer.

"The transfer of a lease from one party to another must be
registered in the office of the Superintendent, and no transfer will be
valid without such registry.

"1st. Every leaseholder shall appoint a responsible agent to be
resident in the forest during the killing, cutting and rafting seasons.

"On the 1st of December of each year the leaseholders shall make
known to the superintending officer, the number of gangs they intend
to hire for killing trees during the season, and the number and strength
of parties of men and elephants they intend to employ in felling, drag-

ging and rafting in their respective forests, when Government peons, in sufficient numbers to prevent any unnecessary delay or obstruction to the work, will be deputed with proper instruments to place a mark on each tree to be killed and on each log to be brought away.

" The peons shall make report to the superintending officer of the number of trees or logs marked, which report, in order to prevent collusion, shall be countersigned by the agent of the leaseholder in the forest.

" 2nd. The position of the work will determine the killing and felling point, which may be immediately below but not above it.

" Every tree marked shall be killed during the same season, and no tree shall hereafter be killed or felled without first receiving this mark.

" 3rd. Every tree marked shall be girdled by cutting through the sap wood or duramen, to prevent the sap from rising. This is only to be done during the months of January, February, March and April.

" 4th. No tree is to be killed of a less girth than 6 feet, measured at 4 feet from the ground.

" 5th. No tree shall be felled until the lapse of one rainy season after being killed in the manner prescribed by rule 3rd.

" 6th. No raft is to enter the Maulmain waters without a pass, bearing the signature of the agent employed to inspect them.

" 7th. For every tree felled or log brought away three young trees shall be planted out on their timber sites. This will be effected by persons employed by Government, and the expenses are to be defrayed by the leaseholder.

" The expense of marking the trees and logs as directed by the first rule is to be borne by the leaseholder at the rate of 2 annas for every tree or log marked. Any surplus over the annual outlay on this account will be carried towards defraying the charges for planting provided for by rule 7th.

" *Fines and penalties.*—If any leaseholder should neglect the 1st Rule, no timber shall be allowed to enter the Maulmain waters from his forest during the succeeding year.

" For every breach of the 2nd, 3rd, 4th, 5th and 6th Rules, a fine, not exceeding 500 Rupees, will be levied from the leaseholder. The fines are to be levied at the discretion, and by the decision of the superintending officer.

" Information by letter will be given by the superintending officer to the Assistant Commissioner's court of the amount of fine due to Government by any leaseholder, which letter shall be considered sufficient proof of the validity of the claim, and shall be sufficient warrant for levying the amount of fine by distraint on the property of the lease-holder.

" These rules were sanctioned with the approval of the Government of India, the only alterations made in them being that five young trees instead of three, as provided by Captain Tremenhere, should be planted in the place of every tree felled, and that the Commissioner should exercise appellate jurisdiction in the cases of fines which the Superintendent of Forests might impose for a breach of the rules. The Superintendent of Forests was, at the same time, invested with magisterial powers to enable him to impose fines not exceeding 500 Rupees for every breach of the forest rules. At the same time Government expressed the intention, in the event of granting leases for unoccupied forests, to limit such new leases to 20 years, renewable on the expiration of that time conditionally on the lessee's strict observance of the rules."

We have thus three distinct set of rules or conditions, all sanctioned by Government, under which the licenses or leases for cutting timber in the Attaran Forests were granted.

1st. Mr. Maingy's rules of 1829, without any penalties whatsoever.

2nd. Mr. Blundell's rules of the 12th of April, 1841, imposing the penalty of immediate resumption on the breach of any of the rules.

3rd. Mr. Tremenhere's rules of the 11th July, 1842, substituting fines and penalties for the resumption of the licenses, but making their continuance depend on the lessee's paying the required observance to the rules and keeping up a sufficient establishment for the working of the forests.

33. But it is by no means clear to which of these rules the licenses, leases or grants were to be held amenable. Indeed, it does not appear that the provisions of any of these rules were ever carried out effectively, this may perhaps, to a certain degree, be ascribed to the views taken of the whole question of forest management by the Government of India and at home. The following is an extract from a despatch of the Honorable the Court of

None of the rules observed. Their enforcement discouraged by Government at home and in India.

Directors, taken from the summary of papers on the Tenasserim
Forests quoted above.

"In February, 1842, the orders of the Court of Directors were
received. The Court reviewed the
measures of the Government and the
local authorities for the management of the Teak forests from the earliest
period down to Captain Tremenhere's appointment, and expressed
doubts as to whether the rules which had been framed by him would
be sufficient to meet all the difficulties which had arisen. The Court
were of opinion that a proper survey of the forests was an indispensable
preliminary to any new system, but they thought that it was scarcely
possible for the conservator with the aid of any establishment which
could be allotted to him, to exercise so minute and searching a
superintendence over such extensive forests as would enable him
to prevent the felling of other trees than those selected by himself, or
to see that the business of planting was properly attended to. But
even if such interference were practicable, the Court considered that
it would still be undesirable to commit to any individual powers so
liable to abuse.

"In order to insure the preservation of the forests held by private
persons, the Court were of opinion that it should be the object of
Government to make it the interest of those persons to take care of
them and to remove all temptation to injure them. For this object
long leases should be granted, on condition of the payment of a certain
percentage on all timber felled, and under an obligation not to clear
the land for cultivation or to employ it for any other purposes besides
plantation. The felling of timber below a certain size should be
strictly prohibited, and a modification of the duty might be made to
check the wasteful practice of cutting up large timber.

"The farmer would then have an interest in the improvement of
his forests, and would probably be inclined to plant, of his own accord.
Even if he neglected to do so, the self-sown plants which he would no
longer have any object in destroying would, in most other situations,
insure to some extent the perpetuation of the forests. The Court also
suggested that it should be made obligatory on the farmer to supply
the places of the trees felled by him by forming new nurseries and
carefully rearing the young plants until they attained maturity; that
Government should reserve to itself the right of forming nurseries at

Page 119.

the farmer's expense in the event of his failing to do so, and that the conservator should be allowed to exercise such a limited controul over private forests as would merely enable him to see that these conditions of the lease were observed. The conservator should also attend to the forests retained for the public service, and Government should reserve to itself a resource independent of the market by selecting for itself from the ungranted forests such as were conveniently situated and sufficiently extensive for all purposes, and placing them under proper management, so as to afford a constant supply of timber both of Teak and of other useful kinds indigenous in the country."

34. One point in this passage deserves particular notice. This is

Fallacy of the supposition that private parties in India will take care of their forests.

the idea that it would be possible to make it the interest of private parties to take care of the forests and to remove all temptation to injure them. This is a fallacy as regards India, where the prospective interests of private parties, Europeans at least, are necessarily of very short duration. Even on the Continent of Europe, where private interests are of a much more permanent character than in India, forest property is not considered safe in the hands of private parties, unless placed under certain rules to guard against their devastation.

The general forest rules of many of the States in Germany may, from an exclusively free trade point-of-view, be considered as an interference with private rights, but they ensure to the country at large a certain supply of an indispensable commodity, and tend to prevent a deterioration of climate and soil which even in a temperate climate too often is the result of hilly tracts or sandy plains being denuded of their forests.

In Burmah, the conservation of the forests merely to ensure the retention of moisture, or the fixing of the soil, so as to prevent its being washed away, is of no great importance to the general welfare of the country as long as the greater part of it is clothed with one unbroken forest. But the preservation of the valuable kinds of wood growing in the same is a matter of general and prospective importance; however, the measures required for ensuring the preservation of Teak in the forests, demand nothing short of an actual sacrifice of immediate returns and, in India, private parties cannot be expected to make this sacrifice.

12

The law of supply and demand can scarcely be supposed to regulate the management of Teak forests in this country. The negotiable value of forests must mainly depend on the immediate outturn they will yield. And supposing the proprietor undertook the establishment of plantations, he could not expect to recover his outlay by an adequate increase in the market value of his forest. At home the growth of trees keeps pace with the accumulating interest of the capital expended on plantations. Here, with a rate of interest of from 12 to 36 per cent. per annum, there is no proportion between the sums expended on plantations and their ultimate results. One thousand rupees expended in planting and rearing 500 Teak trees will, if the interest is constantly added to the capital at 4 per cent. in 62 years have increased to 11,378 Rupees when the trees may, under favorable circumstances, be expected to bring the owner a profit of 22 Rupees each. But if instead of planting the trees the principal were put out at 6 per cent. it would have increased to 37,064 Rupees in 62 years, which would much exceed the value of the 500 trees of that age.

The difficulty of access of the forests and the uncertainty of all estimates of their contents, on account of their scattered and varied character, add another serious obstacle to the chances of considerably improving the market value of a forest by plantation or by other measures for its protection or improvement.

Similar views to those here adverted to are expressed in a subsequent despatch dated 26th June, 1844, para. 89 of summary.

"In September, 1844, a despatch was received, dated the 26th June, in which the Court noticed Captain Tremenhere's revised rules of 1842,

Page 126.

and approved generally of them, but they objected to those clauses which required leaseholders to report at the beginning of each season, the number of men and animals each proposed to employ in his forests, and placed restrictions in regard to the felling of trees. These regulations the Court remarked must often prove exceedingly vexatious and they can only be enforced by means of a number of petty officers invested with powers which ought not to be placed in such hands. They therefore repeated their suggestion for giving long leases on such conditions as would make it the interest of the leaseholders to preserve the forests and maintain a succession of timber trees on their lands. The Court at the same time expressed their approval of the intention of Government to retain the ungranted forests in the Tenasserim Provinces for the supply of the wants of the public service."

35. In September, 1845, Captain Guthrie succeeded Captain Tremenhere as Superintendent of Forests. He found the same reckless disregard of Forest rules as his predecessor, and with the Commissioner's (then Captain Durand) approval resumed summarily several forests under the penalty clause of 1841. Against these proceedings Cockerell and Company, and Mackey and Company, of Calcutta, as the holders of extensive forest grants, appealed to Government. Afterwards several merchants of Moulmain petitioned the Commissioner on the same subject. The Commissioner, however, upheld the measures of Captain Guthrie and reported to Government his having done so.

Captain Guthrie's administration. Several of the forests resumed for breach of forest rules.

36. But Captain Guthrie's measures were entirely disapproved of by the Deputy Governor of Bengal and the Commissioner was directed "to lose no time in redressing the injury which had been sustained by ejected parties, and in reinstating them in their rights, of which they ought not, in such a summary manner or on such insufficient grounds, to have been divested."

Captain Guthrie's measures cancelled.

Page 147.

In the same despatch it was stated "that no confirmation of the penalty can be traced in the records of Government, and it was intimated to the Commissioner that it was not intended to monopolize the forests, or to restrain the free trader, or to trench on the rights of grantees or lessees of the forest lands." These orders of Government have had the effect of altogether frustrating every further attempt to enforce the observance of the forest rules. Since that time the holders of forests might have been justified in considering themselves as bonâ fide proprietors of the Teak in their forests, and not merely as holders of licenses revocable at will.

37. It is, however, of importance to notice that the Court of Directors did not altogether concur in Sir Herbert Maddock's opinion regarding forest management. (Despatch, dated 20th October, 1847.) We extract the following passages from the summary of papers.

The Court of Directors are of opinion that it is not altogether safe to leave forests to the management of private parties.

"We are aware that you do not appear to admit the necessity for this precaution, and you observe that the Government interests will be best served by attracting private capital and enterpize to work the forests and trusting for Government supplies to the market, but we do not concur in this opinion. It is quite possible that not only lease-holders for 99 years, but even leaseholders in perpetuity may not think it worth while to form plantations which must remain for eighty years without yielding any returns of value, and that after felling the timber on their estates they may leave them waste or bring them under the plough."

Page 150.

This is the first acknowledgement on the part of Government recorded in the correspondence regarding the Attaran Forest, that it might not always be safe to leave the management of forests to private parties.

From this time, the history of the Attaran Forests began in a great measure to lose its practical interest as regards the general welfare of Moulmain. The supply of Teak timber from the Attaran fell to less than 1000 tons per annum, the forests on the Thoungyeen and those on the upper Salween in the Siamese and Karenee country having entirely taken the place of the Attaran Forests as the main resource of the Moulmain timber trade. Mr. Colvin, who succeeded Captain Durand as Commissioner of the Tenasserim Provinces on the 29th December, 1846, considered, it would appear, the lapse of the greater part of the Attaran Forests as a *fait accompli* which could not well be altered.

38. He proposed to retain for Government purposes two forests for which no licenses had as yet been granted : the Thinganeennoung on the Winyeo, and the Mittigate Kyouk-taga in the Zimmay division, it being supposed at this time that they were well suited to be reserved for the purposes of having a large growth of timber at command. He also proposed that extensive plantations should be established for the renovation of these forests, and his application for a person capable of superintending the same, resulted in the deputation to Maulmain of Dr. Falconer, Superintendent, Hon'ble Company's Botanical Garden in Calcutta, in January, 1849.

Mr. Colvin proposes to retain two forests as Government property, and to grant long leases for all others.

For the other forests, which were held under licenses by private parties, he proposed to grant long leases, strongly recommending the cession in perpetuity to the holders of Lethmats or licenses of all locations which were occupied by them.

Mr. Colvin does not support this proposal by any very sanguine expectations regarding measures of preservation or improvement of the forests to be effected by the holders: on the contrary, he observes with reference to the despatch from the Court of Directors dated 20th October, 1847, "I feel there is much truth in the remark of the Hon'ble

Page 170.

Court that even holders in perpetuity may not think it worth while to form plantations or provide for fresh growth of trees which must remain for 80 years or even more without yielding to them any returns of value. But the question here is not, whether it is desirable to part with forest lands to private persons, but whether, having parted with them, it is not better that the transfer to such persons should be on the most secure and acceptable tenure."

However, the proposal for granting leases in perpetuity was not approved of by the Court of Directors, and it is evident from the extract of despatch dated 12th September, 1849, given below, that by this time the necessity of making the lease of forest tracts depend on the observance of certain rules regarding the planting of young trees in the place of those felled was fully recognized by the Government at home.

"We cannot accede to any recommendation which would alienate from Government in perpetuity the proprietary right in these forests. We

Page 171.

attach little importance to the argument urged by the Commissioner, as we are of opinion, that where the prospect of obtaining any remuneration for the labour and expense bestowed on the forests is so distant as must necessarily be the case in regard to the plantation of young Teak trees, a perpetual tenure would have little, if any, advantage over a 99 years' lease in inducing the grantees voluntarily to incur that labour and expense where there exists no express condition to that effect. We consider that a far more effectual plan for securing a renewal of the forests on the tracts occupied by the present holders would have been to make it a condition of the lease that three seedlings should be planted wherever a tree had been cut down, and that any default in this respect (which might be ascertained by periodical inspections), should render the grant liable to resumption. Such a condition if faithfully performed, would secure for the future a constant supply of Teak timber, and it might be held out as an inducement to the lessees to exert themselves for the improvement of the forests, that if they were successful in that object, they might look forward to a renewal of the lease at the expiration of the present term." Under Mr. Colvin's administration the rate of duty to be levied on Attaran timber was fixed at 4 Rupees per log all round, and the duty on all other timber imported into Moulmain at Rs. 2-12. Up to that time, duty had been levied at the rate of 15 per cent. on the assumed value of the timber.

No further steps appear to have been taken by Mr. Colvin with reference to the forest holdings on the Attaran, with the exception of the lease granted for the lower Mittigate and Mittigate Codogway, alluded to above in para. 22. Maps and lists of the Attaran Forests were at this time prepared by Mr. A. Hobday, Assistant Forest Department. Copies of the lists are given in Statements Nos. VIII. and IX. and the principal data for the sketch maps of the Attaran Forests attached hereto are taken from the same source.

At a later date, about 1853, a number of permits in the hands of native forest holders who, it appears, had for some time past entirely neglected their forests, not even bringing timber down, were cancelled by order of Sir A. Bogle, then Commissioner of Maulmain. A list is given in Statement No. X.

39. The question of renewing the Attaran Forests by planting had entered by this time a new phase.

Dr. Falconer's Report.

Dr. Falconer was deputed to Maulmain to examine the Attaran Forests, and particularly to report on the localities to be selected and method to be pursued in the establishment of plantations in the same.

It appears that Mr. Colvin intended in the first instance to plant within the limits of the Government reserved forests, but that at the same time he contemplated the possibility of making the experiment on other localities to be made over for the purpose by private holders.

He also anticipated that the forest holders would profit " by such practical directions as Dr. Falconer might be able to give as to the manner in which experiments for the artificial growth of Teak could be made."

Dr. Falconer left Maulmain for the forests on the 30th January and returned on the 9th March, 1849. His report, dated 23rd January, 1851, gives a complete review of the whole subject.

After discussing the general distribution of Teak over the Tenasserim Provinces (paras. 1 to 13) Dr. Falconer gives an abstract of the history of the Attaran forests since the occupation of the provinces (paras. 14 to 23). After this follow general remarks on the mode of occurrence and growth of the tree, the value of its timber as compared with that from Malabar and other countries, and the sources of injury to Teak during its growth (paras. 24 to 43), further a description of the different forests visited (paras. 44 to 59).

The question of the insufficiency of natural propagation of Teak is next discussed (paras. 60 to 73). Dr. Falconer observes that although the tree produces an immense quantity of seed, yet the number of seedlings springing up naturally is very small. He ascribes this to the peculiarity of the seed which, while it has a prolonged vitality, does not germinate readily.

A large proportion of seed also is washed away by the floods, or burnt by the jungle fires, which occur after the nuts are shed and before they can germinate. The greater proportion of seedlings in other forests, particularly in the Thoungyeen, as compared with the Attaran, Dr. Falconer ascribes to the different nature of the surface, which being more broken and hilly in the Thoungyeen, offers more abundant opportunities for the springing up of the seeds. At the same time, however, he observes that the occurrence of large numbers of young Teak trees from 20 to 25 years of age indicates that before the working of the Attaran forests was begun and before wood-cutters commenced systematically to set fire to the jungle, the springing up of seedlings was not so scarce as it was considered to be at the time of his visit.

This explanation is certainly a correct one, but it must not be overlooked that the proportion of seedlings in the Attaran Forest has been considerably underrated by all former observers. For seedlings, although occurring less frequently on a given area than in most other forests, are, by no means, entirely wanting. The survey of the forest shows that the number of seedlings on the square mile in the Attaran (976) is equal or larger than in

The Southern Forests, ... 977

  ,, Upper Salween, ... 844

  ,, Lower ditto, ... 720

  ,, ditto Thoungyeen, ... 168

It is true that most of these seedlings have sprung up since the time of Dr. Falconer's visit (in 1848) ; and it is likely that the proportion destroyed by the jungle fires was larger before that time, the forests being worked more actively.

But the number of third class trees from 10 to 37 years old, which must be supposed to have sprung up between 1821 and 1848 was found to amount to 1105 per square mile, which number considerably exceeds that observed in the

Southern Forests, ... 823
Upper Salween ditto, ... 722
Lower Salween ditto, ... 672
Middle Thoungyeen, ... 474
Lower ditto,....................................... 177

Indeed the per mille statement, shows that the proportion of third class trees in the Attaran, with reference to the other classes is above the average, so that the number of seedlings springing up with reference to the larger trees cannot have been unusually low between the years of 1821 and 1848. It is thus probable that the natural propagation in the Attaran Forests is not as deficient as Dr. Falconer supposed it to be. It is, however, a remarkable fact that with the exception of a group of seedlings described by Dr. Falconer in the Marzettie Forests (para. 46) and a few instances of seedlings recorded by Mr. Salmond and Captain O'Brien, all observers since Dr. Wallich, agree in recording the scarcity and in some instances total absence of seedlings. This can only be ascribed to the circumstance that all surveys were made in the dry season, when it is not always easy to recognize Teak seedlings. A similar instance happened in the Prome Forests in Pegu where Dr. McClelland found no seedlings in 1855, although large numbers were discovered by me in 1856 (Pegu Report for 1856, para. 27). Dr. Falconer closes his report by discussing the method to be observed in the establishment of plantations, but this will be noticed in a separate chapter of this Report.

40. It is a question of interest in connexion with the history of the Attaran Forests to determine the original state of these forests before the working commenced. Dr.

Estimate of the original condition of the Attaran Forests from Dr. Wallich's description.

Wallich's report offers a few data which may serve to give an idea of the original state of the forests.

Below the mouth of the Mittigate, on the 30th March, Dr. Wallich examined a forest on the left bank of the Zimmay, and computed that he saw from 180 to 200 capital Teak trees, within half a mile in one direction and three quarters of a mile in another direction, on high and even ground. The average girth from 22 measurements approached nearly to 10 feet.

This forest was probably near the Maon Choung, perhaps the same locality as that examined by Mr. I. Barker on the 16th August, 1858. The Lower Zimmay Forests, of which this forms a part, have given us on the square mile :

    First class in girth above 7′ 6″, ...   47 trees.

    Ditto ditto between 6′ and 7′ 6″ ....   378 ditto.

Dr. Wallich estimates from 180 to 200 trees, with an average girth of 10′, on ⅜ square mile, or about 500 on the square mile. Of another locality, near the lower Mittigate on the Kyoonben Choung, Dr. Wallich writes as follows :—

" Of all the forests which I have seen, this is by far the largest and best deserving of the name of a Teak forest. In a line of less than two miles in extent, we counted somewhat more than 250 excellent Teaks, including only those that were standing within 40 yards of our path. The results of Dr. Wallich's measurements in this forest were an average girth of 11′ 4″, with clear stems of 25′ and 30′, and sometimes of 50′ and 60′ ; one tree had a girth of 24′ 3″."

This would give 250 trees, with an average girth of 11′ 4″, on $\frac{1}{11}$ square mile, or 2,750 on the square mile. The Mittigate Forests below the Kyouktaga have been found to contain at present on the square mile :

    First class trees above 7′ 6″ in girth,............   224

    Ditto ditto between 6′ and 7′ 6″ ditto, ...   58.

It is evident from these instances that, since Dr. Wallich's visit, the state of the forests has been considerably changed. Dr. Wallich, however, describes only small plots particularly rich in fine timber, and his report may be considered not to convey a correct idea of the condition of the Attaran Forests at the time of his visit.

41. The result of our own forest surveys may serve to give us a more general idea of what the forests were before their working commenced. They, however, fully bear out Dr. Wallich's description.

From the present forest surveys.

13

The age of Teak trees above 7' 6" in girth may be assumed to be above 100 years. Thirty years ago they were above 70 years old, and their girth was above 6'. All the trees therefore that are now above 7' 6" in girth were first class trees when the working of the forests commenced.

We know further the number of Nathat and girdled trees. A portion of these were first class trees 30 years ago; but how many, it would be impossible to determine.

Also the number of stumps in the forests can approximately be determined by doubling the number observed. Of these stumps a portion are the remains of such trees as were thirty years ago below 6' in girth, but how many cannot be ascertained.

By excluding the number of Nathat and girdled trees observed, and taking the whole number of stumps, we may consider any gross errors eliminated.

We thus obtain from the Lower Zimmay forests

Trees in girth above 7' 6", ... 47 per square mile
No. of stumps doubled, ... 1168 ditto ditto

Total, 1215

which is the probable number of first class trees per square mile in the Lower Zimmay forests before the working of the forests commenced.

In the case of two forest groups, viz. the Mittigate Codogway and Kyouktaga forests, the calculation is based on somewhat different data. Here a large proportion of the dead and killed timber has been left standing, and the number of stumps would not give even an approximate idea of the number of first class trees before the working commenced. Here stumps and logs have been neglected, and the number of Nathat and girdled trees taken instead, thus—

Mittigate Codogway.	*No. of Trees.*
In girth above 7' 6", ...	200
No. of Nathat trees, ...	487
Girdled, ...	4,825

Total, 5,512 first class trees

per square mile.

From these data the following results are obtained.

Estimated Number of first class trees per square mile.

Forests	in 1827	in 1858
Lower Winyeo Forest, ...	593	528
Upper ditto, ...	1629	621
Megway Tseikgyee, &c., ...	3552	642
Kyoon Choung, ...	4687	936
Upper Zimmay, ...	1128	389
Mittigate Codogway, ...	5512	989
Mittigate below Kyouktaga, ...	2416	282
Mittigate above ditto, ...	1968	318
Lower Zimmay, ...	1215	425
Attaran Forests,	1962	544

We may thus assume that before 1827, the whole of the Attaran forests contained on 100 square miles 196,200 first class trees.

It would be presumption to venture upon an estimate of what the other classes of trees may have been before the working of the forests was commenced. It is, however, probable that they were similar to what they are now, except that the proportion of seedlings is likely to have been somewhat larger.

We may be justified in assuming that the total of second and third class trees was about equal to the number of first class trees. It is here the place to allude to the estimates of Teak trees in the Attaran forests by Mr. Salmond in 1846 and by Mr. Hobday in 1851, the number of first class trees above 6' in girth are given in their estimates at 22,870 and 10,995, which figures are evidently too low. It is not stated what system was pursued in making out their estimates. See Statements VIII. IX. XVI. and XVII.

42. There are several forests among those surveyed in other

Attaran Forests in their original state compared with other Forest Districts.

parts of the country which at present are in a condition similar to what we may suppose the Attaran forests to have been before their working was commenced.

They are the following :—

Name of Forests.	Area Square Miles.	No. of First class trees estimated.
Moong and Padah,...........................	16.	39,552
Youkthawah and Thoukyaghat, ...	34.	54,136
Kannee and Koonoong,....................	24.	121,296
Beeling, ...	9.166	81,584
Youngzaleen, ...	12.	29,354
Doomdamee, ...	41.25	71,238
A portion of the Tharawaddee Forests,	100.	150,000
	236.416	547,160

Besides these there are numerous forest tracts of a similar character, but not included in the present survey, for instance the Sitang forests near the frontier, Swah, Bimbyay and others.

But none of these forest tracts is situated so near to a seaport and offers such facilities for the removal of the timber as the Attaran Forests.

The whole of the forests on the Sitang river are very inconveniently situated for the removal of the timber, which can be brought to Maulmain or Rangoon only through a series of narrow and tortuous canals, open during a few months of the rainy season only. The Beeling forests in the Martaban provinces labour under a similar disadvantage, and those of the Tharawaddie and Prome forests where any large quantity of timber is left, are situated on hill streams, the lower part of which, at the place where they enter the plains, is almost entirely obstructed.

The Youngzaleen and Doomdamee forests are, of those here enumerated, the easiest for working, but the distance of the timber localities from the main stream is, in most instances, considerably greater than on the Attaran.

The destruction of the Attaran forests therefore has undoubtedly been a great loss for the country ; although it may on the other hand be considered to have proved a benefit, as the abundant supply of timber from thence and the certainty with which it could be calculated upon has given a start to the timber trade and ship-building at

Maulmain, for which other forests more distant and less accessible, might not so easily have afforded the means.

43. From the data given above, it will now be possible to form an estimate of the quantity of timber brought down from the Attaran to Maulmain.

Estimate of the Timber removed from the Attaran Forests.

The records of the timber revenue office from which Statement VII. is compiled only go as far back as 1843-44. Before that time, certain general statements only are available, which are neither complete nor sufficiently accurate. Indeed for one year, 1842-43, no records at all are available, and the return was filled in by taking the mean of the preceding and following years.

The number of stumps estimated as remaining in the whole of the Attaran forests amounts to 171,400. At first sight it would appear that this figure might at once be taken as representing the number of trees or tons of timber removed from the Attaran Forests, but the following remarks lead to a different result.

The number of first class trees in 1827 has been shown to have been 196,200. Assuming the number of second class trees to have been equal to that at present observed, 85,100, there would have been, in 1858, at least 281,300 first class trees, if the forests had not been worked. The second class trees require only 25 years to attain the size of the first class, ... 281,300

Deduct No. of 1st class trees remaining in the Forests, ... 54,400
Ditto No. of trees Nathat and girdled, ... 30,800 = 85,200

Number of trees or tons removed, ... 196,100

This does not include the undersized trees removed. It is, however, a much higher figure than either that obtained from taking the number of stumps (171,400) or the result of Statement VII. (137,947). Assuming, however, the number of stumps as the figure most likely to be correct and considering the returns of the timber revenue office since 1848-49 as reliable, we obtain the number of trees brought down up to 30th April, 1848, ... 161,765

Which gives the annual average for 19 years, ... 7,461 tons
Instead of, as per Statement VII., ... 6,753 „

44. It remains now to show what outturn the Attaran Forests

Estimate of the yield of the Attaran Forests if worked on a regular system. might have yielded, if they had from the beginning been subjected to a regular system of management and worked with a view to maintaining them in their original condition.

The principles laid down for the management of the Pegu Forests are—

1st. Only first class trees to be removed.

2nd. The number of first class trees removed within a given time, to be less than the number of trees of smaller classes which may be expected to attain the standard of the first class within the same time.

From all observations available we conclude that fourth class trees require 10 years, in order to attain the standard of the 3rd class, further that trees of the 3rd class require 27 years in order to attain the standard of the second, and lastly that the smallest second class tree grows up to be a first class tree within 25 years.

If, for instance, the first and second class trees are equal in number, the number of third class trees must be larger in the proportion of 27 to 25, in order to justify a removal of all first class trees within 25 years. The fourth class trees require only 10 years in order to attain the size of the third class trees, but their number is so much subject to diminution from fires and other causes, that to ensure the perpetuation of the forest, it should be at least as large as that of the third class.

In a large portion of the Pegu Forests, viz. the greater part of the Prome, Tharawaddie and Southern Forests, the number of second class trees is equal to, or larger than, that of the first, and the number of third class trees considerably larger than that of the second, while the number of seedlings exceeds the number of trees in any of the other classes. These forests are C Forests, and thirty years have been fixed as the average time during which all first class trees may be removed from a forest tract; five years being allowed above the time required, in order to guard against all contingencies. It must, however, be understood that C Forests can be worked on a short rotation of 30 or 40 years in such localities only as bear a sufficiency of trees to warrant their being worked at all. Many C Forests, like the Attaran, must remain fallow for a considerable time before they can be worked.

But there are many forests where a different proportion prevails, the number of second class trees being considerably smaller than that of the first. In such forests, a longer time must be fixed for the removal of all first class trees. In the Martaban Beeling forests, for instance, the number of first class trees is 8,902, the total of second and third class trees 12,139. It will be necessary here to allow 52 or perhaps even 60 years for the removal of the first class trees, as by that time their place will have been supplied by those of the second and third class trees attaining the standard of the first class.

A list is given on the margin showing how much timber may be removed from several of the forests annually per square mile, without injuring or deteriorating their condition ; but it must be understood that the application of this rule necessarily varies according to circumstances in each separate Teak-producing locality.

	Trees.	
Tharawaddie,..................1·40	24	
Southern Forests,..............1·30	19	
Moong and Padah, ...1·60	41	per Square Mile.
Youkthawah & Thoukyaghat, 1·60	25	
Kannee and Koonoong, ...1·60	84	
Beeling, ...1·60	148	
Youngzaleen,...................1·60	40	
Doomdamee,...................1·60	28	
Middle Thoungyeen, ...1·30	20	

The Attaran Forests, before the working commenced, would appear to have belonged to the same class as the Beeling Forests, and others of a similar character, in which the first class trees more than twice exceed those of the second class. On this supposition one-sixtieth of the first class trees, or 3,270 trees per annum might have been removed without any risk of deteriorating the condition of the forest. For the whole period from 1827 to 1858 this would amount to 101,370 trees or tons, which is 70,000 tons less than the amount actually supposed to have been brought away during that time.

This timber could of course only have been removed without endangering the forests, if the trees to be felled had been carefully selected, and not cut down at random, wherever it appeared most convenient to the wood-cutters.

It would, for instance, not have insured the preservation of the forests if the 32 trees to be removed in one year from one square mile had been cut on one spot, say from a group of Teak trees on the banks of a creek ; for it would have deprived this locality of seedling trees and afforded other kinds an opportunity of coming in and taking up the place of Teak in the forests. But, a regular system once introduced, the same amount of timber might have been removed from the forest annually without diminution; whereas now the supply of timber from the Attaran is come down to less than 1000 trees.

This instance is sufficient to show that protecting the forests is not identical with stopping all supply of timber from the same; yet it makes a great difference in the welfare of a forest, whether a large quantity of timber is removed from the same *at once*, or gradually. The Attaran Forests have been exhausted, not so much through the quantity of timber removed, as through the improvident and irregular manner in which this timber was selected.

45. The earliest Teak plantations in the Attaran Forests were

Captain Tremenheere's plantations unsuccessful.

established by Captain Tremenheere. Nurseries were formed in 1842 in the Natchoung, Mittigate and Kjoon Choung Forests, where about 22,000 seeds were sown. It is not recorded how large a portion of them germinated; but it appears from Captain Guthrie's Report that in 1845 no trace of them remained, with the exception of a single tree at Natchoung.

Another nursery was established near the village of Klay on the Lhineboay river by Captain Tremenheere, in the year 1843; where seeds were sown and seedlings came up. The seeds are represented as having grown well; but the plants were burnt up in the annual fires. Many recovered and flourished on the rains setting in; but were subsequently destroyed by a heavy inundation (page 136 of report).

46. No further attempt was made till 1856, when operations

Thinganneennoung Nursery established in 1856.

were commenced on the Winyeo below its confluence with the Thinganneennoung stream. This is one of the localities proposed by Mr. Colvin, and afterwards recommended by Dr. Falconer in his report (para. 44), the other being in the Mittigate Kyouktaga Forest, in the angle between the Koon Choung and the main stream, and along the banks of the former (para. 55).

A nursery of great extent (192,431 square feet or 4⅜ acres) was prepared. The ground, which had been covered with dense evergreen forest, was cleared; the stumps rooted out; the ground levelled and trenched 1 foot deep; and the nursery drained by a system of open ditches. The soil of the plot selected was remarkably rich, the result of the occupancy for ages by the evergreen forest, never disturbed by the impoverishing inroads of jungle fires.

As far as can be gathered from the information available, 65 baskets of seed were sown. These may be estimated to have contained (at the rate of 15,000 per basket) 907,500 nuts. The operation of sowing was carried on from the 24th March to the 10th April. The seed was not steeped or otherwise prepared, but only the outer leafy covering removed.

It appears that the seed germinated freely and that the plants grew up very satisfactorily. No reliable information can be traced of the number of plants alive one year after sowing, but the following gives an approximate figure. On the 31st July, 1858, the whole of the plants on the two portions, each 28 feet wide and 66 feet long, were counted. The result was as follows.

Number of Teak seedlings counted on 3696 square feet.

Class.	Girth 12″ from ground.	Height of plants.	Number.	
			Well stocked.	Badly stocked.
I.	9″ to 13″	27′ to 32′	17	1
II.	6 to 9	20 to 27	70	38
III.	3 to 6	10 to 20	183	178
IV.	below 3	1 to 10	571	37
			841	254

The two portions were so selected as to be likely to give a correct idea of the whole on the ground. The total number of plants on the ground in July, 1858, may thus be estimated at 57,200 plants; of which about 5,616 had a girth of from 9″ to 13″ and a height of from 27′ to 32′.

But, before 1858, a large number of plants had been transplanted, viz. :

	Plants.	On right side of Winyeo.	On left side of Winyeo.
From 18th April to 9th June, 1857,	10,000	2000	8000
In May 1858,	4,220	4,220	.
	14,220 = 6,220 + 8000		
add, ...	57,200		

This brings the total No., ... 71,420 of plants raised from seed.

14

Many more had undoubtedly germinated, but had perished, being choked by having been allowed to remain too long so close together.

The percentage of plants raised on the quantity of seed thrown out has been comparatively high, viz. 7·9 per cent.; higher than in any other instance in the Teak plantations of these provinces, as will be seen from Statement XIII. attached to this report.

47. During the dry season of 1857 preparations for transplanting were made. A considerable extent of ground was cleared, both immediately around the nursery, on the right bank of the Winyeo, and opposite to it on the left bank. The two sides are very different, as regards the nature of soil and character of the forest. On the right the whole was covered with dense evergreen forest, forming a belt round the ground cleared, which was thus effectually protected from the inroads of jungle fires. However in 1858 a dense mass of herbaceous plants was found to have sprung up between the transplanted seedlings, greatly impeding their development. Here 2000 were planted out in 1857.

A portion transplanted in 1857.

On the left side the ground is higher, more dry and less fertile, it is covered with open mixed forest. A much greater proportion of transplanted seedlings has perished here : partly by the fires, whose sway over this part was unrestrained, partly by the very luxuriant growth of bamboos and grasses.

The number of plants put in here in 1857 was 8000. It is very much to be regretted that the transplanting operations of 1857 were not carried on further, nearly the whole of the plants from the nursery ought to have been removed at that time. It would appear that the operations were interrupted by sickness breaking out among the coolies, which compelled the late Mr. Smith, who was in charge of the work, to return to town, as he found himself deserted by his men. It had been found impossible to induce either Burmans or Karens to work at the plantation, and therefore several hundred Madras coolies had been engaged. The journey to Thinganneennoung took about eight days, of which the last three had to be made by land. There were no villages within less than a day's march, and from these even no provisions could be obtained. Every thing, including rice, had to be brought up from Maulmain. These are difficulties unavoidably connected with an undertaking like this in the interior of the forests.

There is only one time in the year when Teak may be transplanted with success in this country, and that is at the beginning of the rains, and if at that time the operations are interrupted, the whole undertaking is a failure.

The trees were planted, some in quincunx, some in rows; a distance of 10 feet or 20 feet being left between the rows or plants. It is very much to be regretted that they were not planted closer together, for it is quite impossible that plants placed so far apart should be able successfully to struggle with the luxuriant growth of weeds and grasses around them. Had they been placed nearer to each other, say at a distance of 3 feet between plants and of 10 feet between the rows, they would within two years have covered the soil, so far as to destroy all vegetation of weeds and grasses in their neighbourhood.

Dense planting is more necessary in this country than in a temperate climate, on account of the much greater difficulty here in keeping the ground clear of weeds and brushwood; moreover if they grow up close together, the young trees are compelled to form tall and straight stems, and to clear themselves early of their lower branches. These are advantages which fully counterbalance the expense of planting a larger number, which must afterwards be removed by thinning. In May, 1858, the plantation was visited by Mr. Barker, Mr. Smith's successor, who transplanted 4220 more on the right bank of the river, and at the time of my visit from 31st July to 3rd August, an experiment on a small scale with close planting was made. A small patch to the north of the nursery, and originally cleared for a second nursery was covered with transplanted seedlings in rows 10 feet apart and the transplants in the rows 2 feet apart, 2300 trees were thus transplanted. But the plants were then more than 2 years old, and the time of the year, viz. the height of the rains, very unfavorable. No great success therefore can be anticipated from this experiment.

Teak, like oak, first produces a long taproot, which, with plants 2 years old, has a length of from 2 to 4 feet. Only after the tree has attained a certain size, (the exact age has not yet been ascertained) the taproot gradually dies away, and the side branches of the root expand.

The best time for transplanting Teak seedlings is when they are only a few months old. If a year old or more, from 12 to 44 per cent.

usually perish, as will be seen from Statement XIV., showing the results of transplanting Teak at Rangoon. To ensure better success, the seed ought to be sown in April, and transplanted in June of the same year, as recommended in the memorandum describing the method of planting in the Nelumboor Government plantations (Appendix to Dr. Falconer's report No. 2).

48. Had this recommendation been followed out, when the

> Amount that might have been realized, if the transplanting had been completed.
>
> * 1452 seedlings at 3 feet apart, in rows 10 feet apart, fill one acre.

Thinganneennoung plantation was established, it would have been possible to cover an area of 49 acres* with transplanted seedlings. This area would, after successive thinnings, and after the lapse of 62 years, have borne 3675 trees of the first class (in girth above 6 feet). This assumes 75 first class trees per acre, and a distance between the trees of 24 feet. Dr. Falconer only allows 48.4 trees per acre, for second class timber, but there are many localities in the forests where first class trees are found closer together than 24 feet. The total amount of revenue which Government might have expected to realize, including thinnings, would have been as follows.

	Years old.	Trees.	Girth below	Remarks.
Proceeds of thinning before the trees are,	10	726	18	Profit of two first thinnings absorbed by expense of thinning & watching the forest.
,,	22	363	3	
,,	37	181	4' 6''	Revenue Rs. 90-8 per acre at 8 As. a piece.
,,	62	107	6'	Revenue Rs. 428 per acre at Rs. 4 per piece.
No. of full-sized trees remaining.		75		
		1452		

The amount of revenue to be realized from the remaining 75 trees will naturally vary according to the system which may be adopted for working the forest. As it would have become a forest consisting solely of Teak it might be placed under a regular rotation. Supposing the length of rotation were fixed at 62 years, the ground might suitably be divided into 5 divisions which would be cleared in succession of all trees in intervals of 15 years, so as to allow the free space to be stocked with seedlings from the adjoining tracts. The average annual revenue for 10 acres would then be the value of 12 trees 6 feet in girth plus the revenue to be realized from thinnings in those tracts which have not yet attained maturity. The timber growing close to the river, and hence not requiring to be dragged might be expected to sell on the spot at 20 Rupees per tree, so that the annual revenue per acre might be estimated at

Sale of full grown trees, ...Rs. 24 0 0
By proceeds of thinnings ¼, ... 6 0 0

Total Rupees, 30 0 0

Annual revenue per acre.

Or it might be preferred to cut down the whole of the trees on their attaining maturity, in which case the revenue at the end of 62 years would amount to Rupees 1,500 per acre, but in this case, artificial planting would again have to be resorted to, if Teak were again to be produced on the same locality.

49. As the Thinganneennoung plantation stands at present, it is difficult to estimate what the outturn is likely to be. It consists of a nursery 4¼ acres with about 57,200 plants, transplants on both sides of the Winyeo on about 32 acres with 14,220 plants put out, of which a small portion only may be expected to arrive at maturity. The nursery is likely to yield at the rate stated above, viz. thinnings before 37 years, at the rate of Rs. 90-8 per acre.* The transplants are not likely to yield any revenue by way of thinning, and only one-half of the ultimate result after 62 years, or 750 Rupees per acre. The result of the whole after 62 years is not likely to exceed 325 trees on the nursery and 1184 trees on the plantation.

Proceeds likely to be realized by the plantation in its actual condition.

* Before 62 years Rs. 428 per acre and value of full-sized trees at 62 years, 1500 per acre.

Attached is a plan of the Thinganneennoung plantation and forests in its immediate neighbourhood. In May, 1859, another attempt was made at transplanting the plants remaining in the nursery, and it was expected that it would be possible to obtain Karen coolies from the villages on the Winyeo for the work. This has proved a failure, the people were afraid to remain there, and 4000 young trees only were transplanted. The plants being now 4 years old, further attempts would only be a source of expenditure with very doubtful success.

It is necessary here to observe, that since no boundaries were ever laid down between the Government reserved forest of Thinganneennoung and the adjacent forests in the hands of private parties, the Teak trees raised on the plantation may be hereafter claimed by the holders of the latter.

50. Two other plantations have been established by Mr. Gemmer in the Tenasserim provinces, one on Koloon island, another near Shoaegoon, both on the banks of the Salween at a distance of about 60 miles from Maulmain. These localities have the advantage of being far easier accessible than Thinganneennoung, and of being more healthy and situated in the proximity of large villages. But the soil is very inferior. It is a poor loose soil covered with open dry forest containing a fair proportion of Teak, but the stature of the trees is short and they are not very straight. On the east side of the Koloon island, a nursery of 4 or 5 acres was formed in 1855, but owing to the unusually high rise of the river that season most of the plants perished. In 1856 a new nursery was formed on a higher situation, covering about 3 acres. The ground was cleared, levelled, trenched and drained in the usual manner. The number of plants was esti-mated in 1858 to be 25,000. A few only had been transplanted in 1856 and 1857. In April, 1859, I examined the nursery and found that the largest trees had attained a height of 13′. I made arrangements for transplanting the greater portion to the ground adjoining. This was only partially accomplished, as the coolies refused to stay long enough to complete the whole. The plantation comprises now about 7 acres with upwards of 20,000 plants and may thus be expected after 62 years to have 525 first class trees.

On the east bank of the Salween river, above the village of Shoaegoon a nursery was established in 1856. Its size is 4½ acres.

Plantations on the Salween.

The amount of seeds sown was 70 baskets, but only 13,725 plants were found in November, 1856. When last examined (April, 1859,) it was found to contain 11,000 plants, equal in size to those on Koloon island. It may be expected to yield about 338 first class trees in the year 1918.

The probable results of thinning operations on the two plantations on the Salween may be estimated as follows.

On area of 11¼ acres stand 31,000 plants.

Girth below.

Proceeds of thinning before 10 years old	20,000	18′	}	Proceeds absorbed by expenses.
,,	22	6,000	3′	}
,,	37	3,000	4′6″	} Revenue Rs. 1,500 at Rs. 8 a tree.
,,	62	1,137	6′	} Revenue Rs. 4,548 at Rs. 4 per tree.
No. of full sized trees remaining 62 yrs. old,	863	6′	} Proceeds Rs. 17,260 at Rs. 20 per tree.

31,000

51. The total amount expended on account of the plantations up to the 30th September, 1859, when the operations were closed, was Rupees 22,291-6-8. This does not include the pay of the regular establishment of the Forest Department, but it includes all amounts expended on account of travelling allowance and travelling expenses of assistants and subordinates. The different plantations should be charged in the following proportion.

Expenditure incurred in the Tenasserim plantations.

Thinganneennoung, ...	14,965	10	8
Koloon, ...	3,538	15	8
Shoaegoon, ...	3,786	12	4
Total,	22,291	6	8

It will be seen that these figures do not quite correspond with the proportions of full-sized trees expected to be raised on the three plantations.

		Number of 1st class trees expected.	Amount expended on one tree.
For we have on the Thinganneennoung plantation,		1509	Rs. 9-14
Koloon	,,	525	6-11
Shoaegoon	,,	338	11-2
Total,		2372	

The average may be put down at 10 Rupees per tree or at 750 Rupees per acre. This rate of expenditure is much too high, for we have seen above that the ultimate annual revenue will amount only to 30 Rupees per acre commencing when the plantations are 62 years old, and that before that time the thinnings are only likely to produce 518-8 per acre for the entire period.

It is true that the expenditure would be less disproportionate if the seedlings had been transplanted in due time, and thus the area covered with Teak had been increased; but even supposing the area had been doubled the amount expended would still appear too high, if it is borne in mind that the amount expended on a plantation is a capital sunk, to which compound interest must be added until the plantation commences to yield any returns.

52. It is of importance fully to exhaust the question to what

What amount may be expended on Teak plantations without making them unprofitable.

amount the expenditure per acre must be reduced, in order to render Teak plantations remunerative in the Attaran Forests.

We have seen that if a rotation of 62 years is adopted, the annual revenue of an acre of pure Teak forest is not likely to exceed 30 Rupees, to commence when the plantation is 62 years old. Assuming 6 per cent. to be the rate of interest, the value of one acre of forest land would, after the lapse of 62 years, amount to 500 Rupees. We call this the prospective value of the forest. But if the whole timber standing on it is to be felled and sold, the value appears much higher, viz. $75 \times 20 = 1500$ Rupees, we call this the present value of a forest. The difference between the present and prospective value of the forest is of course only apparent: the fact is that the annual yield of an acre of Teak forest in Burmah (30 Rs.) amounts to only 2 per cent. on its value, 1500 Rupees. In Europe where every stick produced in a forest is valuable, the proceeds of thinning considerably increase the rent to be obtained from forest land.

To either, the amount of proceeds from the thinning operations must be added, amounting to

Rs. 90-8, to be realized at about 30 years after establishment of the plantation.

Rs. 428,   ditto   ditto   50   ditto   ditto.

.In order to express what these amounts are worth after 62 years, compound interest must be added, which gives, assuming the rate to be 6 per cent,—

Value of first thinning at the end of 62 years, ...	315
,, second ,, ,, ...	685
,, of 75 full-sized trees,..............................	1,500
Total,	2,500

The principal which may be sunk, in order to realize this sum after 62 years, amounts to 67½ Rupees. If compound interest at the rate of 6 per cent. is added to 67½, it will, in the course of 62 years, increase to 2,500 Rupees.

If the prospective value is taken, then the amount which may be expended on one acre will amount to 40½ Rupees only. Until therefore the expenditure for raising 1,452 Teak seedlings, or any number which may be found sufficient, and for planting them out on one acre can be reduced to respectively Rs. 67½ or 40½, Teak plantations cannot be said to be a profitable undertaking. In the Tenasserim provinces, the expenditure has hitherto amounted to more than ten times this amount, but then the circumstances were exceedingly unfavorable: no villages near the plantation, no provisions to be had, great unhealthiness of the forest, and difficulty of access. If such localities are avoided, success may not be despaired of, provided subordinates can be obtained who are trained to the work, and who do not make a point of wasting public money.

Plantations, on a small scale, should therefore continue to be established with a view to ascertain how the expenditure can be reduced, but it should be distinctly understood that they must not be looked upon as revenue speculations; but as likely to afford us the means to become more intimately acquainted with the mode of growth, the laws of increase, and the general habits of the Teak trees : in short we should at the present time expect plantations to yield the material for observation and experiment, which will enable us, or our successors at a future period, to establish a more rational system of forest management. At the same time these experimental plantations on a small scale will serve to train the subordinates of the Department to this work, and to impress upon them the necessity of husbanding the expenditure on the same.

53. If the Teak on the Attaran forests were Government property, a new and peculiar method of artificially cultivating Teak might be adopted, which of all others is likely to prove least expensive. This is to induce the Toungya cultivators to sow Teak seed together with paddy on their Toungyas. The plan was first proposed in para. 154 of my Report on the Pegu Forests for 1856, a copy of which is given in Appendix No. 7, but hitherto only the Karen inhabitants of the Attaran districts have shown any inclination to adopt it, provided they are permitted to consider the trees raised by themselves as their own property. This request I much regretted not being able to comply with at the time, the ownership of the Teak in the forests not being settled. The proposal was first made by the Tsokays of Tagoondine and other villages situated not far above the junction of both rivers, where the inhabitants cultivate paddy-fields besides their Toungyas, and have no wandering habits; but from conversations I had on the subject with the headmen of other villages, I have no doubt that the measure, if it can be carried out, will be generally acceptable to most of them.

Teak plantations in Toungyas.

54. We now proceed to discuss the future prospects of the forests. These will be of a different nature, should they be left, as they at present are, in the hands of private parties, from what they would be if resumed by Government and brought under a regular system of management.

Prospects of the Attaran Forests, if they were to be resumed by Government.

The latter alternative will be considered first. The first operation in this case would be the removal and disposal by sale of the old seasoned timber in the forests. According to the surveys available this may be estimated to consist of logs and pieces lying on the ground (16,900). These ought, in all fairness, to remain at the disposal of former holders.

Further of Nathat trees,.................... 8,400
Girdled trees, ... 22,400

Total of seasoned trees, 30,800; few of them of any value, except those in the Mittigate Codogway, and not likely all to come down.

These 30,800 trees may, at the highest, be expected to yield a revenue of 2 Rupees per piece, or, upon the whole, of 61,600 Rupees. They would probably yield one-half or two-thirds of this sum by way of duty if brought down by private parties.

After the removal of the seasoned timber, however, the forests ought to have complete rest for 40 years, so as to enable all trees now 22 years old and above, viz. the second and one-half of the third class to attain the standard of first class trees. At the expiration of this period we may expect to have on the square mile,—

Trees at present of the first class, ... 544
ditto   second ditto, ... 851
One half of third, those above 3 cubits in girth and of more
    than 22 years age,... 550

1,945
Deduct 10 per cent. for Nathat, ... 194

Trees,.............. 1,751

The second class would, at the same time, consist of what are
    now the second half of the third and the fourth class
    trees or 550+976 = ... 1,526
From which must be deducted for Nathat trees and the de-
    struction by Jungle fires, 30 per cent., ... 508

Number of second class trees at the end of 40 years,............ 1,018
The forest would then belong to Class B. and might be worked in a rotation of 60 years. It would thus yield an annual outturn of 29 logs per square mile, or 2,900 for the whole forest. If hereafter the number of second class trees were found to increase considerably, so as to exceed that of the first class, the time of rotation might be reduced to 40 or 30 years, and a corresponding increase in the outturns would then be realized.

Instead of letting the forests lie fallow for 40 years, it might be proposed to give up attempting to bring them back to their original condition, and to work them at once, keeping them in the state in which they are now (544 trees per square mile). It might be urged that, in the same manner as the Southern Pegu Forest, they might be worked in a short rotation of 30 years, and yield an annual outturn of 18 logs per square mile. But the two forest tracts are very differently constituted. Those parts of the Southern Pegu Forests which alone are worked, have not as a whole suffered any very material change from their original condition. They have never probably had a much greater number of first class trees on the square mile than they have now, and although large quantities of timber had been obtained from them before they were placed entirely under the control of the Forest Department, yet most of the first class trees remaining are good and sound. Teak on the hills of the Southern Pegu Forests, wherever it has not been destroyed by Toungya cultivation, probably bears nearly the same proportion to other trees as it did before. It may therefore be worked, provided the forest is always maintained in the same state.

The Attaran Forests, however, have within a short time entirely changed their character. Teak never was scattered here over wide extents of dry hilly country, but congregated in patches, where it formed a comparatively large proportion of the trees in the forest. Nearly the whole of the second large trees have been removed. What remains is of no value as timber, and of very little value as yielding seed. The number of trees attacked with epiphytic ficus alone amounts to one-seventh of the whole first class trees in the forests, and in some of those sections where most timber is left (Mittigate and Kyoon Choung) the greater half of the first class trees are attacked with it. One half at least of the first class trees must be considered as of no value for the maintenance of the forests. If the Attaran therefore were to be worked with the view of merely maintaining it in its present condition, 9 trees per square mile, or 900 trees for the whole, would be the limit up to which timber might be removed from the same.

55. In the hands of private parties, the Attaran forests have **Prospects of the Forests if in the hands of private parties.** yielded 983 trees per annum since 1848. They may hereafter occasionally yield a higher outturn, according to the demand for timber in the

market, or other circumstances of an accidental nature, but a higher yield than 900 trees annually cannot be expected to last for any length of time. And even this yield is not likely to be lasting, unless the holders pursue a regular system of selecting the trees to be felled. The chief value of the Attaran forests has of late consisted in the crooked timber which they have produced for ship-building. From 1848 to 1858 they have yielded ships' crooks, ... 17,989

Full-sized logs,........................ 5,681

It is of importance for the ship building at Maulmain that the supply of crooks from the Attaran should not decrease; for the forests on the Thoungyeen and Upper Salween (above the rapids), whence at present the principal supplies of straight timber are brought, are not likely to yield crooks in large quantities, as the floating down of the same is more difficult in the irregular channel of the Salween, than the floating of large logs; and, as on the other hand, their value is too small to bear great expenses on that account. Maulmain therefore must obtain a supply of crooks corresponding to the quantity of straight timber, from the forests below the Salween rapids. The numerous irregular and deformed trees remaining in these forests, are likely to yield a considerable amount of this kind of timber, and a large quantity may also be obtained from branches and the upper part of trees left on the ground by the former workers.

Should Government take the forests into their own hands, it would be difficult to devise measures so as to leave the bringing away of crooks as free and unfettered as it might be desirable for the ship-building interest at Maulmain. This is an important consideration in favour of not resuming the forests, at least not until another source of crooked timber has been opened. At present the only other sources for crooked timber are the Hlinebong and Lower Salween forests, both of very limited extent and with very little timber remaining.

56. It remains now to consider whether the forest-holdings on the Attaran can, in justice, be resumed by Government.

Can the Forest-holdings be resumed by Government?

The number of forest-holders who actually make use of their license, and work their forest regularly is very small. Signs of working were found, in 1858, in five forest tracts only. Besides these, there may be from 10 to 20 more forest-holdings claimed by license-holders, but it is certain that more than one half of the 54 holdings enumerated in Mr. Hobday's list, is vacant. Some of them were cancelled in 1853 (See Statement No. X.), others have lapsed on account of the death of the owner: for instance No. 6, Dooncan's and No. 7 Shoaey-Yah's forest. However, those forests that are claimed, are far more extensive and contain more timber than the others. We have seen above, that the original licenses granted by Mr. Maingy or renewed by Mr. Blundell can scarcely be considered any longer as subject to any penalty clause of the forest rules promulgated at different times. But on the other hand the licenses were from the beginning considered as revocable at will, and the question is only what will constitute sufficient cause for resuming them. The holders have enjoyed the exclusive privilege of cutting timber in a certain locality; what have they done, it may be asked, to merit a continuation of this privilege? No instance is on record in which they have incurred any outlay to improve their forests. Leaving plantations entirely out of the question, they have not even done so much as to facilitate the carriage of their own timber. They have not observed any rules regarding transfer of their licenses; they have disposed of their holdings by sale or otherwise, without registering the transfer, or giving any intimation whatever to the proper authorities. They have not worked the forests with a view to make the best of the produce, but they have constantly brought down green and badly seasoned timber, and have thereby endangered the reputation of Attaran Teak. They have not looked towards husbanding the resources of the forests, but have, in the most reckless manner, cut down trees large and small, and frequently after taking a small piece out of a large tree, they have, left the remainder to be burnt. Even the bringing down of timber from their forests has, in many instances, been entirely neglected by them, they have killed hundreds of trees without making an attempt at removing them; in short they have treated their privilege as a matter of no value whatsoever. Common justice to other parties, who are not forest-holders, would appear to demand that the privilege of cutting timber in a certain locality to the exclusion of all others, if granted, as it was, revocable at will, should be recalled, whenever it is not used, or whenever it is misused. Although therefore none of the penalty clauses of the rules are now of any avail, yet for forests which are not worked in a satisfactory manner the privilege might justly be cancelled.

On the other hand it is urged by the forest-holders that Government has not only practically abandoned the penalty clauses, but has led them to believe that the licenses would never be resumed, and that their permission was not dependent on the fulfilment of any conditions whatsoever.

The holders state that by old usage they are now looked upon as bonâ fide proprietors of the Teak in the forests, and that their right is sold and bought, and has a certain market value; so that in case Government resolved to take possession of the forests, their rights ought to be redeemed by the payment of a certain amount as compensation.

57. The development of the legal consequences of this question is foreign to this report, but the following preliminary measures may be recommended as being likely to prove beneficial to the interests of the forests in these provinces generally.

The decision on this point referred to higher authority : preliminary measures proposed.

First. The Attaran forests will be left to be worked by private parties, and will not be resumed by Government.

Second. None of the licenses to cut timber in the Attaran forests are recognized as conveying an exclusive right to Teak or any other timber in the forest districts, unless such right is distinctly granted by the terms of the license or grant, and unless the boundaries of the tract within which such rights may be exercised are clearly laid down in that document.

Third. All holders of licenses or grants are to prove their claims before a committee appointed for the purpose, within six months; after which time, no claims will be received or recognized.

Fourth. Any one who may plant at his own expense Teak trees on an area not less than one acre, and the plants not less than 10′ apart (or at the rate of 430 plants per acre) will be considered as the owner of all Teak trees thus sown or planted, and such person may claim the right of conveying his timber to the nearest Choung by which timber can be floated.

These measures are naturally only of a preliminary nature. Further steps must be considered when the claims of holders shall have been registered, and their extent is known. But it is necessary at once to declare that the mere fact of a person being considered a forest-holder does not give him the right of disposal over trees planted by others, or of interfering with cultivators, if they cut down any timber which he may wish to use himself.

But, these two points provided for, there appears to be no reason why the present Forest holders, or such of them as are able to prove their claims, should not be left in possession of the right of felling Teak timber in certain localities. The duration of this right may either be fixed at 99 years or at a shorter period. But it must be clearly understood that the inhabitants of the Forest are to exercise fully the same rights as Forest holders, and that the duty fixed for Attaran timber, viz. 4 Rupees per log, remains unchanged.

58. Whatever may be decided regarding the conditions of the

Boundaries between different Forest licenses to cut, the boundaries of the
tracts to be settled. tracts for which the licenses are given
must be defined.

As early as April, 1837, Mr. Blundell pointed out the inconvenience arising from the want of defined boundaries between the different grants and the unsatisfactory nature of the suits in Court arising out of the same.

Mr. Hobday's map of 1851 gives the general situation of the different forest tracts, but does not lay down any defined boundary lines. Hence lawsuits occasionally occur. One instance is given above of a suit between Mr. Darwood and Mr. Rushbrook regarding the upper portion of the Megwa forests.

It may be urged that there is no necessity for interfering with the boundaries, that whenever a dispute arises, it can easily be settled in Court in the regular way. If this objection were correct, it would be much preferable to issue no licenses at all for particular localities, but to let any one cut where he liked. But this would evidently lead to much dispute and confusion.

On the other hand it cannot be denied that in the absence of all principles regulating the laying down of these boundaries, and in the absence of sufficiently detailed and correct maps, the settlement of these cases must always remain a most unsatisfactory one.

The regulation of the boundaries would not be a work of much difficulty, numerous lines being given by the natural configuration of the country and others being easily obtained by the application of a few general principles.

The whole of the forests are divided into two unequal portions, the Zimmay and Winyeo, separated beyond the possibility of a dispute by the water-shed between these two rivers.

Again each of these is easily subdivided into the forests on the east and on the west bank of the main stream. And as the main forest tracts are situated along some of the principal feeders of the main stream, a further subdivision could be carried out according to the drainage into these different feeders, and in a few instances only will it be necessary to introduce artificial lines of demarcation.

A survey of the whole would certainly be required, but as it is of no importance correctly to ascertain the area of the different tracts, four routes, surveyed with prismatic compass and chain only, and laid so as to pass through the principal forests in each of the four large divisions, joined occasionally by transverse routes and checked by bearings taken across the valleys from the hills on either side, would probably be found sufficient.

59. Those parts of the forests which are not held by any one, *The ungranted portions of the forest how to be disposed of.* may be given away in a similar manner. I would recommend that not only those forests which have been vacated through the death of the holders or the licenses for which have been cancelled, should be disposed of, but also those known as the "Government reserved forests," including the Government plantation Thinganneennoung. It is a fallacy to think that these districts will ever be of any value to Government. In the first instance, the number of growing trees on them is very small, and supposing any timber of value were left, there would not be the least security against its being worked out by parties from the adjoining forests at their own convenience, and without regard to its being the produce of a "Government reserved forest," as has been hitherto the practice. Government forests ought to be altogether separate, and not, as the reserved Attaran forests are, at the head-waters of streams, the lower course of which runs through forests in the hands of private parties.

The experiment might be tried to put up the licenses of cutting timber in some of the unoccupied forests, to public competition, but in case this method should not answer, the principle might be introduced of granting licenses to such parties only as have planted a certain area with Teak. I have little doubt that this would soon

16

induce a considerable number of Tsokays of the Karen villages to plant Teak on their Toungyas.

It is true they would not be likely to husband the Teak trees thus planted, they would cut them down wholesale as soon as opportunity offered, but it would level the way towards establishing Teak plant-ations in other parts of the country. Against this supposition it may be urged, that most of the inhabitants of the Attaran are Karens, who are an exceedingly migratory race, and less likely than any others, to establish plantations of trees. But we find the Karens on the whole of the mountainous districts between Sitang and Salween busily engaged in planting groves of the "gigantic bamboo" and making extensive plantations of betel palms. It is true they require the former for the erection of their houses, and the latter for their own consump-tion, besides which both yield returns within 15 years. But the possi-bility of obtaining Teak for the construction of their houses or of selling it to merchants from Maulmain, is likely to prove a great attraction to them, and, although naturally indolent, they will work if an object takes their fancy. At the same time having considerable numbers of elephants, they are well able to work the forests. Indeed most foresters from Maulmain, who now go up into the Attaran, hire the elephants for dragging timber from the Karens.

60. It is here the place to add a few words regarding the inhabi-tants of the Attaran valleys. The Attaran, like the Thoungyeen and other valleys in the Tenasserim Provinces, was originally inhabited by Talines. Old groves of jack and other fruit trees of immense size and the remains of pagodas and rude fortifications indicate in many places the site of their former villages both in the valley of the Winyeo and Zimmay.

Inhabitants of the Attaran.

But no other traces of this old population remain above the junc-tion of the two rivers. The Talines were driven out of their country during the Siamese wars in the latter part of the 18th century, and the forests on the Winyeo and Zimmay rivers, appear to have been utterly uninhabited until the time when the country became a British province. Since then there has been a gradually increasing immigra-tion of Karens and others from the neighbouring country.

The accompanying Statement XII. shows the number of villages as found in July and August, 1858, and the different nationalities are indicated on the map.

According to the statement of some of the oldest inhabitants, the number of villages before 1830 were 8; by 1840 they had increased to 14; by 1850 to 35; and the remainder have sprung up since.

The first immigrants were Pho or Taline Karens, and they form at present by far the larger portion of the inhabitants. They have mostly come in from that portion of the Siamese territory which immediately adjoins the south frontier of the Tenasserim Provinces. The Sgau or Ayine Karens have come across from the Thoungyeen, or from Rangoon. The Pho Karens here are Buddhists, and their priests Talines. Of the Sgau, a few are Christians, converted by the American Baptist Missionaries.

Only a few of these villages have Kwengs with permanent paddy cultivation. They are marked yellow on the map, and are entirely confined to the lower portion of the valley near the junction of the two rivers.

Higher up, Toungyas form the only mode of cultivation: the jungle is cleared away, burnt when dry, and after the first rainfall, paddy is sown. The principal operation after this is keeping the ground clear of weeds, and certainly the Karens in the Attaran excel in the care which they bestow on this work. But they are surpassed by the Shans from Bankok, and the Lawa people. The villages which have wet or permanent paddy cultivation, have considerable herds of buffaloes, but almost all Toungya-cultivating villages possess large numbers of elephants which they purchase in the Shan country beyond Kyoukoung. The use of these animals to them is very limited, they employ them for carrying down their plantains, sugarcanes or other produce to the landing-places of the merchant boats from Maulmain; or for the removal of the unburnt felled trees from Toungyas, or occasionally for timber work, but they seem principally to value them as an ornament, and as a proof of their wealth.

A peculiar feature in the agriculture of the Attaran is the attention paid to the cultivation of plantains, which form a second crop after the paddy is reaped.

Paddy is sown (10 corns in a hole) in holes from 12 to 18 inches apart. Between these, about 9' apart, plantains are put in. No less than thirteen varieties, and some of them of excellent quality, are cultivated in the Attaran forests. In some places the soil is so fertile that a plantain garden will continue to yield valuable fruit for 9 or 10 years in succession, fresh sprouts coming out constantly from the old roots. In other places sugarcane is cultivated. They cultivate six varieties, and the stems attain an unusually large girth.

Several kind of cucumbers are cultivated in a similar manner. They are generally planted near the unburnt trees, which strew the ground, and cover them afterwards with their foliage. Trees that were left standing or stumps of felled trees are covered with the luxuriant foliage of several kinds of yam (Dioscorea, sp). In moist localities is Caladium esculentum, and besides these there are scattered on the Toungyas Asclepias curassavica, Ricinus communis and several species of capsicum.

Very little cotton, and no silk or tobacco, is cultivated in the Attaran. The inhabitants purchase their whole supply of tobacco from Kyoukoung across the frontier. The absence of cotton is remarkable, as both soil and climate appear suitable for this plant. The climate is less dry than in Pegu, rain being of more frequent occurrence during the dry season and the dews very heavy.

The soil is exceedingly fertile in the upper part of the valley. The cultivation of valuable kinds of plantains is principally carried on in the Zimmay valley above the mouth of the Mittigate.

The trade in this article is very considerable. The traders come up during the rains and settle their bargain by making advances on the plantains long before they are ripe. In the dry season they return to conclude their purchases and to carry them down to Maulmain.

The whole area of Toungyas which are annually cut in the Attaran may be estimated at 6 square miles. If it is assumed that deserted Toungyas require 15 years to return to the original state of forest. There

Note.—52 villages at 75 acres each give 3,900 acres or about 6 square miles or 1.2 per cent. of the whole area.

are about 45 square miles with Toungyas at present under cultivation or deserted. These would be twice that amount, if the greater part of the inhabitants had not come in within the last 15 years.

It is impossible that such extensive Toungya clearings should remain without an injurious effect on the Teak forests, unless restricted by forest rules, but there is comparatively little Teak left in the Attaran forest to be damaged by Toungya cultivation, and I consider it to be an additional advantage of making over the forests entirely to private parties, that, in this instance at least, there will be no necessity for interference with the extension of cultivation.

61. India is not the country, where the advantage of a provi-

dent management of forests is generally understood. The interests of a few
persons only in this country reach beyond a limited number of years.
And this feeling of exclusive regard for the interests immediately before
them easily communicates itself to public servants as well as to private
parties.

We must therefore expect that from time to time violent outcries
will be raised in India against the administration of forests by Government.

By proposing to leave the Attaran forests entirely in the hands
of private parties, we give fair play to the other side, and can afterwards draw the comparison between the results of both systems.

The Attaran forests made over to private enterprize, will, it is
hoped, prove the safety-valve for forest administration in India.

No. 167.

FROM

CAPTAIN HENRY HOPKINSON,·

Commissioner Tenasserim and Martaban Provinces,

To

CECIL BEADON, ESQUIRE,

Secretary to the Government of India, Foreign Department, Fort William,
Dated, Maulmain the 6th September, 1860.

SIR,

       I have the honor to submit herewith for the consideration
and orders of Government, a report
by Dr. Brandis on the Attaran forests

Forests.

prepared in obedience to instructions from this office under date the
1st July, 1858. Dr. Brandis' report having been completed in March
last, I wished to have seen him on it, before I forwarded it, and I
trusted that he would have been at Maulmain during this or the past
month at latest; but his local engagements have not apparently allowed
him to have his head quarters in the Tharrawaddie district, and I am
unwilling to encounter further delay by waiting for him any longer.

    2. When I requested Dr. Brandis to oblige me with a report
on the Attaran forests, I had in view merely that, after inspecting
them, he should let me have his opinion as to what should be done
with them : whether the State should take the whole or a portion of
them under any and what sort of management; or whether it should
resign all interest in them unconditionally, or conditionally, making
some bargain or terms with the persons in whom it recognized pre-
existing rights to them or to whom it was willing to cede rights in
them, or thirdly whether its action should be a mixed one, keeping
some forests itself, acknowledging a proprietary right in others, ceding
a third class, and perhaps abandoning a fourth class neither worth
working itself nor any body else working. I also wished the Teak
plantation question determined. These were the points upon which
my predecessor's despatch, No. 9 of the 30th November 1855, chiefly
sought orders, and which the Forest Rules which have been approved

and the appointment of a Superintendent of Forests to which you refer in your letter, No. 1098 of the 14th March, 1859, did not dispose of.

3. Dr. Brandis has not given me the information I wanted in precisely the shape I looked to have it; but he has done much more, he has drawn up a most valuable report, which he is very anxious to publish, and which I trust the Government will allow to be published, and which embraces a dissertation on the general character of the Teak forests in Burmah and the mode of surveying them; secondly, a history of the Attaran forests, commencing in 1827, when Dr. Wallich first visited them, down to the present time; thirdly, an account of the various attempts at Teak plantation, and their probable result; and lastly an estimate of the future prospects of the forests, accordingly as they may be left in the hands of private parties or brought under State management.

4. I cannot regret the elaborate character of Dr. Brandis' report, it will be found, I believe, a mine of information on the subject of which it treats, but my present duty would have been an easier one had he confined himself to a succinct recommendation of the future course to be pursued on the points indicated in my 3rd paragraph, nevertheless his opinion on them has been indicated with sufficient clearness, on the plantation question at part 3rd of his report, beginning with para. 45, and ending at para. 53, and as to the course to be adopted with regard to the Attaran forests, beginning at para. 54 and ending at para. 60.

5. The principle on which my predecessor, Sir Archibald Bogle, proceeded was "that the Government is the only party capable of restoring the forests of Tenasserim" and that to this end Government should proceed to the resumption of all permits to work Teak in the Attaran, and then take their management into their own hands, and push on vigorously the planting them anew. Or if the Government were averse from the resumption of permits, they were then to confirm them with stipulation providing for the work of planting being done by the permit holders. This is the substance of the propositions contained in Sir Archibald Bogle's No. 9 of the 30th November, 1855, to which I before sought an answer.

6. Dr. Brandis' views may be almost said to be diametrically opposed to those of Sir A. Bogle. He does not encourage the idea

of planting on a large scale with the view to the general renovation of the forests, and he would abandon them to the present permit holders. In fact it would seem that he thinks that the best use which can be now made of the Attaran forests is as an example to all India of the deplorable results of private management.

7. I think that Dr. Brandis has clearly and ably made out his case against the planting scheme; to begin, he shows that, in the Tenasserim provinces, the expenditure on Teak planting per acre has hitherto amounted to about ten times the sum which put out at compound interest at 6 per cent. per annum would give an increase, equal to the value of the Teak trees when they reached maturity, supposing all went well with them, or, in other words, that Government have been spending at the rate of Rupees 750 per acre to obtain a possible return in the course of the next 62 years of 2,500 rupees, he shows also that the annual revenue of an acre of pure Teak forest is not likely to exceed 30 rupees, to commence when the plantation is 62 years old, and that could the cost of planting be reduced from 750 rupees per acre and so low as 40½ rupees, the Government would still be getting only 6 per cent. for their money. He tells us also what "the difficulties unavoidably connected with an undertaking" such as that of planting in the interior of the forests are: that Burmese and Karens cannot be induced to work on the plantation, that it is a day's journey from the nearest village, that all provisions have to be brought up from Maulmain, and that it is deadly sickly, so that the Madras coolies who go up there get frightened and desert, lastly the plantation is constantly imperilled by the rank vegetation which the rains raise to choke the young plants, or which, dried up by the succeeding drought, feeds the jungle fires which consume them.

8. I fancy, however, that it was not in the way of a revenue speculation, that the Government desired the renovation of the forests. Government have nothing to do with such speculations, and if they desired to have, the Tenasserim provinces offer better speculations than Teak planting. I rather imagine that the Government would be actuated by the idea of preserving a valuable object of the trade and industry of the people, but even on this supposition, the sacrifice they are called upon to make, seems too great.

9. All then that Dr. Brandis proposes to do is to keep up plantations on a small scale for the purpose of studying the Teak plant and its law of growth, &c., and so to accumulate a stock of

knowledge which may be applied to operations on a large scale, if hereafter found expedient. I agree with Dr. Brandis in this proposition, and recommend that the Government adopt it and direct that all planting operations be henceforward confined within the limits it suggests.

10. In his 53rd paragraph, Dr. Brandis indeed points out how, if the Teak in the Attaran forests were declared Government property, their renovation might, to some extent, be provided for through the agency of the Toungya or bush-cultivators, among whom some of the Karens have shown themselves willing to grow Teak, if their right of property in it were recognized. Dr. Brandis seems to think that he was not able to make this guarantee, and perhaps as Superintendent of Forests he is right, but the Deputy Commissioner might, I believe, without contravening the spirit of our existing revenue rules give anybody who cleared waste land and planted Teak on it the assurance that his right of property would be preserved to him or to his descendants when it arrived at maturity. I do not myself, however, augur any very positive results from anything the present migratory dwellers in the forests are likely to do in the way of Teak planting.

11. I now proceed to a brief expression of my opinion on the question of resumption, or abandonment of the Attaran forests by the Government.

12. The difficulty which has hitherto been supposed to beset this question is the nature of the rights of the permit holders, but the impression the examination of the records of its past discussion gives me is that the determination to solve it has always been wanting. From first to last I should suppose that the Government of India and the Honorable the Court of Directors saw clearly enough that the permit holders had, I will not say, no legal, but no equitable title to what they claimed; but on the other hand, there were those among them whose resentment was a matter worth the regarding. The Hon'ble Court therefore, while unwilling to surrender what they felt were their just rights, yet liked as little to give an opportunity to the clamour always ready to be urged against them that they stood between the British capitalist and his enterprise, and which, in this instance, might be raised by voices unusually powerful; a stronger Government, however, may follow a bolder policy.

17

13., As stated by Dr. Brandis, the holders would no doubt be still ready to insist upon what they would term their prescriptive right, and show how the permits have been bought and sold, and have always had a certain market value attached to them ; but I believe that no holder was ever deceived as to the real value of his permit, or reckoned in buying it on any other assurance than the Government would not venture to deprive him of it.

14. Sir Archibald's letter to which I have before referred, contains an exhaustive analysis of the nature of the title of the permit holders, and his conclusion upon it is given at paragraphs 34 and 35 of the letter : it runs as follows :—

" 34. I have been at some pains to ascertain this," (the permit title,) " and I have no hesitation in saying that from the beginning it has never been anything more than a permission to cut within certain localities, revocable at will, and that the let-mats or licenses never contained any proprietary right whatever.

" 35. Although a disposition has frequently been shewn by different authorities, including the Bengal Government, to regard the fact of lengthened occupation, occupancy, or use, as conveying a prescriptive right, the Government and the Court of Directors have as frequently shewn that they did not recognize any such claim as of right, and have over and over again in correspondence as well as in Rules, maintained the right of resumption, which I hold to be incontestable. There certainly does not exist any deed or contract showing that the foresters have any right to be continued in unrestricted occupation."

15. I am of opinion that this is an incontrovertible judgment upon the facts of the case, and that if it were a matter of expediency to resume the permits, the Government would have also justice on their side in resuming them.

16. But I do not think it expedient that they should be resumed : the time when it might have been worth while to bring the permit holders to an issue has passed : during the period of indecision, the forests have been so thoroughly gutted, that they are no longer worth the attention of the Government : to oust the permit-holders now would be but the vindication of a bare right, bringing little profit with it : this at least is the inference to which I am led by the fourth and concluding division of Dr. Brandis' report. It begins, to be sure, by an estimate of an immediate profit to Government of 61,000

rupees, but the Government could not avail themselves of the principal source of this profit; most assuredly they could not seize the 22,400 girdled trees estimated to yield 44,800 rupees; trees girdled under the permits; they might confiscate the permits but they could not confiscate them retrospectively, and disregarding a right of property already acquired under them, seize girdled trees.

17. This splendid bonus of 61,000 rupees therefore had better not be allowed to distract attention from the main prospect which Dr. Brandis holds out, if the Attaran forests be resumed, viz.:

1st. The expense of nursing them for 40 years in a state of absolute rest, not a log to be taken out of them, with the prospect of an outturn at the end of that period of 29 logs a square mile, or 2,900 for the whole forests.

2nd. The immediate working them with an annual return of 9 logs the square mile! or 900 trees for the whole, which is equal to between 1 and 2 per cent. on the foreign Teak annually imported into Maulmain, and I may here remark in passing that notwithstanding all that has been said about the reckless extravagant way in which the Attaran forests have been worked, they have not since 1828, when the 1st log was taken out of them, up to the present time yielded altogether in the 32 years as many logs as sometimes have been imported in a single year of foreign timber, and this may be easily understood when we remember that Dr. Brandis tells us that they do not cover an area of more than a hundred square miles, and that it is a good Teak forest in which Teak is found in the proportion of 1-10 to the other trees. The fact is "much cry and little wool" has been from first to last the attribute of the Attaran forests.

18. An annual outturn of 2,900 logs per annum after 40 years, or a present annual outturn of 900 logs! Is this a speculation into which a great Government can be called upon to enter, at a time too when the finances are heavily pressed for the discharge of inevitable obligations? As to the other light, not as a speculation, in which the question may be viewed, Teak will not perish out of the world because the Attaran forests are yielded up to waste. If the enchanter's wand could restore them to their virgin luxuriance, the supply that could be withdrawn from them under Dr. Brandis' best management would not have an appreciable effect upon the Teak market. I say therefore, Let them go.

19. On the other hand it seems that if Government resumed the forests it would be difficult to devise measures so as to leave the bringing away of crooks as free and unfettered as it might be desirable for the ship-building interest at Maulmain; that the chief value of the Attaran forests has of late consisted in their crooked timber, and that in that article the foreign forests cannot compete with them.

20. This is not all, Government Teak preserves have an effect like the game preserves of the Ameers of Scinde, in checking the settlement of population and interfering with cultivation. I solicit particular attention to Dr. Brandis' interesting account of the increase of villages, agricultural produce, and trade therein going on in the Attaran, and I ask if the renewal of a population is not more desirable than the renewal of a forest.

21. Adopting Dr. Brandis' suggestions, I therefore propose as follows:

1st. That a declaration be made by Government renouncing its claims to all Teak trees, the growth of tracts now in the occupation of permit-holders in the Attaran forest.

2nd. That all holders of permits shall produce the same, and every person claiming to work any forest in the Attaran under colour of any title shall exhibit such title before a Committee appointed to examine the authenticity of all such permits or titles within six months from a date to be hereafter notified, and after which date no permits or titles which have not been so produced or exhibited shall be deemed valid.

3rd. The Committee shall consist of the Deputy Commissioner of Province Amherst, as President, the Local Superintendent of Forests, and a non-official member, who shall be named by the Commissioner of the Tenasserim and Martaban Provinces.

4th. The Committee shall give in exchange for every permit or title approved by it, a fresh permit which shall be transferable and shall convey to the holder, the right to fell Teak trees in the locality named in the permit for a period of 99 years, but such permit shall be strictly construed, and shall not be held to convey any other right than that expressly named in it.

5th. Every Teak tree felled under a permit obtained in the manner provided for by Rule 4 shall become the property of the holder of such permit.

6th. No permit shall be held to convey any right to fell any Teak tree sown or planted by any private person intending his own benefit or advantage, or of those representing him, neither shall any permit be held to restrain the grant by competent authority of any waste land for the purpose of cultivation, or for any other purpose, according to the rules which from time to time may be in force for the grant of waste lands in the Tenasserim and Martaban Provinces, and notwithstanding that the land the subject of the grant may have Teak trees growing on it, and may be situated within the locality described in the permit, but the Teak trees growing on the land shall go with the land in the grant.

6th. There shall be a survey made of the boundaries of every tract, for which a permit has been given for the felling of Teak trees therein; and the survey shall be conducted by the officers of the Forest Department, and the boundaries of the tract as ascertained by the survey shall be entered in the "fresh permits" granted in respect to the tract under Rule 4 of those rules.

7th. A permit under those rules may be given for the felling of Teak trees within any tract for which no permit has been previously given, or for which any permit, previously given, has lapsed.

8th. The right of the Government to levy any tax or duty on Teak timber, the produce of the Attaran forests is not abridged or limited by any thing contained in those rules.

22. I believe that those rules will be found to embody all Dr. Brandis' suggestions and to meet sufficiently the exigencies of the case, and I have the hope that in the event of the Government adopting them, they may set a long vexed question finally at rest.

———

No. 8.

From

DOCTOR D. BRANDIS,

Supdt. of Forests, Pegu, Tenasserim and Martaban Provinces.

To

CAPTAIN H. HOPKINSON,

Commissioner, Tenasserim and Martaban Provinces, Maulmain.

Dated Myoduin the 6th March, 1860.

Sir,

I have the honor to submit herewith my report on the Attaran Forests, and although I regret the delay which has attended its preparation, yet I must say that this delay has been unavoidable.

2. In compliance with your letter No. 8, dated 22nd March, 1859, I have embodied my views on the Attaran Forests in a separate report, but I could not well help touching on several questions referring to Teak forests generally, and illustrating them by the results of my researches throughout the provinces, the forests of which have been placed under my control.

3. I have been obliged to review the principles on which my system of forest survey and forest management in these provinces is based, and as the report has thus received a more general character, it appears desirable that it should be printed as soon as possible, so as to enable me to place in the hands of my assistants and others interested in the subject, the result of four years' labour in the forests of British Burmah. I have repeatedly had reason to regret, that my first report on the Pegu Forests was never published; but if Government should be pleased to order the printing of my Attaran report, the inconvenience felt, will, in a measure, be obviated. I shall therefore consider it a favour if you will, together with this report, submit a copy of this letter to Government.

STATEMENTS.

Statement I.

Extract from the Forest Day-Books of the Officers of the Forest Department of different classes, observed during 1857,

FORESTS.			Year of Survey.	By whom Surveyed.
1 Pegu Section, ...		I. Div. Tharawaddy Forest,	Jan. to April, 1857 & 1858.	Dr. Brandis & Lieut. Mandel, 14th M. N. I.
2 „		IV. Div. Southern ditto, ...	Jan. to April, 1859.	Dr. Brandis.
3 „	VI. Eastern Sitang Forests.	„ Moong and Padah,...	Dec. to Feb. 1859.	Ditto & Mr. Clemen.
4 „		„ Youkthawah & Thoukyaghat, ...	Jan. to Feb. 1859.	Ditto ditto.
5 „		„ Kannee & Koonoung,	Mar. to May. „	Mr. E. Clemen.
6 Moulmain do.	Martaban Province.	Beeling, ...	Feb. to April. „	Mr. J. Barker.
7 „		Yoonzaleen, ...	„	Dr. Brandis & Mr. Barker.
8 „		Upper Salween, ...	„	Dr. Brandis.
9 „		Lower Salween, ...	„	Ditto & Mr. Barker.
10 „		Doomdamee, ...	„	Mr. J. Barker.
11 Moulmain do.	Tenasserim Province.	Thoungyeen middle, ...	„	Dr. Brandis & Mr. Barker.
12 „		Ditto lower, ...	„	Dr. Brandis.
13 „		Attaran (excluding Mittigate Codogway and Mittigate Kyouktaga,...............	July & Augt. 1858.	Dr. Brandis & Mr. Barker.
			Total, ...	

Total number of green Teak trees

Statement exhibiting the proportion of the different sections

NAMES OF FORESTS.

Moung and Padah, ...
Youkthawah and Thoukyaghat, ...
Kannee and Koonoung, ...
Upper Salween, ...
Middle Thoungyeen, ...
Lower Thoungyeen, ...

Office of the Supdt. of Forests in Pegu,
H. M. Flat "Punlang,"
3rd Feb., 1860.

Pegu, Tenasserim and Martaban Provinces, shewing the number of Teak trees 1858 & 1859, in different parts of the Forests.

No. of Forest tracts surveyed.	TEAK TREES.							Logs good.	Logs burnt or useless.	Stumps.	Teak trees attacked with Ficus.	Area surveyed in sq. miles.	REMARKS.
	1st Class above 4 cubits.	2nd from 3 to 4 cubits.	3rd from 1 to 3 cubits.	4th below 1 cubit.	Nathat.	Fallen.	Girdled.						
59	12,461	9,432	22,331	32,242	112	0	0	0	0	0	0	12.560	
22	2,619	2,895	3,705	4,399	0	0	0	0	0	0	8	4.499	Not observed.
16	3,441	2,065	2,138	2,287	206	351	92	326	165	811	581	1.3925	
15	3,163	1,437	3,012	3,736	103	121	51	119	74	442	350	2.1018	
14	8,577	3,747	11,355	24,419	285	256	9	402	6	960	559	1.697	
7	5,514	2,212	5,307	2,131	122	326	1,292	412	92	331	1,119	6.195	
13	3,618	1,431	4,645	3,560	150	363	624	284	229	631	350	1.479	
25	2,472	1,717	3,248	3,793	166	226	448	166	137	742	81	4.494	
7	685	1,080	1,922	2,060	11	42	441	61	42	719	118	2.86	
12	4,732	2,014	4,361	3,650	11	253	1,515	404	199	778	807	2.7482	
18	2,262	755	1,773	4,821	251	245	357	113	79	537	209	3.74	
9	378	198	179	170	34	35	46	4	3	251	47	1.01	
33	1,756	2,640	3,558	3,141	272	0	721	546	0	2,756	268	3.2175	
250	51,678	31,623	67,567	90,412	1,723	2,218	5,599	2,810	1,026	9,011	4,497	42.4185	

observed,...................... 2,40,299

of the 1st class trees observed in the different Forests.

FIRST CLASS.			Total.
Above 6 cub.	Above 5 cub.	Above 4 cub.	
889	920	1,682	3,441
1,064	757	1,342	3,163
2,721	3,212	2,644	8,577
459	810	1,203	2,472
676	655	931	2,262
103	130	145	378

(Sd.) D. BRANDIS,
Supdt. of Forests in Pegu, Tenasserim and Martaban Provinces.

Statement shewing the proportions of Teak Trees of different classes in the Tracts surveyed in the Forests of the Pegu, Tenasserim and Martaban Provinces.

Name of Forest.	Class of Forest.	First Class.	Second Class.	Third Class.	Fourth Class.	Total.	Proportion of stumps to 1,000 trees of all classes.	Remarks.
1 Pegu Sec., I. Div. Tharawaddie Forest,	B⁹	163	123	293	421	1,000	...	} Not observed.
2 " IV. Div. Southern Forest,	C⁵	193	213	272	322	1,000	...	
3 " VI. Div. Moung and Padah,	B²⁴	346	207	215	232	1,000	82	
4 " Youkthawah Thoukyaghat,	A¹⁵	278	127	267	328	1,000	39	
5 " Kannee and Koonoung,	A⁵⁰	78	79	236	507	1,000	19	
6 Maulmain Sec. Martaban Province, Beeling,	A⁸⁹	363	145	350	142	1,000	22	
7 " Yoonzaleen,	A²⁴	273	107	351	269	1,000	47	Average per miles of the different sections of the four classes.
8 " Upper Salween,	B⁵	238	149	283	330	1,000	66	
9 " Lower Salween,	C⁹	118	188	335	359	1,000	130	
10 " Doomdamee,	A¹	322	136	295	247	1,000	52	
11 Tenasserim Provinces, Upper Thoungyeen,	A⁶	236	78	185	501	1,000	58	
12 " Lower ditto,	B³	409	215	193	183	1,000	271	
13 " Attaran (excluding Mittigate Codogway and Mittigate Kyouktags,)	C⁴	156	238	321	285	1,000	248	
Calculated from total No. of trees estimated in Statement 3, average per mile,	...	202	189	282	377	1,000		
Same, doubling number of fourth class trees,	...	147	100	205	548	1,000		

Class and Size.	No. of 4th class trees doubled.	No. of 4th class trees not doubled.
1st Class above 9' Girth,	42	58
Ditto ditto 7' 6" ditto,	47	65
Ditto ditto 6' ditto,	58	79
2nd ditto ditto 4' 6" ditto,	100	139
3rd ditto ditto 3' ditto,	103	142
Ditto ditto 1' 6" ditto,	102	140
4th ditto small trees,	548	377
Total,	1,000	1,000

Office of the Supdt. of Forests in Pegu, H. M. Flat "Panlang," 4th Feb., 1860.

(Sd.) D. BRANDIS, Supdt. of Forests, Pegu, Tenasserim and Martaban Provinces.

Statement showing the number of Teak Trees of the different classes, estimated to stand on one square mile of Teak localities in different parts of the Forests in Pegu, Tenasserim and Martaban Provinces.

No.	Name of Forests.		Class of Forests.	1st Class.	2nd Class.	3rd Class.	4th Class.	Total.
1	Pegu Section,	I. Div. Tharawaddie,	B⁹	992	751	1,778	2,567	6,088
2	"	IV. Div. Southern Forests,	C³	584	643	823	977	3,027
3	Eastern Sitang Province.	VI. Div. Moong and Pedah,	B²⁴	2,472	1,483	1,535	1,643	7,133
4	"	" Younkthawah & Thou-kyaghat,	A¹⁶	1,594	683	1,447	1,777	5,411
5	"	" Kamee & Koonoung,	A⁵⁰	5,054	2,208	6,691	14,448	28,391
6	Martaban Province.	Moulmain Section, Beeling,	A⁸⁹	8,902	3,571	8,568	3,445	24,486
7	"	Yoonzaleen,	A²⁴	2,446	967	3,140	2,407	8,960
8	"	Upper Salween,	B⁵	550	360	723	844	2,477
9	"	Lower ditto,	C²	239	377	672	720	2,008
10	"	Doomdamee,	A¹⁷	1,727	782	1,587	1,324	5,370
11	Tenasserim Province.	Middle Thoungyem,	A⁶	605	201	474	1,289	2,569
12	"	Lower ditto,	B³	374	196	177	168	915
13	"	Attaran (excluding Mittigate Codogway and Mittigate Kyouktagg,	C⁵	544	851	1,105	976	3,476

Remarks.

Average per square mile of the different sections of the 4 classes.

Class and Size.	Per square mile.	Per 10 acres.
1st Class above 9' girth, ...	284	4
Ditto ditto 7' 6" ditto, ...	314	5
Ditto ditto 6' ditto,	385	6
2nd Class ditto 4' 6" ditto,	684	10
3rd Class ditto 3' ditto,	689	11
Ditto ditto 1' 6" ditto, ...	683	10
4th Class small trees, ...	1,840	29
Total, ...	4,879	74
or doubling the small trees,	3,680	56

Statement exhibiting the proportion of the different sections of the III. Class trees observed in the Tharrawaddie Forests.

Name of Forests.	IIIa. 1 Cubit.	IIIb. 2 Cubits.	Total.
Beeling,	1,689	1,232	2,921
Minhla,	878	725	1,603
Htoo,	6,664	7,362	14,026
Kadoke,	74	51	125
Boabin,	87	89	176
Tounyo,	195	185	380
Total, ...	9,587	9,644	19,281
or per mille,	498	502	1,000

(Sd.)　D. BRANDIS,
Supdt. of Forests, Pegu,
Tenasserim & Martaban Provinces.

Office of the Supdt. of Forests in Pegu, }
H. M. Flat "Panlang,"
3rd Feb., 1860.

Statement IV.

Statement showing the number of Green Trees estimated to be growing in different parts of the Forests, Pegu, Tenasserim and Martaban Provinces.

Name of Forests.	Estimated area of Teak localities in Square Miles.	Area Surveyed.	First class above IV Cubits.	Second class above III Cubits.	Third class above I Cubit.	Fourth class under I Cubit.	Total.	Remarks.
1 Pegu Sec., I Div. Tharrawaddie Forests, ...	580.	12.56	5,75,360	4,35,580	1,081,240	1,488,860	3,531,040	
2 " IV " Southern, ...	355.6	4.499	205,795	2,27,364	2,91,012	3,45,467	1,069,638	
3 " VI " Moung and Padah, ...	16.	1.3925	39,552	23,728	24,560	26,288	114,128	
4 " Eastern Stang " Youkthawah and Thoukyaghat, ..	34.	2.1018	51,136	23,222	49,198	60,962	184,518	
5 " " Kannee and Koonoung, ...	24.	1.697	1,21,296	52,992	1,60,584	3,46,752	681,624	
6 Moulmain Sec. Martaban Forests Beeling, ...	9.166	0.6195	81,584	32,226	78,521	31,574	223,905	
" " Yoonzaleen, ...	12.	1.479	29,354	11,610	37,686	28,884	107,534	
" " Upper Salween, ...	106.25	4.494	58,437	40,607	76,712	89,675	265,431	
" " Lower Doomdamee and Salween, ...	60.	2.86	14,340	22,620	40,320	42,200	120,480	
" " Doomdamees, ...	41.25	2.7482	71,238	80,195	65,463	54,615	221,511	
" Tenasserim ditto Middle Thoungyeen, ...	176.	8.74	106,480	35,376	83,424	2,26,864	452,144	
" " Lower Thoungyeen, ...	48.	1.01	17,952	9,408	8,496	8,064	43,920	
" " Attaran (excluding Mittigate Codogway and Mittigate Kyouktaga,	100.	3.2175	54,400	85,100	1,10,500	97,600	847,600	
Total, ...	1561.1266	42.4185	1,426,924	1,030,028	2,067,716	2,848,805	7,963,473	
Average number of Trees per Square Mile in the Forests Surveyed, ...			983	684	1,372	1,840	4,879	
Average number ditto ditto per 10 Acres, ...			15	10	21	28	74	
Average number ditto ditto per Mile, ...			202	189	282	377	1,003	

Office of the Supdt. of Forests in Pegu,
H. M. Flat, "Palang,"
3rd Feby., 1860.

(Sd.) D. BRANDIS,
Supdt. of Forests in Pegu, Tenasserim and Martaban Provinces.

Statement V.

Statement showing the proportion of Teak Trees of different classes observed in the different tracts of the Attaran Forests per mile and on the square mile.

Name of Forests.	Class of Forests.	First Class.	Second Class.	Third Class.	Fourth Class.	Total of Green Trees.	Stumps.	Remarks.
Lower Winyeo Forests,	C⁴	528	1,142	1,647	1,159	4,476	219	
Upper ditto,	B⁴	621	564	640	463	2,288	647	
Megna Tseikgyee Kyoukpya Forest,	C⁴	642	962	1,047	2,256	4,907	1,582	Per Square mile.
Kyoon Choung Forest,	B⁴	936	751	1,263	809	3,759	2,017	
Upper Zimmay Forest,	C³	389	751	973	292	2,406	522	
Mittigate Forest below Kyocktaga,	A²	282	101	92	303	778	1,096	
Lower Zimmay Forest,	C⁴	425	1,213	1,666	1,303	4,607	584	
Lower Winyeo Forests,	C⁴	118	255	368	259	1,000	48	
Upper ditto,	B⁴	271	247	280	202	1,000	282	
Megna Tseikgyee Kyoukpya Forest,	C⁴	130	196	214	460	1,000	322	Per Mile.
Kyoon Choung Forest,	B⁴	249	200	335	216	1,000	536	
Upper Zimmay Forest,	C³	162	313	404	121	1,000	216	
Mittigate Forest below Kyouktaga,	A²	362	130	119	889	1,000	1,574	
Lower Zimmay Forest,	C⁴	92	262	364	282	1,000	126	
Average per mile taken from Statement No. II.,		156	238	321	285	1,000	248	

Proportion of the 2 Divisions of the 1st Class.

Name of Forest.	Above 7½' girth.	Above 6' feet girth.	Total.
Lower Winyeo,	29	71	100
Upper Winyeo,	64	36	100
Megna Tseikgyee and Kyoukpya,	60	40	100
Kyoon Choung,	69	31	100
Upper Zimmay,	21	79	100
Mittigate below Kyouktaga,	79	21	100
Lower Zimmay,	11	89	100
Average,	48	52	100

Office of the Supdt. of Forests in Pegu,
Tenasserim & Martaban Provinces,
Theyetmyo, 20th Feb., 1860.

(Sd.)　D. BRANDIS,
Supdt. of Forests in Pegu,
Tenasserim & Martaban Provinces.

Statement VI.

Statement showing the highest and lowest number of the First Class Teak Trees observed on the square mile in the different tracts of the Forests surveyed, and the number of Forest tracts belonging to each of the three Forest Classes.

Name of Forests.	Number of 1st class Trees on the square mile.			Number of Forest tracts belonging to each of the three Forest Classes.			Remarks.
	Highest.	Lowest.	Difference.	A.	B.	C.	
1 Southern Forests,	2,119	88	2,036	2	4	16	Poor Forests, mostly in dry bamboo jungle; much worked out in the plains.
2 Tharawaddie ditto,	5,908	208	5,700	12	35	11	The northern Forests excellent, protected by obstructions in the rivers.
3 Middle Sitang Forests Moung & Padah,	8,100	366	7,734	5	11	0	Fine Teak localities on dry diluvial soil near the streams, little worked.
4 Do. do. do. Youkthawah & Thoukyaghat,	7,608	73	7,535	6	9	1	Excellent Forest tracts, but some of them much worked.
5 Upper do. do. Kannee and Koonoung,	23,478	1,526	21,952	8	6	0	Ditto ditto.
6 Beeling Forests,	21,339	1,926	19,413	5	2	0	Most on low ground near the river, on excellent soil.
7 Yoongalum ditto,	8,571	122	8,449	5	4	2	The Tsingouay and Tepoon Forest rich, in the others Teak is much scattered.
8 Upper Salween Forests,	1,982	20	1,962	6	9	9	Much injured by Toungya cultivation.
9 Lower do. & Lower Doomdamee Forests,	500	100	400	1	2	4	Very much worked out.
10 Upper Doomdamee Forests,	6,451	167	6,284	7	1	2	Valuable Forest tracts in dry open Forest.
11 Middle Thoungyen ditto,	5,950	15	5,935	17	1	0	Ditto ditto.
12 Lower ditto ditto,	1,100	112	988	4	5	0	Very much worked out, but never very rich.
13 Attaran,	1,840	55	1,785	8	8	22	Very much worked out, at one time very rich.
Total, ...				86	97	67	

Office of the Supdt. of Forests in Pegu,
H. M. Flat "Panlang,"
4th Feb., 1860.

(Sd.) D. BRANDIS,
Supdt. of Forests in Pegu, Tenasserim and Martaban Provinces.

Statement VII.

Statement showing the quantity of Timber brought to Maulmain from the Attaran Forests from 1829 to 30th April, 1858.

Years.	Full sized Logs.	Under sized Logs.	Ship Crooks.	Boat Crooks.	Stem Pieces.	Squares.	Planks.	Slabs.	No. of trees likely to have yielded this timber.	Remarks.
From 1829 to 30th April, 1841.	See Explanatory Remarks,								77,704	See page 116 of Printed Report on Tenasserim Teak Forests, 1853, estimated, no returns being available.
1841-42,	6,936	..	13,563	..	..	461	1,858	..	10,788	
1842-43,	5,000	..	9,000	2,174	..	250	1,000	..	7,550	
1843-44,	4,913	..	4,295	901	..	34	763	157	6,622	
1844-45,	7,870	..	6,763	1,014	..	..	8	14	9,406	
1845-46,	5,188	..	4,268	..	..	73	53	27	6,343	
1846-47,	3,110	208	1,206	..	..	1	..	..	3,560	
1847-48,	4,611	648	4,876	501	5	..	..	255	6,339	Taken from the Returns of the Timber Revenue Department, Maulmain.
1848-49,	1,329	35	4,459	..	2	6	5	690	2,264	
1849-50,	482	23	1,489	24	9	1	..	64	810	
1850-51,	594	27	2,489	..	..	..	..	9	1,128	
1851-52,	488	9	1,152	..	1	..	..	85	727	
1852-53,	385	55	102	..	38	3	..	..	414	
1853-54,	526	9	189	200	..	..	..	..	651	
1854-55,	806	11	1,537	200	..	..	..	..	1,164	
1855-56,	311	..	2,485	..	..	..	..	..	808	
1856-57,	193	..	3,795	..	..	..	..	..	952	
1857-58,	617	42	292	..	..	..	..	..	717	
Total,....	43,309	1,067	61,960	5,014	55	829	3,187	1,301	137,947	

Number of Trees to 30th April, 1841,..............	77,704	Annual average for 12 years,..........	6475.3
Ditto ditto after ditto ditto, ...	60,243	Ditto ditto for 17 ditto,..............	3,543.705
Number of Trees to 30th April, 1848,..........	128,312	Ditto ditto for 19 ditto,..............	6,753.26
Ditto ditto after ditto ditto, ...	9,635	Ditto ditto for 10 ditto,..............	963.5

EXPLANATORY REMARKS.

1. The number of trees removed since 1841-42 is calculated from the timber of different descriptions on the following assumptions, one log, one stem-piece, one square, 2 bend planks and 5 crooks are severally considered to represent one tree. The slabs are left out.

2. The quantity of timber brought in before 30th April, 1841, has been estimated on the following data.

   A. From timber revenue realized.

Total amount of timber revenue realized, including the proceeds of sale of timber levied as duty in kind up to 30th April, 1836., ... 81,031 8 2

Ditto ditto from 1st May, 1836, to 30th April, 1841, ... 111,559 2 9

Total,...... 192,590 10 11

Duty was paid on the timber at the rate of 15 per cent. ad valorem. Assuming the ton was at the time assessed at Rs. 16 (which was afterwards by Government Orders, dated 4th October, 1845 lowered to 14); the duty would have amounted to Rupees 2-6-5 per ton and the above amount would have been paid for Teak timber tons 80,245.

   B. From Exports of timber and ships built at Maulmain.

1. Timber was exported from Maulmain up to 1833 to the amount of, ... Tons 7,309

2. From April, 1833 to April, 1841 (8 years,) .... do. 40,000

Note.—5000 tons are said to have been exported annually in the 9 years preceding 1841.

3. Number of vessels built at Maulmain up to end of 1841, sixty-eight, with a tonnage of 15,680 tons, estimated to have required for construction Teak timber, ... Tons 24,254

4. Timber estimated to have been expended for local consumption at the rate of 300 tons per annum for 12 years, ...Tons 3,600

Total amount of timber,...do. 75,163

Taking the mean of these 2 figures we have the probable amount of timber brought to Maulmain up to 30th April, 1841; tons 77,704. Of this timber a portion was from other Forests. It is impossible to ascertain the exact proportion, but the following data may serve to arrive at approximate figures.

The Attaran was the main source for timber till 1835, when the supply from other Forests became of importance; Thoungyeen and Shan (Siamese) timber was first brought down about 1838. In 1841-42, the Attaran timber formed ¼ of the whole timber brought into Maulmain.

Assuming that it formed one-half from 1835 to 1841 and the whole of the supplies before 1835 three-fourths of the above figure may be put down as Attaran timber, viz.: ....Tons 58,278

Timber from other sources, ... do. 19,426

Total,......... 77,704 Tons.

And as under the mode of working the Forests pursued in the Attaran a ton of timber may fairly be assumed to represent one tree, the number of trees brought away from these Forests previous to 30th April, 1841, may be put down at 137,947.

Office of the Supdt. of Forests in Pegu, ⎫   D. BRANDIS,
   H. M. Flat " Panlang," ⎬   *Supdt. of Forests in Pegu,*
     2nd Feby., 1860. ⎭ *Tenasserim and Martaban Provinces.*

No. of Forest as per Map.	OCCUPIER.	SITUATION OF FOREST.
16	Mrs. Wales,	West banks of both branches of Megwa, ...
19	Ko Bitt, ...	Both banks of Zammee below mouth of Chakat Creek,
20	Mackey & Co.	Natchoung and Chakat Creek,...............................
21	Ditto, ...	Right bank of Zammee at Badayee Island, ...
22	Moung Judah,	Left bank of Zammee above Taropman,................ ..
23	Ko Dya, ...	Goonglay Creek, ...
24	Mackey & Co.	Sources of Goonglay, ...
26	Ditto, ...	Goongee,... ....
27	Unoccupied,	Right bank of Zammee above Mo-oo, ...
28	Moung Waa,	Left bank of Zammee and right bank of Mo-oo, ...
29	Phojah, ...	Right bank of Zammee between Nos. 27 & 54, ...
30	Shaik Abdullah, ...	Left ditto opposite No. 29, ...
35	Pho Soo,......	Both banks of Zammee below mouth of Goongyee,...
36	Taracoon, ...	Choung Byey a feeder of the Goongyee, ...
37	Moung Tan lai, ...	Left bank of Goongyee opposite No. 36,.............
43	Shway Po, ..	Left bank of Zammee at the mouth of Mittigate,......
44	Shway Dong,	Ditto between Mittigate and Megwa Creeks,...........
45	Unoccupied,	Right bund of Zammee ditto ditto,.....................
46	Mackey & Co.	Mouth of Mittigate to Kyouktaga, ...
47	Ditto, ...	The whole of the Mittigate Codogway, ...
48	Unoccupied,	Sources of the Mittigate above the Kyouktaga,........
49	Mackey & Co.	Left or Northern bank of Megwa, ...
50	Ditto, ...	Right bank of Megwa and both banks of Zammee from mouth of Megwa to Kyoukpya and Thalew Creeks,
51	Mr. Pascal,...	Right bank of Zammee from Kyoukpya to Kyon Choung Codogway, ...
52	Mackey & Co.	Ditto from Kyon Choung Codogway to Kyon Choung Cadogway, ...
53	Mrs. Dawood,	Both banks of Zammee from Thaben and Kyon Choung Codogway to above Peng Choung, ...
54	Nga Kaa,......	Right bank of Zammee at the Whagee, ...
		Total number of Trees,......
18	Shaik Abdullah, ...	*Forests not visited.* Dalee Creek, ...
25	Ko Byey,......	Danong Creek, ...
31	Po Thike Ree,	Right bank of Zammee between Nos. 28 & 33, ...

Statement IX.

...ees on the Zammee and its Tributaries.

Estimate area in square miles.	TEAK TREES.						REMARKS.
	Full size.			Under size.			
	Growing.	Felled.	Killed.	Growing.	Felled.	Killed.	
4	20	0	400	200	0	0	The trees in this Forest are of very large growth; straight, smooth bark, and of sound appearance.
¾	50	0	0	300	0	0	These are mostly small trees and crooked. Ko Bitt is dead.
9	0	0	200	1,500	0	350	Ditto ditto.
½	0	0	15	200	0	10	Ditto·ditto. [Forest.
1	0	0	0	150	0	6	Crooked trees, very inferior, old, nearly worked out
¼	15	0	2	50	0	0	Ditto ditto.
1	50	0	30	300	0	0	Fine young trees, straight, of smooth bark. The soil is of a dry nature.
16	500	70	800	2,800	230	400	Some of these growing trees are of great length and if permitted to grow will attain a superior size and quality.
¼	3	0	2	200	0	0	Crooked trees, seemingly sound.
1¼	250	0	0	800	0	0	These are tall handsome trees growing on a hard, dry soil.
1½	100	0	0	300	0	0	Short, sound but not crooked. Phojah is dead.
¾	30	0	0	200	0	0	Ditto ditto.
2	200	0	5	600	0	0	Part of these trees growing near the Zammee are short but the greater number being further from the stream are tall and straight, soil hard and dry.
¾	100	0	0	250	0	0	These are nearly all tall, straight trees.
¼	30	0	10	200	0	0	Ditto ditto.
¼	0	0	0	250	0	0	Crooked trees very inferior.
1	20	0	10	350	0	20	Crooked trees seemingly sound. Shway Dong is dead.
1¼	10	0	0	150	0	0	Ditto ditto.
12	2,000	400	800	2,000	0	400	This timber is superior in size and quality to most others.
7	6	35	190	676	0	100	Some of these killed trees are of immense size and sound, the growing trees are straight, smooth bark and healthy
12	133	343	158	0	0	0	These are almost all extremely large trees, in the column of felled there are 297 Olays or blown fallen trees, the others are lapped; included in the column of killed there are 20 Nathat, but the remainder 138 trees are killed and all are now well seasoned.
8	30	0	310	250	0	0	These are stout, straight trees, smooth bark and sound. [of immense size.
11	400	0	1,400	1,600	0	200	The whole of these are fine trees, among them are some
2	200	0	100	600	0	0	Of good quality.
8	1,400	0	1,400	4,600	0	300	Among these are trees of every description short and tall, some of moderate size, others of very large bulk, but the whole are of good quality. [trees.
11	108	0	19	1,354	0	0	This wood is in patches widely apart, mostly young
¼	100	0	0	400	0	0	These are of short growth, but sound.
...	5,755	848	5,851	20,280	230	1,786	

2nd Feby., 1860.) Tenasserim and Martaban Provinces.

Statement X.

List of the Forests on the Attaran, the leases of which have been resumed.

No.	Lease Holders.	Name of Forests.	No. on the Map.	Where Situated.	Lease by whom granted.	Remarks.
1	Nga Soo, ...	Goonjee, ...	35	L. Zimmay.	Mr. Blundell,	Lhet Mhats resumed about 6 years ago.
2	,, Bitt Shuay Goneg,	Kouk Sareet, ...	19,39 & 40	,, Zimmay.	,,	Ditto.
3	,, Phan, ...	Thitseintoh Shoay Pho Chg,	38	,,	,,	ditto.
4	,, Khai (Nga Yay),	Weyghee, ...	54	,,	,,	ditto.
5	,, Tho Nah, ...	Goongalay, ...	24	,,	,,	ditto.
6	,, Doeng (Nga Thoon),	Me-prahn, ...	5	L. Winyeo.	,,	Said to be destroyed when his house was burnt.
7	,, Cheo, ...	Phayahgalay (M'Oo Chg),	33	,, Zimmay.	,,	Lhet Mhats resumed about 6 years ago.
8	,, Lhat (Nga wah),	M'Oo, ...	28	,,	,,	ditto.
9	,, Nga Khine,	Ditto, ...	34	,,	,,	ditto.
10	,, Doke Kyee (Nga Youk),	Ditto, ...	31	,,	,,	ditto.
11	,, Thite Soo, ...	Ditto, ...	32	,,	,,	ditto.
12	,, Lhaw, ...	Kyat Choung,	42	,,	,,	ditto.
13	,, Byaw, ...	Ditto, ...	41	,,	,,	ditto.
14	,, Moo (Nga Tit),	Phah Byah,	10	L. Winyeo.	,,	ditto.
15	,, Nay, ...	Phahkpooay,	14 I	Ditto.	,,	ditto.
16	,, Myat Thah,	Ditto, ...	14 I	Ditto.	,,	ditto.
17	,, Khan tah (Tohgneo),	Ditto, ...	13 I	Ditto.	,,	ditto.
18	,, Kywet, ...	Kyone Kawoon,	9 I	Ditto.	,,	ditto.

MAULMAIN,
Forest Office,
30th September 1859.

(Sd.) JAMES BARBER,
Head Assistant, Forest Department,
Tenasserim and Martaban Provinces.

19

Statement XI.

Estimated average rate of growth of Teak in the Forests of the Pegu, Tenasserim and Martaban Provinces.

Age of Trees. As assumed in Report for 1856. Years.	Age of Trees as present. Years.	Girth of Tree at 6' from ground.	Diameter of Tree at 6' from ground.	Cubic contents of a pole 30' long calculated on the round log in cubic feet.	Annual increase of girth.	Average annual increase of timber in a pole 30 ft. long in cub. feet.	Oak.	Beach.	Larch.	Teak Age.	Teak Girth.	Teak No.	Where measured.
0	0	0	0	0	1.'8"	0.534	0	0	0	0	0	0	Thinganneenoung Teak Plantation, measured in 1858.
										2	8"	17	Calcutta Botanic Gardens ditto 1856.
										6	1.'4"	9	Near Panko Village Attaran ditto 1858.
										7	1.6	9	
7	10	1.'6"	5"	5°.34	1.5	1.85	23	17	17	14	1.2	...	Bombay Forest plains (communicated by Dr. Gibson.)
										14	8	...	Ditto, Hills, ditto.
18	2	8	11.4	21°.5	1.2	1.78	34	32	27	22	3.4	15	Maulmain Private Garden, measured in 1858.
										25	4.5	9	Sprouts from Stumps Kyoon Choung Forests, Attaran ditto.
										25	3.2	...	Java, taken from Tunghuhu's work on Java, Vol. I. p. 253.
40	37	4.6	17.8	48.25	0.72	1.51	43	41	36				Java see above.
62	62	6	22.1	86.	0.45	1.20	56	56	43	70	6.7	8	Calcutta Botanic Gardens, measured in 1856.
										82	7.10¼	4	Houndrow Forests in the plains, age calculated from No. of annual rings taken from summary of papers on Tenasserim Forests, page 106.
										93	6.9	6	Houndrow Forests in the Hills, ditto ditto.
										100	12.6	..	Java see above.
98	102	7.6	28.7	134.25	0.30	0.98	68	76	70	216	10.7¼	5	Houndrow Forests on the hills (from summary of papers, page 106.)
1??	169	9	34.4	193.25			115	89	110	249	12.8¼	8	Ditto ditto ditto.

REMARKS.

The rate of growth of Teak, like that of all other trees, is exceedingly variable, according to the locality and the soil where it occurs. The tree grows fastest in forests of the first group, in deep alluvial soil. Here the roots can spread far, and the leaves remain green during a considerable part of the dry season. Thus some of the largest seedlings on the Thinganneennoung plantation had within 2 years attained a girth of from 10" to 13" near the root or of 8" at 6' from the ground, which in other localities would correspond to an age of from 4 to 5 years. And in a similar locality on the banks of the Zimmay river (near Punko village), 9 trees were measured stated to be 7 years old with an average girth of 1' 6", usually the size of trees 10 years old. Also the growth of the sprouts from stumps in the Kjoon Choung forests is an instance of unusually fast growth; 9, sprouts estimated to be 25 years old had an average girth of 4' 5" which girth Teak trees generally attain with 35 years only. Further 6 Teak trees of different sizes in girth between 3' and 15' were measured in the Thoukyaghat forests in 1856. The same trees were measured again in 1859, and showed an average annual increase in girth of 1.6 inches, which rate usually is observed only in trees below 3' in girth.

But on the other hand Teak has a very slow growth on arid hills, with poor soil or with rocks near the surface. Here often not a single tree is to be found, exceeding 4' in girth, although the forest has never been interfered with either by cultivators or timber cutters. The large number of Nathat trees shows that the tree remains stunted and dies off before reaching a good size. Teak of this description is found on the hills between the Pah Choung and the Karenee country and on the dry hills of the Prome district near the frontier on both sides of the Irrawaddee. In the Bombay Forests Teak 14 years old is said to attain a girth of 8" in the hills and of 14" in the plains. Both are remarkable instances of slow growth.

This table is intended as far as possible to represent the average rate of growth of Teak in Burmah. But the observations available are as yet very incomplete, and hence a portion of the data have necessarily been fixed in an arbitrary manner. In Europe where the complete rest of vegetation in winter, causes the formation of distinct annual rings, it is easy for the purpose of determining the time of rotation by which a certain forest is to be worked, to ascertain the rate of growth in every locality; here the concentric rings in the wood do not always indicate the age of the tree, although they may do so in some instances. The age of trees 1' 6" and 3' in girth has been fixed higher than was assumed in 1856, because it was found that the growth of Teak trees of small sizes is rather slower than was assumed before. A similar alteration has been made with regard to the growth of trees of the largest size. The growth of Teak as here assumed is remarkably fast during its early age, but slow after it has attained a girth of 4' 6'.

D. BRANDIS,
Superintendent of Forests,
Pegu, Tenasserim & Martaban Provinces.

Office of the Supdt. of Forests,
   CAMP MINGEE,
  The 1st March, 1860.

Statement XII.

Abstract Statement of Villages found in the Winyeo and Zimmay Valley above their junction in July and August, 1858, shewing nationality of inhabitants and time of settlement on the Attaran.

DISTRICT.	Number of Villages.							Number of Villages.				
	Karens Po.	Karens square.	Shans from Bankok.	Shans Lower.	Talings.	Mixed population of Karens, Shans, Talains and Chinese men.	Total.	Immigrated before 1830.	Immigrated before 1840.	Immigrated before 1850.	Immigrated since 1850.	Total.
Zimmay,............... West side, ...	1	1	2	0	0	2	6	0	0	2	4	6
Ditto,.......... .... East side, ...	19	6	1	1	1	2	30	0	6	17	7	30
Winyeo,............... West side, ...	6	2	0	0	0	2	10	7	0	0	3	10
Ditto,............... East side, ...	5	0	0	0	1	0	6	1	0	2	3	6
	31	9	3	1	2	6	52	8	6	21	17	52

D. BRANDIS,

Supdt. of Forests in Pegu, Tenasserim and Martaban Provinces.

Office of the Supdt. of Forests,
Pegu, Tenasserim and Martaban Provinces,
THYETMYO,
The 20th February, 1860.

Statement shewing the number of Teak plants raised from a certain quantity of Teak seed in the different Teak Plantations of the Pegu, Tenasserim and Martaban Provinces.

No.	Locality.	Time when sown.	Number of Baskets sown.	Number of seeds sown.	Number of plants alive.	Time when counted.	Percentage of plants alive on seed sown.	Remarks.
1	Thinganeenoung (Attaran,)	April, 1856,	65	907,500	71,420	April, 1857.	7,9	Sown on nursery beds close together; deep alluvial soil with rich vegetable moulds, ground trenched 1 ft. deep.
2	Tharrawoon,	Ditto,	70	1,050,000	13,725	Nov. 1856.	1,8	Sown on nursery beds close together. Soil poor, ground trenched 1 ft. deep.
3	Prome,	May, 1857,	60	900,000	40,000	April, 1858.	4,4	Sown on nursery beds close together; soil poor, ground trenched 1 ft. deep.
4	Ditto,	Ditto,	30	450,000	14,305	Jan. 1858.	3,1	Sown in holes 2 ft. apart, these in rows 10 ft. distant; soil poor, ground not trenched.
5	Ditto,	June, 1858,	56	840,000	40,100	April, 1859.	4,7	Sown close together; ground ploughed, not trenched.
6	Rangoon,	June, 1858,	4	60,000	3,600	August, 1859.	6,0	Sown in beds close together in a garden; ground carefully prepared, trenched and manured.
7	Ditto,	August, 1859,	4½	67,500	3,060	Nov. 1859.	5,00	Sown in rows, the rows 3 ft. apart; ground dry and weeded but not trenched.

D. BRANDIS,
Superintendent of Forests,
Pegu, Tenaserim and Martaban Provinces.

Office of the Supdt. of Forests,
Pegu, Tenasserim & Martaban Provinces,
THEYETMYO,
The 20th February, 1860.

Statement XIV.

Result of the Transplanting of Teak at Rangoon.

	Total No.	Alive.	Dead.	Per cent. Dead.	Per cent. Alive.
1. Experimental Cotton Garden,	990	555	435	43.94	56.06
2. Private Garden in Town, ...	99	83	16	16.0	84.0
3. Private Garden in Cantonment,	189	165	24	12.69	87.31

The seed was sown in June, 1858, the plants were transplanted in July, 1859, they were then from 1′ to 4′ high, they were counted on the 29th August, 1859.

D. BRANDIS,
Supdt. of Forests in Pegu,
Tenasserim and Martaban Provinces.

Office of the Supdt. of Forests,
Pegu, Tenasserim and Martaban Provinces,
THEYETMYO,
The 20th February, 1860.

Statement XV.

Probable resources of the Teak Forests on the Winyeo river and its Tributaries.

Name of Forests visited.	Approximate extent.	TEAK TREES.						By whom worked.	Remarks.
		Under 6 feet.			Above 6 feet.				
	Miles	Growing.	Felled.	Killed.	Growing.	Felled.	Killed.		
Noocan, ...	4½	342	0	0	18	0	0	Noo-can.	This forest has not been worked for 4 years.
Khantas, ...	4½	900	0	0	0	0	0	Khan-tsa.	Ditto.
Mietus, ...	6	1,440	0	0	480	0	0	Bo-gai-doo.	Ditto.
Ko nai, ...	3	600	132	0	240	168	0	Ko-nai.	This forest worked last year, 300 logs in the Pakoobooai stream.
Moungboon, ...	3	1,844	0	0	120	60	0	Shaik Abdullah.	This forest has not been worked for 6 years.
Allaantras, ...	0	53	0	0	0	0	0	Unoccupied.	
Wales, ...	4½	1,854	181	3	1,026	40	24	Mrs. Wales.	This forest was worked last year.
Ditto, ...	1	160	0	2	0	0	0	Ditto.	This forest has not been worked for 4 years.
Thongananmoung, ...	12	3,986	0	0	3,023	0	0	Unoccupied.	Mrs. Wales, by permission, transported 500 Teak logs killed long ago.
Maru, ...	2	80	0	0	240	0	0	Ditto.	
Phomoo, ...	1½	1,038	0	0	0	0	0	Phomoo.	Worked last year, felled green trees for crooks.
Shosiyaa, ...	2½	2,889	51	0	0	0	0	Shoaiyaa.	Worked last in 1844. Shoaiyaa is dead.
Shosidong, ...	1½	2,418	0	0	78	0	0	Shoaidong.	This forest has not been worked for 3 years.
Tagoondine, ...	2	1,556	0	0	856	0	0	Unoccupied.	} The village of Tagoondine fell small trees which they use for fences.
Ditto, ...	0	200	0	0	0	0	0	Ditto.	
Total,.........	46½	18,810	864	5	5,481	268	24		

MAULMAIN,
Superintendent of Forest's Office, }
March 27th, 1846.

(True Copy.)

(Sd.) CHAS. SALMOND,
Asst. Forest Surveyor.

D. BRANDIS,
Supdt. of Forests in Pegu, Tenasserim and Martaban Provinces.

Statement XVI.

Probable Resources of the Teak Forests on the Zimmay River
and its Tributaries.

NAME OF FOREST VISITED.	Approximate extent in miles.	TEAK TREES.						By whom worked.
		Under 6 feet.			Above 6 feet.			
		Growing.	Felled.	Killed.	Growing.	Felled.	Killed.	
Natchoung,............	4½	3,734	...	486	...	...	...	Captain Chik.
Phojaa, ...	1½	230	77	...	...	...	...	Phojaa,
Ghoongee, ...	4½	5,454	...	174	414	...	...	Mr. J. Richardson.
Phosoo, ...	1½	1,200	...	...	...	...	...	Ditto.
Nga baans, ...	3	300	...	...	...	20	...	Nga baan.
Ko bitt, ...	3	300	...	...	...	...	...	Kobitt's relatives.
Mittigate Codogway No. 1,	1	13	...	...	134	...	64	Unoccupied.
Ditto No. 2, ...	2	480	...	...	211	...	111	Ditto.
Ditto No. 3, ...	2¼	5,147	...	...	604	..	4	Ditto.
Mittigate, ...	10	4,000	...	16	4,000	33	600	Creaton and Co.
Keouktaga, ...	2	1,418	...	...	872	...	120	Unoccupied.
Pothike soo, ...	2	672	...	23	136	...	...	Photheke soo.
Moung choe, ...	2	872	...	...	88	...	...	Shaik Abdullah.
Moung khine,........	2	544	..	37	196	...	50	Chwaman.
Ko lans, ...	2	664	...	...	64	...	...	Kolan.
Ko be nau, ...	2	600	...	..	60	23	...	Kobaraan.
Shoai dong, ...	1½	1,014	...	...	66	...	...	No one.
Meguaa, ...	10	2,000	94	1,520	2,400	90	2,000	Cockerell & Co.
Shoai Poe, ...	1	804	...	...	128	...	...	Shoaipoe.
Koloug, ...	2	1,160	...	...	184	...	...	Kolang.
Koyaa, ...	2	1,160	..	...	184	...	...	Shaik Abdullah.
Po thoke kee, ...	2	840	...	13	504	...	...	His relatives.
Pho tatt, ...	1	600	...	19	312	...	...	Ditto.
Moung Wau, ...	1	600	...	...	312	...	...	Mouing wau.
Not Visited.								
Guongaa Menhe, ...	16	2,560	...	150	1,600	...	640	J. Darwood.
Keon choung, ...	12	2,400	...	1,824	2,880	...	700	Cockerell & Co.
Meo hown and	4	480	...	300	...	...	...	Shaik Abdullah.
Meguaa, ...	2	320	...	.	300	...	...	Ditto.
Shoaelay, ...	2	240	...	...	240	...	...	No one.
Meguaa, ...	4	1,200	...	...	1,200	...	...	Captain Chik.
Dalli choung, ...	3	500	...	350	300	...	450	Shaik Abdullah.
Phaboung, ...	}							
Pha blue, ...	}							Phoglan.
Thaa mue, ...	}							
Total,....	108¾	41,536	171	4,912	17,389	166	4,739	

MAULMAIN,
Superintendent of Forest's Office,
The 27th March, 1846.

REMARKS.

Dead worked and trees killed last year in the rains.
Working now.
Worked last year.
Has not been worked for 3 years.
Has ditto for several years.
Kobitt is dead. Has not been worked for 6 years.
179 trees killed by Mr. Barber 10 years ago.

358 Dead trees and 455 Teak trees killed recently by order.

Is annually worked.
Messrs. Creaton & Co.'s people killed 120 Teak trees, 2 years ago.
Worked last year.
Has not been worked for several years.
Has not been worked for 2 years.
Worked last year.
Has not been worked for 4 years.
Showdong dead long ago and no one resumed the forest.
Is annually worked twice.
Has not worked for a considerable time.
          Ditto.
Worked last year.
Worked last year.
          Ditto.
          Ditto.

Worked last year.
Is annually worked twice.
Has not been worked for 4 years. ⎫
Has not been worked for 2 years. ⎬ Pascal's Estate.

Worked last year.
          Ditto.
⎰   The forests are exhausted. The occupier formed a nursery on the Phaboung
⎱ stream 2 years ago, which is in a flourishing state.

(True Copy.)
D. BRANDIS,
Supdt. of Forests in Pegu,
Tenasserim and Martaban Provinces.

(Sd.)   CHAS. SALMOND,
Assistant Forest Surveyor.

APPENDIX.

APPENDIX, No. I.

I.—In the Tsintsway Forests (Yoonzaleen) one acre was measured out and all trees growing on the same counted. The forest was of the upper mixed forest (third group) with a large proportion of Teak.

No.	Description of Trees and Class.	Size or girth in cubits.	Number observed.	Total.	Per square mile.	REMARKS.
1	Tesk 1st Class, ...	5	5	17	10,880	
	,,	4	12			
	Teak 2nd Class, ...	3	13	13	8,320	
	,, 3rd Class, ...	2 & 1	12	12	7,680	
	,, 4th Class, ...	Small.	1	1	640	
	Total,......			43	27,520	
2	Other trees : Pynkadoe, Inga xylocarpa, ...		11			
	Kyayoe, Vitex sp., ...		2			
	Pæwoon, Berrya mollis, Wall., ...		2			
	Pymmah, Lagerstrœmia regina,......		1			
	Boay Gyin, Bauhinia malabarica, Roxb., ...		1			
	Myayah, Grewia microstemma, ...		1			
	Myoukshaw, Blackwellia tomentosa,		1			
	Gnooben Cassia fistula, ...		1			
	Shawben, Sterculia sp., ...		1			
	Bingah, Nauclea sp., ...		1			
	Pangah, Terminalia chebula, ...		1			
	Yaimein, ...		1	24	15,360	
	Total,		24	15,360		
	Grand Total, ...			67	42,880	

II.—In the same forest eight Teak trees were measured, growing close together on a square $52\frac{1}{2} \times$ by $73' = 3,833$ square feet. The trees had clear stems on an average 50 feet high and their girth varied from 4' 6'' to 6' 5'', the average being 5' 6''.

This gives 91 Teak trees per acre or 58,240 per square mile.

III.—In the Bindah forests Dr. MacClelland found on the space of two acres.

```
Teak trees    1st Class, ⎫
  ,,    ,,    2nd   ,,  ⎬ 12
  ,,    ,,    3rd   ,,  ⎭
  ,, seedlings 4th  ,,     30
                         ____
            Total,    42
```
This corresponds to 13,440 trees per square mile.

No.	Date.	Name of Officer conducting the Survey.	District.	Name and situation of Forest Tract.	Teak trees in girth above.				Fourth small Trees.	Nathat.	Girdled.
					Cubits.						
					1st Class.		2nd Class.	3rd Class.			
					V.	VI.	III.	II. & I.			
1	July 26.	D. Brandis.	Winyeo Lower.	Doon Can No. 6, of Hobday's List.	56	94	253	249	542	37	38
2	July 26.	Do.	Do.	Shoay Doug, No.5, of Hobday's List.	16	76	280	650	192	12	27
3	July 27.	Do.	Do.	Shoay Yah, No. 7, of Hobday's List.	14	59	206	191	88	24	20

Attaran.

Logs.	Stumps.	Attacked with Ficus.	Length.	Width.	Area.	REMARKS.
14	75	0	6	0.05	0.3	*No.* 1. *Locality.*—The forest is situated north west of the present village of Cronkawoon, on a small tributary of the Cronkawoon Choung, on rising, slightly undulated ground. *Soil.*—Light loam; colour, reddish. *Other Trees.*—The forest is clear and open, no bamboo, the ground is covered with long soft grass often 6′ high. *Prevailing trees.*—Pymmah (Lagerstrœmia sp.), Zimbjoon (Dillenia aurea), Bambouay (Careya arborea), Nabhayben. *Scattered*—Yindike (Dalbergia), Myoukshaw (Blackwellia tomentosa.) Pynkadoe (Inga xylocarpa). Thingau (Hopea odorata), Pangah (Terminalia) Yaymein. *Scarce.*—Padouk, but of immense girth. (Pterocarpus Dalbergioides, Roxb.) *Genl. Remarks.*—Growth of Teak trees very inferior. Stems of large trees crooked and branched near the base, frequently forked. Only three (3) trees of good straight growth in girth above 3 cubits are observed. The forest has not been worked for many years. The owner is dead.
6	36	0	·3	0.05	0.15	*No.* 2. *Locality.*—On both banks of the Muprang Choung, commencing about 13 miles from its mouth. *Soil.*—See No. 1. *Other Trees.*—Ditto. *Genl. Remarks.*—Growth as in No. 1. Only 1 tree of 3 cubits in girth of straight growth. The holder is dead. Forest last worked in 1844. (Hobday).
9	32	0	3	0.05	0.15	*No.* 3. *Locality.*—On both sides of the Cronkawoon Choung, on even ground. The forest does not extend to the foot of the hills. *Soil.*—Same as No. 1. *Other Trees.*—Same as No. 1, with the addition of the following trees. *Frequent.*—Pynkadoe, Kjoonboe (Premna pyramidata, Wall.) Taunmag-

No.	Date.	Name of Officer conducting the Survey.	District.	Name and situation of Forest Tract.	Teak trees in girth above.				Fourth small Trees.	Nathat.	Girdled.
					Cubits.						
					1st Class.	2nd Class.	3rd Class.	II. & I.			
					V.	VI.	III.				
4	July 28.	D. Brandis.	Winyeo Lower.	Umogland Forest between the Palyaband Majitto Choung, not mentioned on Map or list.	28	45	101	148	51	11	7
5	August 2.	Moung-shwoelium.	Left bank of Majitto Choung seven miles from its mouth not mentioned on map or List.	Lower Winyeo	3	7	20	0	0	1	0

Attaran—(Continued.)

Logs.	Stumps.	Attacked with Ficus.	Length.	Width.	Area.	REMARKS.
						giben (Albizzia odoratissima). *Scattered* —Ananben (Fagræa sp.) Didoke Lepan (Eriodendron anfractuosum ? fl. albis.) Myayaben (Grewia microstemma), Yemenchben (Gmelina arborea), Tansha, Theinben (Nauclea sp.) Padouk. Ananbo, Marench, Kokohben. *Scarce.*—Tanthanben, (Borassus, sp.) Tanthayet (Mangifera indica β sylvestris.)
						Genl. Remarks.—Growth somewhat better, 9 trees in girth above 3 cubits were found good and straight, the remainder are all crooked or branching. The holder is dead. Forest last worked in 1847. (Hobday.)
3	22		3	0.05	0.15	*No. 4. Locality.*—On a small feeder of the Paljah Choung, on even ground.
						Soil.—Same as No. 1.
						Other Trees.—Same as No. 1, but a large amount of bamboos, Myoukshaw, and Kyoonboe prevailing.
						Genl. Remarks.—Growth superior to the former, many trees of very large girth, but none with tall clear stems. The following are the dimensions of some of the largest :
						Girth 6' from the ground 21', 19', 15', 10', three trees grown into one had a joint girth of 24'. Fifteen straight trees in girth above 3 cubits were observed. Most of the stumps were large. This forest has evidently not been worked for a number of years, and no particulars could be obtained regarding the parties who formerly had worked it.
0	0	0	0	0	0.03	*No. 5. Locality.*—There are numerous isolated small patches of Teak on the upper course of the different tributaries of the Winyeo not far from the foot of the western range of hills. One was observed on the 27th July between Llatshanvill, and Forest No. 4, but as only 2 trees were observed, it has not been entered here The present one is near the headwaters of the Majitto Choung, where it emerges from the hills. The Karens are positive in assert-

21

No.	Date.	Name of Officer conducting the Survey.	District.	Name and situation of Forest Tract.	Teak trees in girth above.				Fourth small Trees.	Nathat.	Girdled.
					Cubits.						
					1st Class.	2nd Class.	3rd Class.	II. & I.			
					V.	IV.	III.				
				Total of Lower Winyeo Forests.	117	281	860	1238	873	85	92
				Per square mile,	528		1142	1647	1159	112	122
6	July 30.	D. Brandis.	Winyeo Upper.	Tounbjan Forest, No. 16.	155 77	373 139	120	179	230	14	20
7	July 31. to August 3.	Do.	Do.	Left side of the Winyeo near its junction with the Thingan-neennoung, No. 16?	*a* 12	2	49	123	19	1	5
					b 3	10	10	12	3	1	1
					c 6	7	60	20	8	1	3

Attaran—(Continued.)

Logs.	Stumps.	Attacked with Ficus.	Length.	Width.	Area.	REMARKS.
132	165				0753	ing that there is no Teak on the hills here, or near the sources of the Pabjah, Croonkawoon and other tributaries of the Winyeo on this side.
42	219					*Genl. Remarks.*—The other trees are those of the mixed forest as in Nos. 1 and 4. The growth of Teak is good, the greater portion of the larger trees being straight.
31	192		6½	0034	0.21	*No. 6. Locality.*—Between the Winyeo Choung and the range of hills forming the watershed between Winyeo and Zimmay, extending from the Pourloung Choung to the north, to the junction of Thinganneenoung and Winyeo to the South. Undulating ground between a number of small streams, falling into the Winyeo. *Soil.*—Light reddish loam. *Other Trees.*—Bamboo abundant (Wanoë) here and there; the other trees are those of the mixed forest. *Genl. Remarks.*—Growth good, almost all trees of 3 and 4 cubits in girth are straight, and without side branches. But all larger trees (of 5 cubits and above) are either embraced by the epiphytic ficus, or hollow, or of so irregular growth, that if felled, they would be perfectly valueless. All large trees of value have been felled, and only the refuse has been left standing. The forest has been worked in a wasteful manner, many logs have been left to be destroyed by the annual fires, and the ground near the stumps is covered with their remains.
6	79*	1	4	0.03	0.02	*No. 7. Locality.*—Teak localities stretch along the left bank of the Winyeo a considerable distance above and below the junction. A series of undulating hills run parallel to the Winyeo river, Teak occurs on the lower slopes of those hills, and on the even ground between them and the stream, (*a*) was observed on the hills below, (*c*) on those
1	11		2	0.03	0.06	
1	9†		2	0.03	0.06	

* Of these 60 undersized.   † 4 of them were undersized.

No.	Date.	Name of Officer conducting the Survey.	District.	Name and situation of Forest Tract.	Teak trees in girth above.				Fourth small Trees.	Nathat.	Girdled.
					Cubits.						
					1st Class.	2nd Class.	3rd Class.				
					V.	IV.	III.	II. & I.			
8	August 2. to August 4.	D. Brandis.	Upper Winyeo.	On the right side of the Winyeo near its junction, No. 17. Thingan-neennoung Reserved Forest.	*a* 40 *b* 25	4 29	8 75	1 30	3 1	3 5	7 29

Attaran—(Continued.)

Logs.	Stumps.	Attacked with Ficus.	Length.	Width.	Area.	REMARKS.
						above the junction, and (*b*) on the even ground opposite the Teak plantation.
						Soil.—White (reddish on the outside). Sandstone similar to that of Maulmein is found cropping out here and there, on it rests ferruginous conglomerate. (Laterite.)
						The soil is of a reddish colour.
						Other Trees.—Mixed forest and dense bamboo jungles (Wajah and Wanoë). When bamboo is wanting, the soft grass of the Teak localities covers the ground.
						Genl. Remarks.—Growth good, most trees straight and clear of branches. The great number of third class trees in (*a*) and of undersized stumps in the same locality is remarkable.
13	35	}	8	0 15	0.12	*No. 8. Locality.*—Teak is found from the Teak plantation (about 1st below the junction) to a considerable distance above it, here it occurs on even ground along the river, but between both rivers, the Thinganneennoung and Winyeo, it was only found in the slopes of hills (*a*) was observed along the right bank of the Winyeo, and Thinganneennoung, and (*b*) on the hills between both streams.
18	43	}				*Soil.*—The white Maulmein sandstone with its red crust underlies the ferruginous conglomerate. With the exception of the river's bank, Teak is not found on alluvial soil here.
						Other Trees.—Teak occurs here in the dense evergreen forest, which here and there alternates with dense bamboo jungle. But the forest in (*a*) consists of old trees mostly of immense size, whereas that in (*b*) is evidently younger. Teak seedlings do not spring up in the dense shade of this kind of forest. It must therefore be assumed, that when Teak first sprung up, the tract was covered with forest of a different kind.
						Genl. Remarks.—The growth of the tree is good,

No.	Date.	Name of Officer conducting the Survey.	District.	Name and situation of Forest Tract.	Teak trees in girth above.				Fourth small Trees.	Nathat.	Girdled.
					Cubits.						
					1st Class.	2nd Class.	3rd Class.				
					V.	IV.	III.	11. & 1.			
				Total of Upper Winyeo Forests. Per square mile.	163 191 621		322 564	365 640	264 463	24 42	64 112
					335	286					
9	August 5.	D. Brandis.	Zimmay, Megwa, Tseikgja, Kyoupja.	Megwa Forest, above and below the Kyouktaga (Nos. 49 and 50)	93	34	121	112	92	15	79

Attaran—Continued.

Logs.	Stumps.	Attacked with Ficus.	Length.	Width.	Area.	REMARKS.
69	369				0.57	but most of the large trees are attacked with ficus, or are hollow, or otherwise useless. The forest has evidently been worked out as much as any other forest, it has been a reserved forest only by name.
121	647					
57	191		3	0023	0069	*No. 9. Locality.*—The Megwa Choung passes through a narrow gorge about 1 mile long between two high ranges of hills, running in a north-west direction, parellel to the Zimmay Choung. The present village of Megwa, is between the gorge and the mouth. Near it, another branch from the north joins the Megwa. On both branches, both in the valley and on the hills Teak is found. The northern parts are said to be best preserved. Below the gorge, the number of large trees is small, but the number of stumps very great. The survey went over the hills near the south branch, and along the course of the Megwa down to the village. *Soil.*—No outer springs of any rocks are observed, the soil on the hills is sandy, in the plains the debris of ferruginous conglomerate are mixed with gravel. *Other Trees.*—The usual trees of the mixed forest, with the addition of the groups of sterculia from which bark rope is made, the red, Shawnee, and the white, Shawbjoo, another kind of Lagerstrœmia, L. cuspidata, Wall. Pymmahljoo, with white bark, and rose-coloured blossoms, coming out in July and August, not in April and May as the Pymmah, Toukkyan (Pentaptera sp.) Taben (Dillenia speciosa). A great variety of bamboo was found, viz. Tinwa, Minwa, near the stream, and Wanoë, Tabendine Wah on the hills.

No.	Date.	Name of Officer conducting the Survey.	District.	Name and situation of Forest Tract.	Teak trees in girth above.				Fourth small Trees.	Nathat.	Girdled.
					Cubits.						
					1st Class.	2nd Class.	3rd Class.				
					V.	IV.	III.	II. & I.			
10	August 6.	D. Brandis.	Zimmay.	Tabew Choung Forest said to belong to No. 50	15	9	41	46	3	4	36

Attaran—Continued.

Logs.	Stumps.	Attacked with Ficus.	Length.	Width.	Area.	REMARKS.
						Genl. Remarks.—The growth of the Teak trees is good; better than in any of the Winyeo forests. The general appearance of the forest is much like those on the Pegu Yomah; however, Teak is more scattered here, it covers only a small portion of the hills. The forest above the gorge has been claimed by Mr. Rushbrook as part of No. 16, by the owners of the Naturad estate, it is considered as a part of their territory, but it is worked by Mrs. Darwood's people, who claim it, apparently, as a portion of the Majyebe forest, No. 53. Found a hut on the banks of the Megwa in which the timber-cutters and elephanteers lived. They expected to get 100 logs by November.
24	59	6	3	0.023	0.069	*No. 10 Locality.*—South of the Megwa, along the course of the Taben Choung and its branches. The Taben Choung is a tributary of the Megwa. The hills commence close to the village of Megwa, with some Teak, then follows Ein forest, on the first terrace. But beyond this, on ground gradually rising to the higher hills, Teak again occurs, scattered throughout the mixed forest. Of the spars and ridges of these hills, a few only are covered with Teak. *Soil.*—Sandstone is frequently observed outcropping, the soil is sandy, but of a red colour. *Other Trees.*—Same as No. 9.—The forest is rather dense and shady, very few seedlings. *Genl. Remarks.*—The large trees remaining are mostly attacked by the parasitic ficus, or of inferior growth, the small timber is straight. Found a party of Burmans at work cutting and dragging. They stated that they had 20 men and 4 elephants, and that their timber would reach Maulmein in February.

22

No.	Date.	Name of Officer conducting the Survey.	District.	Name and situation of Forest Tract.	Teak trees in girth above.				Fourth small Trees.	Nathat.	Girdled.
					Cubits.						
					1st Class.	2nd Class.	3rd Class.	II. & I.			
					V.	IV.	III.				
11	Augt. 7.	D. Brandis.	Zimmay.	Tseikgyee Forest, No. 50.	20	40	116	159	493	7	24

Attaran—(Continued.)

Logs.	Stumps.	Attacked with Ficus.	Length.	Width.	Area.	REMARKS.
32	165	15	4	0.03	0.02	*No.* 11 *Locality.*—This forest extends along the Zimmay near the mouth of the Tseikgyee Choung and up this stream. Only the portion near the main river was surveyed.

Soil.—The influence of the soil on the growth of Teak is very evident here. Further inland there is a belt of deep clay, now in a state of soft mud. All other trees of the mixed forest and bamboos, grow here luxuriantly, but Teak is wanting. As soon as we entered the Teak forest, the mud ceased, and a sandy loam took its place.

Other Trees.—Same as in No. 9, with the addition of Gjaben (Schleichera trijuga ?)

Genl. Remarks.—Before it was brought under the operation of the axe, this forest must have been a most valuable one. The area surveyed was only 76 acres, and on this span were seen 165 stumps, but the grass was so high, that probably only one-fourth of the stumps could be counted. This would give nearly 9 large trees per acre, when the working of the forest was first commenced. The size of these stumps is immense. The following is the measurement of 8, taken at random from among those near the road.

3 at 14′   girth ⎫
2 ,,   17′   ,,   ⎬ The remainder were all of from
1 ,,   21′   ,,   ⎬   6′ to 14′ in girth.
1 ,,   16′ 6″   ,,   ⎬
1 ,,   17′ 6″   ,,   ⎭

All first class trees still standing are either crooked, or branching, or attacked with ficus. Creepers are very numerous in this forest, and have had a most injurious effect on the growth of the trees. A few of the trees girdled were of very small girth, only 2 or 3 cubits; these had evidently been girdled, in order to obtain small crooks from the

No.	Date.	Name of Officer conducting the Survey.	District.	Name and situation of Forest Tract.	Teak trees in girth above. Cubits.				Fourth small Trees.	Nathat.	Girdled.
					1st Class. V.	2nd Class. IV.	3rd Class. III.	11. & I.			
12	Augt. 7.	D. Brandis.	Zimmay.	Kyoukpja Forest, No. 51.	19	13	86	79	265	24	49
				Total of Megwa, Tseikgyee, Kjoukpja Forests,	147	96	364	396	853	50	188
				Per square mile,	642		962	1047	2256	132	497
					388	254					
13	Augt. 9.	Do.	Do.	Kyoon Choung Forest, lower portion near the Zimmay river, No. 52.	35	17	30	84	60	10	25

Attaran—(Continued.)

Logs.	Stumps.	Attacked with Ficus.	Length.	With.	Area.	REMARKS.
						upper end of the stem, which had been bent by the weight of creepers. The number of seedlings is very considerable in this forest, near the banks of the river there were entire groves of the same, in girth 12″ and in height 30′. The forest being clear, without any bamboo or underwood, greatly favors the growth of young Teak in the same. The forest is actively worked, at present 35 dooggies were ready dragged to the bank of the Zimmay.
61	183	0	6	0.02	0.12	*No.* 12 *Locality.*—The right bank of the Zimmay river is occupied by a succession of low undulating hills and on these Teak is found here and there.
						Soil.—Same as in No. 10.—Teak is found only where the ground is comparatively dry, but not when the rain has turned it into mud. *Other Trees.*—Mixed forest with a large proportion of Toukkyan, a large part of the route lay through
174	598	21	0	0	0.378	old deserted toungyas, cultivated about 10 years ago, and on them young trees of different kinds were growing up in large numbers. The young
460	1582	55	0	0	0	Teak trees observed, were found chiefly on such places, and on clear spots in the forest.
						Genl. Remarks.—The growth of Teak is good, but nearly all large trees are useless from being attacked with parasitic ficus, or hollow, or from other causes. The forest is not worked at present.
30	161	31	5	0.02	0.10	*Nos.* 13 and 14 *Locality.*—The Kyoon Choung forest stretches along the course of the Kyoon Choung and its tributaries from its mouth to the hills; the ground is slightly undulated throughout, and a few patches of Teak trees are said to be on the hills.
						Soil.—Light sandy loam, in a few places red gravelly soil, resting on ferruginous conglomerate. *Other Trees.*—The forest is open in the upper part, especially in the neighbourhood of the Kyoon

No.	Date.	Name of Officer conducting the Survey.	District.	Name and situation of Forest Tract.	Teak trees in girth above.				Fourth small Trees.	Nathat.	Girdled.
					Cubits.						
					1st Class.	2nd Class.	3rd Class.	II. & I.			
					V.	IV.	III.				
14	Augt. 11.	D. Brandis.	Zimmay.	Kyoon Choung Forest, upper portion, near the Hills, No. 52.	138	57	160	297	173	30	136

Attaran—Continued.

Logs.	Stumps.	Attacked with Ficus.	Length.	Width.	Area.	REMARKS.
18	477	90	6	0.036	'.216	Choung, the ground is here covered with long soft grass ; the trees are those of the mixed forest, often of immense size. On the hills, bamboo jungle comes in, and near the mouth there is more underwood, and here and there patches of evergreen forest. *Genl. Remarks.*—Growth good, but all trees above 4 cubits in girth with few exceptions are deformed and useless, either attacked with parasite ficus, or hollow, or branching. Only *seven* (7) really fine large trees were found, and these had stems clear up to a height of from 40 to 60 feet. (*Note* 1). Many of the trees of 1, 2, or 3 cubits in girth were off-shoots from stumps. Such trees had evidently been felled green, without previous killing. The stumps, if killed, could not have brought forth these shoots. Similar off-shoots are found wherever trees have been felled green for toungya cultivation, a measurement of stumps and off-shoots is given below. (*Note* 2). Capt. O'Brien mentions the circumstance in his journal. The average age of these off-shoots may be assumed at about 25 years (1833). The forest was not worked when we examined it. It is evidently greatly exposed to the ravages from jungle fires.

Note 1.—Measurement of large Teak trees.

Girth	height of char stin,
14'	60'
15'8	40
7	50
12	50

Note 2.—Measurement of Stumps and offshoots.

Stumps.	Girth.	Offshoots.	Girth.
11'	10''	5'	9''
12		4	8
13	8	5	7
9	8	5	5
11		3	6
12		8	
10		3	6
11		4	6
9	4	5	

Average girth of offshoot 4' 5'.

No.	Date.	Name of Officer conducting the Survey.	District.	Name and situation of Forest Tract.	Teak trees in girth above.				Fourth small Trees.	Nathat.	Girdled.
					Cubits.						
					1st Class.	2nd Class.	3rd Class.				
					V.	IV.	III.	II. & I.			
15	Augt. 9.	Mr. J. Barker.	Zimmay.	North tributary of the Kyoon Choung, (No. 52.)	26	13	40	43	40	4	5
16	Augt. 9.	Do.	Do.	Do. (No. 52.)	27	11	30	13	7	2	0
				Total of Kyoon Choung Forests,	226	98	260	437	280	46	166
				Per square mile.	{956}		751	1263	809	133	479
17	Augt. 9.	Dr. D. Brandis.	Zimmay.	Between the Okdan and Methaban Choung, No. 53.	653 3	283 4	47	26	12	3	5
18	Augt. 10.	Do.	Do.	Prakat Forest, No. 53.	5	18	47	28	8	6	2
19	Augt. 11.	Do.	Do.	Punko Forest, No. 53.	5	21	58	153	40	1	1

Attaran—(Continued.)

Logs.	Stumps.	Attacked with Ficus.	Length.	Width.	Area.	REMARKS.
75	59	7	1	0.015	0.015	*No.* 15 *Locality.*—On a small tributary of the Kyoon Choung, 2 miles from the village of Kheewu, to the left of the main road leading from the three pagodas to the Mittigate. *Soil.*—Mixed sand and clay. *Other Trees.*—Dense bamboo jungle with the trees of the mixed forest. *Genl. Remarks.*—The Teak found here is remarkable for the beauty and regularity of its growth. The forest apparently has not been worked for several years, the stumps are old, and the logs almost consumed by fire.
2	1	3	I	0.015	0.015	*No.* 16 *Locality.*—Beyond No. 15, near the watershed between Kyoon Choung and Mittigate, on the left side of the road. *Soil.*—Dryer than No. 15, and mixed with pebbles and gravel. The Teak was found growing on the slopes of small hills.
125	698	131	0	0	0.346	*Other Trees.*—Same as No. 15.
361	2017	378	0	0	0	*Genl. Remarks.*—This small forest is still more remarkable for the regularity and beauty of the Teak trees. The forest, apparently, has never been worked.
0	0	0	4	0.018	0.072	*Nos.* 17 *to* 20 *Locality.*—Teak occurs on both sides of the upper course of the Zimmay river as far as the Methaban Choung, beyond which there are only a few isolated patches. The country is hilly, but from the low undulating hills, steep and rugged limestone rocks arise, often to a considerable height. The Teak localities are either near the
0	40	2	4	0.018	0.072	banks of the Zimmay, or at the foot of the limestone rocks. *Soil.*—Near the river a sandy loam, higher up, red clay soil, such as is generally found near the
0	51	2	1	0.018	0.036	Tenasserim limestone rocks. *Other Trees.*—The country is covered partly with open mixed forest, partly with evergreen forest,

No.	Date.	Name of Officer conducting the Survey.	District.	Name and situation of Forest Tract.	Teak trees in girth above.				Fourth small Trees.	Nathat.	Girdled.
					Cubits.						
					1st Class.	2nd Class.	3rd Class.				
					V.	IV.	III.	II. & I.			
20	Augt. 18.	Dr. D. Bran-dis.	Zimmay.	Teeklent Forest on a tributary of the Prakat stream, No. 53.	0	17	13	4	0	0	1
21	Augt. 10.	Do.	Do.	Methaban Forest, No. 53.	6	9	5	9	6	10	7
				Total of the upper Zimmay Forests,	19	69	170	220	66	20	16
				Per square mile,	389		751	973	292	88	70
					84	305					
22	Augt. 9.	Mr. J. Bar-ker.	Do.	Mittigate Kodogway, South Tributary,	4	7	10	10	10	10	7
23	Augt. 10.	Do.	Do.	Do. (No. 47.)	0	4	3	0	0	0	0
24	Augt. 9.	Do.	Do.	On the hills S. E. of the Mitt. Kodogway,	20	8	94	72	6	20	206

Attaran—(Continued.)

Logs.	Stumps.	Attacked with Ficus.	Length.	Width.	Area.	REMARKS.
0	2	0	2	0.018	0.036	partly with bamboo jungle. The trees mostly associated with Teak are Toukkyau, Pymmah, Pymmahben, Kunjinben, Thinganben. *Genl. Remarks.*—Most of the large trees left standing of little value, irregular, hollow, or attacked with ficus. A large number of fine tall trees of 3 cubits everywhere.
8	25	4	0	0	001	*No. 21 Locality.*—An isolated patch of Teak on the hills, east of the mouth of the Methaban Choung, at the foot of a steep and high limestone rock, between the Prakat and Methaban Choungs. *Soil.*—A rich black loam. *Other Trees.*—The Teak trees are found in the dense evergreen forest, the seedlings had sprung up further down when the forest was clearer.
8	118	8	0	0	0.226	*Genl. Remarks.*—The trees are tall and of regular growth, but all large trees are on the decline. The
35	522	35	0	0	0	trees that are nathat (or dead from natural causes), have all been blown down, a remarkable fact, for the situation is not exposed, and the soil is apparently deep ; further, Teak is sheltered by other large trees. The only explanation that can be given is, that the green dense forest growing up with them, has gradually smothered them.
4	6	2	0	0	0.015	*No. 22 Locality, &c.*—To the left of the main road from the 3 pagodas to the Mittigate in small patches in the Ein forest.
0	0	0	0	0	0	*No. 23 Locality, &c.*—Near the lower Mephra village.
21	3	23	2m.	0.015	0.03	*Nos. 24 to 26 Locality.*—This is the forest described by Capt. O'Brien as the unexplored forest on the Mittigate Kodogway. It occupies a tract of low hills on the right bank of the stream, and extends to the foot of the high mountain range to the east.

Forest Day Book

No.	Date.	Name of Officer conducting the Survey.	District.	Name and situation of Forest Tract.	Teak trees in girth above. Cubits.				Fourth small Trees.	Nathat.	Girdled.
					1st Class. V.	2nd Class. IV.	3rd Class. III.	II. & I.			
25	Augt. 10.	Mr. J. Barker.	Zimmay.	On the hills S. E. of the Mitt. Kodogway.	8	53	96	62	20	34	166
26	Augt. 11.	Do.	Do.	Do. (No. 47.)	17	72	165	109	10	31	562
				Total of Mittigate Kodogway Forests,	49	144	368	253	46	95	941
				Per square mile,	989		1887	1295	235	487	4825
					257	738					

Attaran—*(Continued.)*

Logs.	Stumps.	Attacked with Ficus.	Length.	Width.	Area.	REMARKS.
45	5	10	3m.	0.015	0.045	*Soil.*—Mixed sand and clay, generally with the addition of gravel, evidently very favorable for the growth of Teak.
110	15	15	7m.	0.015	0.105	*Other Trees.*—The Teak occurs in dense bamboo jungle, with other trees of the mixed forest. Large specimens of the poison tree (Antiaris sp.) with the milk of which arrows are poisoned, were observed.
180	29	50	0	0	0.195	*Genl. Remarks.*—The number of nathat, killed and fallen trees, in this forest is disproportionably large. There are no apparent signs of the forest having been worked for many years back ; the stumps, few in number, are not from felled trees, but the remains of trees burnt down. There are no shaped or lopped logs, but all those noted in the statement,
923	148	256	0	0	0	are fallen trees, mostly killed. Of this timber, thus left neglected to perish in the forest, it is not too much to say, that generally it is the finest I (Mr. J. Barker) have seen, or at least of the best. I measured several of these standing, killed and fallen trees, the result of which is given on the margin (1). Of the 941 killed standing trees, 380 are under 5 cubits or 7½′ in girth, a proportion of the latter are under 5′ in girth. The logs or fallen trees are, with few exceptions, of the class above 5 cubits in girth, a number of these logs have been more or less destroyed by fire. The growing trees are good, tall, straight and regular in growth.

(1.)—Memo. of Measurement of Trees.

2 Killed standing trees, girth,		...	10′	6″	The average height of these trees was esti-
1 ,, ,, ,,		...	9	6	mated at 60′, up to the first branch, including
2 ,, ,, ,,		...	13	6	the trunk as far as it could from the dressed
1 ,, ,, ,,		...	12	0	log. These trees are round, straight and with-
2 ,, ,, ,,		...	11	8	out blemish. These measurements are not ex-
1 ,, ,, ,,		...	9	0	ceptions, but given as a sample of the general
1 ,, ,, ,,		...	8	0	character of the timber.
1 ,, ,, ,,		...	15	0	
1 Growing tree, ,,		...	15	0	forked at 18′ from the ground, the two arms being about 40′ in height and 8′ or 9′ in girth.

No.	Date.	Name of Officer conducting the Survey.	District.	Name and situation of Forest Tract.	Teak trees in girth above.				Fourth small Trees.	Nathat.	Girdeled.
					Cubits.						
					1st Class.	2nd Class.	3rd Class.				
					V.	IV.	III.	II. & I.			
27	Augt. 12	Mr. J. Barker.	Zimmay.	On the left side of the Mittigate Choung, opposite Meekouk village.	30	6	19	10	53	15	63
28	Do.	Dr. D. Brandis.	Do.	Do. (No. 46)	21	5	12	6	9	5	13
29	Augt. 13.	Do.	Do.	Mittigate right side, above Meekouk village.	8	0	9	5	7	1	7

Attaran—(Continued.)

Logs.	Stumps.	Attacked with the Ficus.	Length.	Width.	Area.	REMARKS.
						The bamboo jungle is so dense, that the vision is generally limited to about 20 yards, and often to much less, on the highest points of the hills, it was found impossible to get a more extended view. When Capt. O'Brien visited the forest (16th Feb. 1841) only a small number of trees had been killed. The natives state, that the wholesale girdling of the trees took place about 15 years ago (in 1843). Certainly this forest is a remarkable instance of the care which private parties bestow upon their property if the forests are left in their hands. In 1849, the Mittigate and Mittigate Kodogway forests were granted to Mr. Donald Mackey for a period of 99 years with the whole of the trees and timber on the same, and here is seasoned timber ready for removal, to the value of at least 24,320 Rupees, if we only take the timber actually seen and counted at Rs. 20 the tree, burning away annually.
90	180	36				*Nos. 27 and* 28 *Locality.*—On even ground and low undulating hills along a south tributary of the Mittigate.
						Soil.—Mixed sand and clay.
			6	0.03	0.36	*Other Trees.*—Those of the mixed forest.
					0.18	*Genl. Remarks.*—Growth fine, the stumps of great girth.
5	72	19				
8	78	6	3	0.023	0.069	*Nos. 29 to 30 Locality.*—The Mittigate forests below the Kyouktaga are said to be richer in Teak on the right side. They commence several miles above the mouth, at the Tiwapadon Choung, and extend to within 4 miles from the Kyouktaga. The forest above and below is dense evergreen forest without any trace of Teak.

No.	Date.	Name of Officer. conducting the Survey.	District.	Name and situation of Forest Tract.	Teak trees in girth above.				Fourth small Trees.	Nathat.	Girdled.
					Cubits.						
					1st Class.		2nd Class.	3rd Class.			
					V.	IV.	III.	I. II. &			
30	Augt. 14.	Dr. D. Brandis.	Zimmay.	Mittigate below Meekouk village as far down as the Tiwapadon Choung, No. 46.	45	16	7	22	72	3	51
				Total of Mittigate Forests below Kyouktaga,	104	27	47	43	141	24	134
				Per square mile,	158		56	52	170	29	162
					224	58	101	92	303	52	288
					282						

Attaran—(Continued.)

Logs.	Stumps.	Attacked with Ficus.	Length.	Width.	Area.	REMARKS.
13	180	39	6	0.36	0.216	*Soil.*—Sandy loam. *Other Trees.*—Those of the mixed forest, with the long soft grass underneath. The forest is much more clear in the lower part, hence the large proportion of small trees. *Genl. Remarks.*—Growth good, but all large trees remaining are of very little value, hollow, half burnt, branching, or attacked with ficus. But the large number of stumps proves that the forest has once been a most valuable one. Toungyas are very numerous here, and have added much to the destruction of the Teak in the forests, Teak being cut down indiscriminately with other trees. Many trees are girdled and not removed.
116	510	100	0	0	0.465	
140	618	121	0	0	0	
249	1096	215	0	0	0	

24

No.	Date.	Name of Officer conducting the Survey.	District.	Name and situation of Forest Tract.	Teak trees in girth above.				Fourth small Trees.	Nathat.	Girdled.
					Cubits.						
					1st Class.	2nd Class.	3rd Class.	II. & I.			
					V.	IV.	III.				
31	Augt. 13.	Dr.D. Brandis.	Zimmay.	Mittigate above the Kyouktaga, along the Koon Chg. Gelay (No. 48, reserved Forest.)	17	0	0	0	0	34*	0

Memo. of measurement of Logs.

```
 1 Length 30'  Lower girth 6'  Upper girth 6'
 2   „    64          „    12          „     8
 3   „    23          „    8.8         „     7.4
 4   „    64          „    10.7        „     7
 5   „    30          „    6           „     6
 6   „    33          „    12.5        „     11.4
 7   „    39          „    10.5        „     8
 8   „    41          „    12          „     11
 9   „    80          „    9           „     5.3
10   „    29          „    8           „     6.6
11   „    32          „    9           „     8.4
```

* Of these Nathat trees, 30 were fallen.

Attaran—(Continued.)

Logs.	Stumps.	Attacked with Ficus.	Length.	Width.	Area.	REMARKS.
34*	20	27	4	0.015	0.060	*Nos. 31 to 34 Locality.*—The Mittigate Choung passes through a break in the mountain range, which bounds the Zimmay valley to the east. Above the narrow gorge thus formed, the valley widens into a basin, several miles long and wide, surrounded on all sides by hills of considerable height. The bottom of the basin, and a great portion of the slopes of the hills encircling it, are covered with dense evergreen forests, and in these are found several tracts of Teak. *Soil.*—Deep black alluvial soil, with much vegetable mould. *Other Trees.*—Those of the green forest, most of them unknown to Burmans. *Bomoh*, hard elastic wood used for spear-handles and bows. *Thitcha.* (Quercus, sp.) ; *Kathilben*, (Erythima, sp.) ; *Maneeoga?* *Myouklouk*, (Artocarpus, sp.) ; large specimens of *Pymmah* and *Pymmahben*, with *Thingan, Kanyin* and other trees of the Dipterocarpus family. The underwood, consisting mostly of young trees of the above, is very dense. *Genl. Remarks.*—The Karens state that besides the tracts described sub. (31-34) there are no Teak localities above the Kyouktaga, and as we, in examining the forest have every where penetrated far beyond the localities where Teak occurs, without finding any trees of it either in the valley or on the hills, this statement is likely to be correct. The total area surveyed on the 13th and 14th August was 0.135 square miles, so that, if it be assumed, that we saw one-fifth of the whole, 0.665 of a square mile appears to be a more correct estimate

* Of these logs, 16 were above 6′ cub. middle girth.
        18 below,   6 ,,   ,,

No.	Date.	Name of Officer conducting the Survey.	District.	Name and situation of Forest Tract.	Teak trees in girth above.				Fourth small Trees.	Nathat.	Girdled.
					Cubits.						
					1st Class.	2nd Class.	3rd Class.	II. & I.			
					V.	IV.	III.				
32	Augt. 14.	Dr. D. Brandis.	Zimmay.	Mittigate above the Kyouktaga, right bank of the Mittigate, below the Teekine Choung.	5	0	2	0	0	41*	3
33	Do.	Do.	Do.	Do. above the Teekine Choung.	6	0	0	0	0	90†	9

Memo. of measurement of Logs.

1	Length	51′	Lower girth	11′4	Upper girth	8′9	13	Length	40′	Lower girth	9′	Upper girth	6′
2	,,	53	,,	8	,,	6	14	,,	35	,,	9	,,	7
3	,,	40	,,	8	,,	6.7	15	,,	50	,,	12	,,	8
4	,,	51	,,	8	,,	7	16	,,	31	,,	8	,,	6
5	,,	23	,,	10	,,	8	17	,,	30	,,	8	,,	6
6	,,	55	,,	10.4	,,	8	18	,,	40	,,	12	,,	8
7	,,	23	,,	10	,,	10	19	,,	40	,,	7	,,	5
8	,,	60	,,	7	,,	5	20	,,	64	,,	13	,,	7.6
9	,,	52	,,	11	,,	8	21	,,	18	,,	8.6	,,	8.6
10	,,	32	,,	8	,,	6	22	,,	32	,,	10.6	,,	9
11	,,	40	,,	8	,,	6	23	,,	50	,,	10	,,	8
12	,,	42	,,	8	,,	7							

* These Nathat trees are all fallen trees.
† These Nathat trees were all blown down.

Attaran—(Continued.)

Logs.	Stumps.	Attacked with Ficus.	Length.	Width.	Area.	REMARKS.
34*	1	5				of the area covered with Teak, containing forest above the Mittigate Kyouktaga, than 12 square miles, as given in the list of the Zimmay forests of 25th May, 1851. The general character of the Kyouktaga forest is
			4	0015	006	well described in Capt. O'Brien's journal and in Dr. Falconer's report, paras. 54, 55. A few isolated old Teak trees, still alive, of immense size, mostly attacked by huge parasitical ficus, and evidently dying off. No Teak trees of smaller size, and no
0	0	6				trace of seedlings. But numerous dead trees (Nathat) standing or fallen, a few killed and felled. The timber which in some places may be said to strew the ground, is exposed to no danger, except the axe of the wood-cutter, as no jungle fires penetrate the dense evergreen forest. Much of it is still perfectly sound, but in very large pieces, the core of the tree is frequently hollow.

Many of the best logs have, however, been removed by stray-workers from the neighbouring forests, a practice, which without a local forest establishment, it is not possible to prevent. Yet the value of the remainder is very considerable. The number of seasoned timber observed, was :—

Nathat, standing and fallen, ... 211
Logs (more or less trimmed,) ... 76
Girdled Trees, ... 12
___
299. The value of these at Maulmain may be estimated at Rs. 30 each, or Rs. 8,970, but the Revenue which Govern-

___
* Of these logs, 23 were above 6 cubits.
11 „ under „
___
34

No.	Date.	Name of Officer conducting the Survey.	District.	Name and situation of Forest Tract.	Teak trees in girth above.				Fourth small Trees.	Nathat.	Girdled.
					Cubits.						
					1st Class.	2nd Class.	3rd Class.	II. & I.			
					V.	IV.	III.				
31	Augt. 14.	Mr. J. Barker.	Zimmay.	Mittigate above the Teekine Choung, left bank of Mittigate, below No. 32.	5	0	0	0	0	46*	0
				Total of Mittigate Kyoukta-ga Forests,	43	0	2	0	0	211	12
				Or per square mile,	318	0	14	0	0	1562	88
				Or for the whole tract, estimated at 0.665 sq. mile,	215	0	10	0	0	1055	60

* These Nathat trees are all blown down.

Memo. of measurement of Logs.

1	Length 17'	Lower girth 13'	Upper girth, 13'	(a Log 31'	Long taken away from this)
2	„ 14	„ 9	„ 9	(a Log 48	„	„	„	„)
3	„ 27	„ 9	„ 9	(a Log 30	„	„	„	„)
4	„ 41	„ 15	„ 8.6	
5	„ 51	„ 14	„ 10	

Attaran—Continued.

Logs.	Stumps.	Attacked with Ficus.	Length.	Width.	Area.	REMARKS.
8	0	5	1	0.015	0.015	ment might realise from the same, would probably not exceed Rs. 4 duty at Kadai Rs. 5 purchase money in the forest.
76	21	43	0	0	0.135	Rs. 9 per tree or log or Rs. 2,691 upon the whole. These figures, if the above estimate of the area of the forest is correct, must be multiplied by 5. But as a source for future supplies, the Kyouktaga forest is without value. The whole of the Teak is dying out fast, and as long as the ground is covered with its present dense vegetation, there is no chance of propagation of Teak. It is an interesting instance of a Teak forest, which, at one time may have been vigorously thriving here being affected and at last stopped in its develope-
562	155	318	0	0	0	ment by the rise of a vegetation of different trees on the same spot. When Teak first sprung up here, perhaps one or two centuries ago, the forest must have been altogether of a different character. The cessation of jungle fires for a few years, either caused by rain-fall during the dry season, or by
380	105	215	0	0	0	other causes of a more accidental nature, want of travellers for a season, who ignite the dry masses by the remains of their camp fires—may have permit-ted the accumulation of vegetable mould, and fa-vored the springing up of a new class of trees among the Teak trees. Let these trees of the dense evergreen forest once take possession of the ground, so as to keep off jungle fires, and the progress of their growth is irresistible. Their first effect on the Teak is a beneficial one. Grow-ing up in close vicinity to other trees, the Teak is obliged to clear itself of its side branches, and is gradually drawn up to that stately height, which is the character of the trees of the green forest. But here the beneficial influence ends. The spring-ing up of Teak seedlings in the dense shady forest

No.	Date.	Name of Officer conducting the Survey.	District.	Name and situation of Forest Tract.	Teak trees in girth above.				Fourth small Trees.	Nathat.	Girdled.
					Cubits.						
					1st Class.	2nd Class.	3rd Class.	II. & I.			
					V.	IV.	III.				
35	Augt. 16.	Mr. J. Barker.	Zimmay.	Mo. oulhz Forest, No. 28. Moung Waa's Forest.	7	65	135	80	183	3	4
36	Augt. 17.	Shwoag Tha.	Do.	Eingtha (Moung Indah's Forest) No. 22.	4	36	122	435	200	2	1
37	Augt. 16.	Dr. D. Brandis.	Do.	Danoong Forest, No. 25.	7	38	126	110	143	2	5

Attaran—Continued.

Logs.	Stumps.	Attacked with Ficus.	Length.	With.	Area.	REMARKS.
						is out of the question, and the Teak dies of old age without any chance of propagation.
						The Kyouktaga forest, like a portion of those near the Thingannccnnoung and Mithaban Choungs (Nos. 8 and 21) are in the last stage of their combat, so to say, with the dense evergreen forest.
2	42	3	5	0.03	0.15	*No.* 35 *Locality.*—Between the Zimmay river and the Moon Choung and above the mouth of the latter along the path from Danoongjoia to Karaso on the Winyeo. *Soil*—Light sandy loam. *Other Trees.*—Those of the mixed forest, with Kjoomboe in great abundance. *Genl. Remarks.*—The Teak found here, is generally of good regular growth, tall and straight, other trees are not of large size nor is the forest dense. The ground is covered here and there with grass used for thatching (Thekkay). Forest not worked, lethmat resumed.
8	132	0	3	0023	0069	*No.* 36 *Locality.*—Opposite Kapah village, on the left bank of the Zimmay, about one mile from the river, between small hills. *Genl. Remarks.*—Growth middling, only 15 trees in girth above 3 cubits, had tall stems without side branches low down. Many of the stumps are undersized.
5	48*	1	35	0023	0805	*No.* 37 *Locality.*—The Danoong forests stretch from the banks of the Zimmay to the sources of the Danoong Choung up to the Ein forest, which covers wide tracts between the Goongul and Goongaby Choung. *Soil.*—White sandstone, forming a light sandy soil, here and there ferruginous conglomerate. *Other Trees.*—Those of the mixed forests, with a large proportion of bamboos.

* Of these stumps, most were undersized, the girth of one was 16′.

N°	Date.	Name of Officer conducting the Survey.	District.	Name and situation of Forest Tract.	Teak trees in girth above.				Fourth small Trees.	Nathat.	Girdled.
					Cubits.						
					1st Class. V.	2nd Class. IV.	3rd Class. III.	II. & I.			
38	Augt. 16.	Dr. D. Brandis.	Zimmay.	Goongee below the gorge, No. 26 and 36.	2	24	201	216	105	10	41*
39	Augt. 16.	Do.	Do.	Goongee above the gorge, No. 26.	5	30	33	18	33	6	10
				Total of the Lower Zimmay forests,	25	193	617	859	664	23	61
				Or per square mile,	47	378	1213	1666	1303	45	118
					425						

40 Memo. of Teak trees counted from the boat in going down the Zimmay river from the mouth of the Mittigate to the junction of Winyeo and Zimmay.

August. 17.	Dr. D. Brandis.	Zimmay.		*Eastside.*	*Westside.*
			Mittigate to Goongee,	210	190 trees of different sizes mostly of the second class (3 cub. in girth.)
			Goongee to Mo Oo,	120	140 do. do. do.
			Mo Oo to Nat. Chg.	72	54 do. do. do.
			Near Yakat Choung,	30	6 do. do. do.
			Above Dahi Choung,	34	0 do. do. do.
			Total,	466	390 do. do. do.

* Of these girdled trees only 20 are full sized.

Attaran—(Continued.)

Logs.	Stumps.	Attacked with Ficus.	Length.	Width.	Area.	REMARKS.
						Genl. Remarks.—The trees are of very good growth ; to judge from the size of the stumps, the forest must have yielded much undersized timber. The forest has not been worked lately.
3	44*	1	4	0 03	0.12	*No. 38 Locality.*—The lower Goongee forests occupy the banks of the Goongee river below the gorge, through which it leaves the hills. The Teak localities are interrupted by belts of Ein forest, which occupy the high ground covered with gravel between the Goongee and Goongiby streams The undulating hills, on which Teak occurs, are sometimes higher, sometimes lower, than the Ein forest.
						Soil. *Other Trees.* *Genl. Remarks.* } Same as No. 37, but the forest more clear, less bamboos.
4	32†	3	3	0.03	0.09	*No. 39 Locality.*—The valley of the Goongee opens into a basin of considerable extent above the gorge, surrounded by hills on all sides. The road to the Handrau leads through this basin, and there are several Karen settlements in it, with a large amount of Toungya cultivation. Teak occurs on undulated ground near the different branches of the stream.
22	298	8	0	0	5095	*Soil.*—Light sandy loam. *Other Trees.*—A belt of dense evergreen forest surrounds the localities where Teak is found, associated with bamboo and the trees of the mixed forest.
43	584	15	0	0	0	*Genl. Remarks.*—The forest has suffered some injury from Toungya cultivation, and is at present actively worked. We found a party employed with 4 elephants. They had cut 150 logs within the last 2 months, and were engaged in dragging the timber down the bed of the stream below the gorge, where there is sufficient water to float it. The growth of Teak is good here.

* Of these stumps only 24 are full sized.
† Of these stumps only 20 are full sized.

Abstract.

No.	Names of Forests.	Teak trees. Size in Cubits. 1st Class. V.	1st Class. IV.	2nd Class. III.	3rd Class. II. & I.	4th Class small Trees.	Nathat.	Girdled.	Logs.	Stumps.	Attacked with Ficus.	Area.
1	Lower Winyeo,	117	281	860	1238	873	85	92	32	165		0·753
2	Upper Winyeo,	163	191	322	365	264	24	64	69	369	21	0·57
3	Megway Tseikgyee Kyoukpyo,	147	96	364	396	853	50	188	174	598	131	0·378
4	Kyoon Choung Forests,	226	98	260	437	280	46	166	125	698	8	0·316
5	Upper Zimmay,	19	69	170	220	66	20	16	8	118	8	0·226
6	Mittigate Forests below Kyouktaga,	104	27	47	43	141	24	134	116	510	100	0·465
7	Lower Zimmay,	25	193	617	859	664	23	61	22	298	8	0·5095
	Total,	801	955	2640	3558	3141	272	721	546	2756	268	3·2175
	Average per square mile,	248 {1756	296}	851	1105	976	84	224	169	857	83	
	Mittigate Codogway,	49 {544	144}	368	253	46	95	941	180	29	50	0·125
	Mittigate Kyouktaga,	42		2			21	112	76	21	43	0·135
	Grand Total,	893	1099	3010	3811	3187	388	1744	802	2806	361	3·5475

Note.—The groups of the Mittigate Codogway and Kyouktaga being of an exceptional character, their survey has not been included in the statements exhibiting the general results of Forest surveys.

APPENDIX, No. 3.

———

EXTRACT FROM FOREST DAY BOOKS.

Southern Forests.
Tharawaddee Forests.
Eastern Sittang Forests.
Beeling ditto.
Yoonzaleen ditto.
Salween ditto.
Doomdamee ditto.
Thoungyeen ditto.
1857 to 1859.

I.—Southern Forests.

No. of Forest Day Book.	Month and Date.	Name of Officer conducting the Survey.	District.	Name of situation of Forest Tract.	1st Class. Ft. In. 6 0	2nd Class. Ft. In. 4 6	3rd Class. Ft. In. 1 6	4th Class. Small Trees.	Stumps.	Attacked with Ficus.	Area.	Class of Forests.	REMARKS.
1	1858, Feb. to May.	Dr. Brandis.	Thoungzin.	Kroukdala, ...	80	55	23	21		8	0.36	B. 2	Third group on arid hills, worked but little.
2	,,	,,	,,	Nyaeekyo, ...	178	90	90	265			0.184	B. 9	Fourth group on good soil.
3	,,	,,	,,	Kodogway, ...	275	127	260	240			0.30	A. 5	Third group on arid hills, worked but little.
4	,,	,,	,,	Thabalew, ...	56	67	85	75			0.15	B. 3	Fourth group much worked.
5	,,	,,	,,	Natoo Choung, ...	51	26	126	270			0.138	B. 3	Ditto ditto.
6	,,	,,	,,	Kyekgalaytoung, ...	151	63	182	15			0.230	A. 6	Ditto worked but little.
8	,,	,,	,,	Thabyew Choung, ...	390	520	410	530			0.181	C. 21	Third group on arid hills, worked moderately.
9	,,	,,	,,	Tenay Choung, ...	297	394	311	250			0.15	C. 19	Ditto ditto ditto.
11	,,	,,	,,	Kodogway Junugoung, ...	234	258	260	240			0.138	C. 16	Ditto ditto on a South branch of No. 3 but worked more. [rd more.
12	,,	,,	Pounglin.	Natoo Choung, ...	37	40	126	270			0.115	C. 3	Ditto ditto near No. 5.
13	,,	,,	Magayee.	Wazway Kadin, ...	10	25	25	80			0.30	C. 0	Ditto ditto much worked.
14	,,	,,	,,	Doodoung, ...	33	46	150	330			0.230	C. 1	Second group on undulated ground with some of Third class.
15	,,	,,	,,	Kayoo Choung (upper), ...	39	86	117	140			0.092	C. 4	Third group and fourth class. [First class.
16	,,	,,	,,	Legla Choung (lower), ...	61	74	88	52			0.138	C. 4	First group and second class.
17	,,	,,	,,	Kayoo Choung, ...	70	120	92	90			0.184	C. 3	Third group on arid hills.
18	,,	,,	Oakkan.	Dhasjeing, ...	40	50	120	150			0.138	C. 2	Ditto ditto.
19	,,	,,	Pegu.	Lepang Choung, ...	20	30	0	80			0.24	C. 0	A few straggling trees scattered over a wide extent of mixed Forest.
20	,,	,,	,,	South of Taidoo Choung, ...	22	30	150	270			0.138	C. 1	Ditto ditto.
21	,,	,,	,,	North ditto, ...	146	186	230	75			0.184	C. 7	Third group on arid hills.
22	,,	,,	,,	Kyouktaga, ...	59	123	160	300			0.18	C. 3	Ditto ditto.
23	,,	,,	,,	Kwago Choung, ...	208	356	440	46			0.276	C. 7	Ditto ditto.
7	,,	,,	Thoungzai.	Nana Pouk, ...	162	135	260	600			0.45	B. 3	Ditto ditto.
				Total, ...	2619	2895	3706	4399	0	8	4.499		
				Or per square mile,	584	643	823	977					

Stumps — Not observed.

II.—Tharawaddee Forests.

No.	Date	By whom surveyed	Range	Forest	I	II	III	IV	Per sq. mile	Class	Remarks
31	April, 1858.		Boben.	Yangyoung,	475	37	72	33	0.138	A. 34	Fourth group, Forest never worked.
32	,,		,,	Ditto,	403	40	60	30	0.23	A. 26	Ditto ditto.
33	,,		,,	Ditto,	214	29	48	26	0.23	A. 33	Ditto ditto.
35	,,		Kokee.	Kneebyagyo,	767	30	53	14	0.12	A. 11	Ditto ditto.
36	,,		Kudoke.	.....,	140	35	133	67	0.23	B. 2	Third group worked but little.
37	,,		Toungo.	Kaugintan,	49	25	3	63	0.184	A. 7	Ditto ditto.
38	,,		,,	Singolaytoung,	141	30	85	25	0.90	A. 4	Ditto ditto.
27	,,		,,	Quay Gyoung,	400	129	200	224	0.115	B. 4	Ditto ditto.
28	,,		Fitoo.	Myoung Gyoung,	57	45	57	45	0.24	A. 8	Ditto ditto.
29	,,		,,	Ditto,	199	79	200	0	0.18	B. 2	Ditto ditto.
39	March to April, 1857.		Kudoke.	Zugah Taw,	49	35	32	61	0.90	A. 12	Second group, low undulated hills.
			Utno.	Tain Hmyeouke,	1,141	381	882	1,519	0.90		
34	April, 1858.		Toungo.	Myoyah,	84	63	92	116	0.115	B. 7	Fourth group.
40	January to March, 1857.	Dr. Brandis and Lieut. Maude.	Minboo.	Phayagnee,	1,218	489	1,455	3,018	0.75	A. 16	Fourth group and first class.
41	,,		Minlah.	Tsan Cooktan,	383	228	414	786	0.60	B. 6	Ditto ditto.
42	Mar., 1858.	Dr. Brandis.	Minboo.	Ginardyuktan,	686	167	586	1,780	0.460	A. 14	Fourth group, little worked.
21	,,		Koombeling.	Kyekgdaytoung,	56	70	124	40	0.24	B. 2	Fourth group, ditto ditto (near No. 6.)
26	,,		Minlah.	Shawbreur,	131	115	220	57	0.138	B. 9	Ditto ditto.
43	January to March, 1857.	Lt. Mando & Dr. Brandis.	Beeling.	Shadow Taw,	514	426	1,129	4,687	1.150	B. 4	First group on even ground.
44	,,		,,	Ditto,	604	436	1,022	4,687	1.380	B. 4	Ditto ditto.
45*	..		,,	Ditto,	197	178	232	2,464	0.460	B. 4	Ditto ditto.
46	,,		Mekkha.	Tabine Dut, South East,	252	580	866	1,755	0.460	C. 5	First group and fourth group.
47	,,		Minhla.	Ditto ditto,	167	151	408	390	0.60	B. 2	Fourth group.
48	,,		,,	Ditto ditto,	150	117	267	352	0.60	B. 2	Ditto ditto.
49	,,		Htoo.	Tain Hmyouke,	2,836	2,976	8,753	8,110	0.480	C. 59	On even ground (first group) with undulating hills between (second group).
50	,,		,,	Ditto,	519	1,835	3,625	158	0.60	C. 9	The largest trees are found on the hills.
51	,,		,,	Eingheen Goung,	183	404	509	457	0.60	C. 3	Fourth group.
52	,,		Minboo.	Phayagyee,	417	302	807	1,278	0.460	B. 9	Ditto.
				Total, ...	12,461	9,432	22,334	32,242	12.56		
				Or per square mile,	992	751	1,778	2,567			

* Note.—The surveys No. 39-52 are the results of several surveys.

III.—*Middle Sittang Forests Moung and Padah.*

No. of Forest Day Book.	Month and Date.	Name of Officer conducting the Survey.	District.	Name of Situation of Forest Tract.	1st Class. Ft. In. 6 0	2nd Class. Ft. In. 4 6	3rd Class. Ft. In. 1 6	4th Class. Small trees.	Stumps.	Attacked with Ficus.	Area.	Class of Trees.	REMARKS.
1	January 6,	Dr. Brandis.	Padah.	Kyattluin,	84	21	44	204	43	1	0.092	A⁹	Fourth group.
2	,, 7,	,,	Moung.	Tikola,	115	55	29	364	185	4	0.06	A¹⁹	First group and some second (reserved forest).
3	,, 8,	,,	,,	Yaiboo West,	65	21	21	30	9	15	0.06	B³	Second group undulated hills.
4	,, 8,	,,	,,	Ditto East,	22	13	40	30	2	7	0.06	B³	Ditto ditto.
5	,, 9,	,,	,,	Llaelomyoung,	28	17	8	0	0	4	0.046	B⁶	Fourth group.
6	,, 10,	,,	,,	Pocheekotoung,	294	62	63	6	80	8	0.0805	A³⁶	Fourth group dense Bamboo forest, no seedlings.
7	,, 15,	,,	,,	Kyouktaniewond,	141	105	35	25	69	6	0.092	B¹⁵	Fourth group.
8	,, 16,	,,	,,	Ditto,	33	4	8	12	6	6	0.023	A¹⁴	Ditto.
1 Cl.	,, 5,	Mr. Clemen.	Padah.	Near Bopay,	230	173	160	197	58	48	0.012	B¹⁹	Mostly first and second group.
2 Cl.	,, 11,	,,	,,	Ditto,	111	94	49	67	48	63	0.06	B¹⁸	Ditto ditto.
3 Cl.	,, 12,	,,	,,	Right bank,	167	105	183	233	7	93	0.09	B¹⁸	Ditto ditto.
4 Cl.	,, 18,	,,	,,	May Poo Chg.,	729	390	481	402	111	85	0.09	B⁸¹	Ditto ditto.
5 Cl.	,, 24,	,,	,,	Right bank of Pada Choung,	192	141	200	287	45	54	0.115	B¹⁹	Ditto ditto.
6 Cl.	,, 25,	,,	,,	Ditto,	192	141	200	287	45	51	0.18	B¹⁰	Ditto ditto.
7 Cl.	,, 26,	,,	,,	Toung below,	267	230	205	83	28	83	0.09	B²⁹	Ditto ditto.
8 Cl.	,, 27,	,,	,,	Ditto East,	771	493	412	572	75	54	0.134	B⁵⁷	Ditto ditto.
				Total, ...	3,441	2,065	2,136	2,287	811	581	1.3925		
				Or per square mile,	2,472	1,483	1,537	1,613					

IV.—Middle Sittang Forests, Youktawah and Thoukyaghat.

No.	Date (1859)	Surveyor	Location	Forest								Code	Remarks
	9 January 22,	Dr. Brandis.	Youktawah.	Between the Kaugni choung and Youktawah, ...	124	64	87	212	149	2	0.45	B²	First and Third group. Forest much changed, by extensive Toungya clearing.
10	„ 24,	„	„	Bimbay Forest, ...	129	56	90	163	47	3	0.06	A²¹	First group on level ground between the Kin Forest and the Youktawah Choung.
11	„ 31,	„	Thoukyaghat.	Maybalan Forest, ...	78	42	50	70	20	11	0.069	B¹³	Fourth group, much of the Teak occurring on the Kin Forest.
11a	„ „	„	„	N.E. side of road to choung Magnay,...	221	40	98	136	11	19	0.069	A³⁵	Fourth group, very shady, excellent large trees but few Seedlings.
12	February 1,	„	„	Kyoukoo Forest,......	265	34	197	163	35	22	0.138	A¹⁹	Fourth group, a most valuable tract (Reserved Forest).
13	„ 5,	Mr. Clemen.	„	Choung Magnay, ... East of Maybalceen choung, ...	96	37	102	137	23	10	0.0598	A¹⁴	Mostly First group, some of it Fourth (on the hill).
9	„ 9,	„	„	Ditto West, ...	163	47	83	216	19	9	0.069	A²³	Mostly Fourth group, some First and Third.
10	„ 6,	„	„	Eastern ditto,.........	197	117	123	285	8	16	0.076	B²⁵	Ditto ditto ditto.
11	„ 28,	„	„	Northern ditto,.........	254	140	120	431	12	52	0.069	B²⁶	Ditto ditto ditto.
12	March 1,	„	„	North and East of Magnay choung,...	387	100	568	597	0	120	0.138	A²⁸	Ditto ditto ditto.
13	„ 2,	„	„	East and West of Thaeba choung...	397	227	670	422	46	38	0.092	B⁴³	Ditto ditto ditto.
14	„ 8,	„	„	Kyay choung,...	700	401	895	657	25	27	0.092	B⁷⁶	Ditto ditto ditto.
71	May 21,	Dr. Brandis.	„	Ditto,.........	11	11	8	8	6	5	0.15	B⁰	Fourth group forest, completely changed by Toungya clearings, wherever the slope admits of cultivation; in its original state only, where the slope exceeds 35°. Teak is found here as high as 2700' elevation.
72	„ „	„	„	Natulee,.........	20	18	21	35	9	4	0.15	C⁰	
73	„ 23,	„	„	Paylows to Bauco village,.........	23	25	39	158	6	2	0.30		
74	„ 24,	„	„	....	98	75	92	46	26	10	0.12	B⁸	Fourth group. Teak of excellent growth.
				Total,......	3163	1137	3012	3736	442	350	2.1018		
				Or per square mile,	1504	683	1447	1777	211	166			

(On the Hills East of Toungoo.)

No. 4. Upper Sittang Forests, Kanuee & Koonoung.

No.	Date	Surveyor	Location	Forest								Code	Remarks
15	March,	Mr. Clemen.	Kanuee.	Gueben, ...	223	68	142	165	31	43	0.06	A³⁷	Character of forest stated to be principally that of the Third group.
16	„	„	„	Teikadoung Forest,	178	75	180	235	16	74	0.069	A²⁵	Occasionally Fourth group, patches very rich in Teak, but of limited extent.
17	„	„	„	Meencedoung, ...	165	72	495	411	17	37	0.046	A³⁵	Ditto.
				Carried forward,	566	215	820	811	58	151	0.175		

No.	Month and Date.	Name of Officer conducting the Survey.	District.	Name of situation of Forest Tract.	1st Class. Ft. In. 6 0	2nd Class. Ft. In. 4 6	3rd Class. Ft. In. 1 6	4th Class. Small trees.	Stumps.	Attacked with Ficus.	Area.	Class of Forest.	REMARKS.
				Brought over,	566	215	820	811	58	154	0.175	B^{76}	Character of Forest stated to be principally that of the Third group, occasionally Fourth group. Patches very rich in Teak, but of limited extent.
18	1859. March 16,	Mr. Clemen.	Kannee.	Goweeing, ...	177	150	357	450	12	37	0.023	B^{13}	
18a	,, 17,	,,	,,	Ditto, ...	953	740	1009	3325	24	28	0.069	A^{45}	
19	April	,,	,,	Wedjobo choung, ..	1045	431	1262	10781	117	68	0.230	A^{48}	Ditto.
20	,,	,,	,,	Majan East & North,	265	129	469	510	56	37	0.069	B^{26}	Ditto.
21	,,	,,	,,	Motjeebo, ...	185	98	500	570	39	39	0.069	B^{26}	Ditto.
22	,,	,,	,,	Upper Sebinechoung,	117	78	350	980	30	96	0.046	$^{.25}$	Ditto.
23	,,	,,	,,	Karen Choung, ...	2621	645	3764	3422	432	96	0.368	A^{71}	Ditto.
24	,,	,,	Koonoung.	Thoukyan Forest, ...	458	269	641	861	48	26	0.30	B^{15}	Ditto.
25	,,	,,	,,	Latuya choung, ...	1052	434	1096	1450	20	58	0.21	A^{50}	Ditto.
26	,,	,,	,,	Nioung Kyoung, ..	598	370	681	753	42	0	0.115	B^{52}	Ditto.
27	,,	,,	,,	Sveay deya choung,....	540	138	356	506	82	16	0.023	A^{234}	Ditto.
				Total,......	8577	3747	11355	24419	960	559	1.697		
				Or per square mile,	5054	2208	6691	14448	565	325			

V.—*Beeling Forests.*

No.	Month and Date.	Name of Officer conducting the Survey.	District.	Name of situation of Forest Tract.	1st Class. Ft. In. 6 0	2nd Class. Ft. In. 4 6	3rd Class. Ft. In. 1 6	4th Class. Small trees.	Stumps.	Attacked with Ficus.	Area.	Class of Forest.	REMARKS.
11	Feby. 16,	Mr. Barker.	Beeling.	Mayenieng,.........	2326	534	1000	221	20	539	0.109	A^{213}	Mostly First Class. One of the richest forests in the country.
12	17,	,,	,,	Beeling river, West side,..........	1100	800	2000	800	110	258	0.156	B^{70}	Ditto.
13	March 8,	,,	,,	Myotin, East of do.,	700	500	1400	400	13	123	0.046	B^{152}	Ditto.
14	,,	,,	,,	Kyouktoung, West side ditto,	650	100	150	63	103	14	0.109	A^{59}	Ditto.
15	,, 9,	,,	,,	Maynolan on West side ditto,	450	200	500	505	50	80	0.078	A^{57}	Ditto.
16	Feby. 20,	,,	,,	Somekkee, East side ditto, ...	78	13	97	4	16	10	0.0125	A^{62}	Ditto.
17	,, 21,	,,	,,	Maynaunooai, East,	210	65	160	141	16	95	0.109	A^{19}	Ditto.
				Total,......	5514	2212	5307	2134	384	1119	0.6195		
				Or per square mile,	8902	3571	8568	3445	5391	1806			

VI.—Yoonzaleen Forests.

No.	Date	Surveyor	Region	Locality							Area (sq. mi.)	Code	Remarks
18	Feby 25,	Mr. Barker.	Yoonzaleen.	Kandaray, East side of Yoozaleen, ...	61	42	123	191	14	40	Area not given.	A^{40}	Mostly First group, a valuable forest along the Yoonzaleen below Papoon.
19	" 24,	"	"	Methu, ditto, ...	1000	400	3000	2200	157	131	0.25	A^{40}	
20	" 27,	"	"	Khwaygeo tadal, ...	71	53	200	130	30	30	0.016	B^{15}	A small forest much injured by Toungya clearings, originally Second group.
21	" "	"	"	Winpah Forest, West side Yoonzaleen, ...	84	4	20	12	14	5	Area not given.		
22	March 15,	"	"	Koon choung, do., ...	750	220	420	330	100	60	0.125	A^{60}	Surveys of the Suizonay forest, a most valuable tract on the west side of the Yoonzaleen. The forest is dry and open, belonging almost exclusively to the Third group, it is surrounded by wide tracts of Ein forest and green bamboo jungle (Fourth group). Teak occurs in both on the outskirts of the forest.
23	" 16,	"	"	Surzway choung, do., ...	900	300	420	220	100	50	0.213	A^{37}	
24	" 17,	Dr. Brandis.	"	Khweloe choung, do., ...	300	50	200	100	40	1	0.035	A^{85}	
49	April 29,	Dr. Brandis.	Yoonzaleen.	Suizonay, ...	90	110	0	31	6	18	0.03	C^{30}	
50	" 30,	"	"	Ditto, ...	196	126	80	176	45	11	0.06	B^{32}	
51	May 2,	"	"	Khwaygeo tadal, ...	62	56	65	39	18	8	0.06	B^{10}	See No. 20.
59	" 9,	"	"	Between Papoon and Kandway, ...	55	10	34	16	4	1	0.45	A^{7}	Third group, arid bamboo forest.
60	" "	"	"	Above Kandway rapids, ...	21	33	43	98	10	0	0.12	C^{1}	Ditto ditto.
61	" "	"	"	Tilisolo, ...	28	27	40	20	3	0	0.06	B^{4}	The highest Teak forest in the Yoonzaleen valley, elevation 1000'. Third group.
				Total, ...	3618	1431	4615	3560	631	350	1.479		
				Or per square mile,	2446	967	3140	2107	426	236			

VII.—Upper Salween Forests.

No.	Date	Surveyor	Region	Locality							Area (sq. mi.)	Code	Remarks
62	May 11,	Dr. Brandis.	Upper Salween.	Tsampokolo choung,	55	45	83	72	3	1	0.15	B^{5}	Teak occurs on the steep slopes of the hills, occasionally at the bottom of the valleys, or on top of the spurs and ridges. On the summit Ein forest is prevailing, on the slopes green bamboo forest of the Fourth group, but wherever the slope is easy, its character is totally changed by long continued Toungya clearings. The Teak in the Ein forest is generally very stunted, that on the slopes and at the bottom of the valley of good growth. This is the general
63	" "	Tsauthla.	"	Ditto, ...	119	0	0	0	0	0	0.0	C^{8}	
64	" "	Dr. Brandis.	"	Tsolo, ...	42	47	163	327	48	2	0.05	C^{9}	
65	" 13,	"	"	Kolodo, ...	60	75	203	361	44	1	0.3	C^{1}	
66	" "	"	"	Ditto as far as Pah choung, ...	39	42	102	197	10	2	0.24	C^{1}	
67	" 14,	"	"	Ditto to Bullock road Nga choung, ...	13	46	91	128	9	0	0.18	C^{0}	
68	" "	"	"	Nga choung to Kymapioo, ...	31	49	113	146	16	0	0.36	C^{0}	
				Carried forward,	359	304	755	1231	130	6	1.28		

No.	Month and Date.	Name of Officer conducting the Survey.	District.	Name of Situation of Forest Tracts.	1st Class. Ft. In. 6 0	2nd Class. Ft. In. 4 6	3rd Class. Ft. In. 1 6	4th Class. Small trees.	Stumps.	Attacked with Ficus.	Area.	Class of Forest.	REMARKS.
69	1859. May 15,	Dr. Brandis.	Upper Salween.	Brought over,	359	304	755	1234	130		61.28		character of the upper Salween Forests. The timber would be valuable, if the greater number of trees had not become deformed by the destructive practices of Toungya cultivators. Most of the trees remaining are forked or crooked.
70	", 15	"	"	Kymapioo, ...	81	66	182	330	38	9	0.36	B[2]	
3	Feby. 22,	"	"	Ditto, ...	53	56	141	136	35	3	0.12	C[4]	
4	", 24,	"	"	Above Kolodo, ...	46	54	66	61	0	0	0.18	C[2]	
5	", 25,	"	"	Below ditto, ...	48	71	184	106	11	0	0.24	O[2]	
6	March 2,	"	"	Near the Salween, ...	3	0	135	110	0	0	0.15	1[0]	
				Mintabu chg. both sides, ...	114	45	195	240	26	3	0.18	1[6]	Some good trees on slopes covered with green bamboo (Fourth group).
7	", 5,	Tsauthla.	"	North of Natchoung,	46	25	34	41	0	5	0.03	B[15]	The most valuable forest examined on the Salween, the hills are low, and the growth of the trees excellent, much of the forest is dry bamboo jungle (Third group).
8	", 7,	"	"	Dalgunzeik Natchoung, ...									
9	", 9,	Dr. Brandis.	"	Natchoung Forest, ...	106	54	142	234	24	2	0.24	B[4]	
10	", 10,	Tsauthla.	"	Dalgunzeik, ...	242	142	268	50	73	2	0.42	B[5]	
11	"	"	"	North of Ouma chg,	117	66	121	201	54	2	0.24	B[4]	
12	", 12,	Dr. Brandis.	"	Below Kyoukenin,	37	40	62	30	6	0	0.24	C[1]	On steep slopes.
52	May 4,	Moung Shway Moung.	"	Kaber, ...	20	4	1	4	7	2	0.03	A[6]	Ditto ditto.
				Below Maykouta, ...	892	664	679	650	246	35	0.45	B[10]	Maytharouk forest good, wherever the slopes [exceed 30°.
53	", 5,	Dr. Brandis.	"	Above ditto, ...	111	23	183	275	66	7	0.12	A[9]	Ditto ditto.
54	"	"	"	Tinoqui choung to Mingah choung, ..	45	13	48	22	15	0	0.03	A[15]	Ditto ditto.
55	", 6,	"	"	Above Mingah chg.,	93	50	12	26	6	5	0.069	B[13]	Ditto ditto.
56	"	"	"	Pahipeo with sides of,	0	0	0	0	0	0	...		
57	"	"	"	Maitharouk from	26	26	20	15	5	0	0.023	B[11]	A small forest on level ground, near the Maytharouk (Third group).
58	"	"	"	Outan choung, ...	40	9	20	25	0	0	0.092	A[4]	Fourth group.
				Total, ...	2472	1717	3248	3793	742	81	4.494		
				Or per square mile,	550	860	723	844	160	18			

VIII.—Lower Salween and Lower Doomdamee Forests.

No.	Date	Surveyor	Locality									Class
44	April 14,	Dr. Brandis.	Lower Salween.	Hline boay,	14	44	12	0	28	2	0.06	C[2]
46	" 15,	Moung Shway Moung,	"	Dondan,	160	180	460	280	200	0	0.48	C[3]
47	" , 16,	Dr. Brandis.	"	Ditto,	80	160	0	10	220	0	0.16	B[5]
48	" ,	Moung Shway Moung.	"	Ditto,	76	20	60	20	0	0	0.16	A[4]
1	January 5,	Mr. Barker.	"	Thagert,	110	300	600	800	0	45	0.25	C[4]
3	" 20,	Ditto.	"	Bailoin,	94	263	470	400	170	34	.9375	C[1]
4	" 21,	Ditto.	"	Ditto,	151	113	320	550	131	37	0.8125	B[1]
				Total,	**685**	**1080**	**1922**	**2060**	**749**	**118**	**2.86**	
				Or per square mile,	289	377	672	720	261	41		

The lower Salween and Hline boay forests, are dry, open forests enclosed generally by Ein forests. Group of trees very inferior. Stems short and branching close to the ground. They mostly belong to Third group.

IX.—Upper Doomdamee Forests.

No.	Date	Surveyor	District	Locality								Class
2	January 9,	Mr. Barker.	Doomdamee.	Hlinegë-ay,	0	0	17	18	0	0	0.0625	C[1]
5	" 23,		Kroung Seay.	Kroung Seay,	149	150	200	71	36	0.7812		C[1]
6	" 24,		"	Ditto,	94	253	518	101	45	0.5625		A[25]
7	" 27,		"	Ounkajee,	600	250	315	55	82	0.156		A[25]
7	" 28,		"	Ditto,	877	310	597	354	140	302	0.25	A[64]
7	" 29,		"	Ditto,	400	150	300	354	41	44	0.062	A[9]
7	Feby. 2,		"	Ditto,	90	26	180	40	15	28	0.093	A[8]
8	" 2,		"	Beelakajee,	608	128	541	186	47	59	0.156	B[16]
8	" 8,		"	Ditto,	407	233	740	630	136	130	0.25	A[22]
9	January 30,		"	Noung Phomolo,	800	200	432	658	108	30	0.125	A[66]
9	" 31,		"	Doomdamee,	700	308	986	371	46	36		
10	" 31,		"	Thamelan,	7	6	97	7	0	15	"	"
				Total,	**4732**	**2014**	**4361**	**3650**	**778**	**807**	**2.7482**	
				Or per square mile,	1727	732	1587	1824	283	393		

Mostly belonging to the Third Class. Ditto. Ditto. Ditto. Ditto. Ditto. Ditto. Ditto. Ditto. Ditto. Ditto. Ditto.

X.—*Middle Thoungyeen Forests.*

No.	Month and Date.	Name of Officer conducting the Survey.	District.	Name of situation of Forest Tract.	1st Class. Ft. In. 6 0	2nd Class. Ft. In. 4 6	3rd Class. Ft. In. 1 6	4th Class. Small Trees.	Stumps.	Attacked with Ficus.	Area.	Class of Forests.	REMARKS.
20	1859. March 24,	Dr. Brandis.	Thoungyeen.	Raigelee choung, ..	213	80	100	141	10	12	0.18	A^{11}	Fourth group some Teak on the Ein forest.
21	" 25,	Tsauthla.	"	Lepoklo choung, ..	337	97	156	79	30	35	0.18	A^{18}	Ditto.
22	" 25,	Dr. Brandis.	"	Road from Lepoklo choung to Tseepay village, .	61	28	13	9	25	6	0.09	A^{7}	Ditto.
23	"	"	"	Hills near Bothulo choung, ...	47	9	1	0	0	0	0.09	A^{5}	Ditto and Third group.
24	" 26,	"	"	On the road to Meerawaddee, ...	363	164	86	153	38	36	0.40	A^{9}	Third group.
25	"	"	"	Between Meerawaddee and Kyoukett,	3	0	0	820	3	2	0.20	A^{0}	Open dry forest.
26	" 30,	"	"	Ditto, ...	45	22	73	160	6	8	0.60	A^{0}	Third group, patches of bamboo jungle with Teak between tracts of Ein forest.
27	" 31,	Mr. Barker.	"	Ditto, ...	34	13	45	70	24	6	0.08	A^{4}	Ditto.
28	"	Dr. Brandis.	"	Podokooill to Lupo choung, ...	182	37	69	273	25	17	0.33	A^{5}	Third group ditto.
30	April 2,	"	"	Along the Thoungyeen below mouth of Meplar, ...	357	76	801	1470	214	12	0.06	A^{69}	Third group, a portion in the Evergreen forest.

29	,,	,,	1	,,	,,	Luko Choung to Pohobas vill., ...	109	21	64	209	53	11	0.18	A⁶	Fourth group green bamboo jungle.
33	,,	,,	2	,,	,,	Between Pohobas vill. and bank of Thoungyeen, ...	43	10	0	10	10	0	0.09	A⁴	Third group, the Teak localities intervening between tracts of Ein forest.
34	,,	,,	5	,,	,,	Between Meeplay & Theetsantay, ...	16	3	4	3	0	2	0.18	A²³	Ditto.
35			6	,,	,,	Between Theetsantay and Thekara Choungs	186	83	161	950	44	81	0.36	A⁵	Ditto.
36			6	,,	,,	Along Thekara Choung, ...	23	4	21	120	3	4	0.12	A¹	Ditto.
37			7	,,	,,	Between Thekara and Manpashee Choung, ...	75	16	63	15	15	10	0.18	A⁴	Ditto.
						Kamokis, ...	98	62	96	200	40	10	0.30	B³	Ditto.
38			7	,,	,,	Between Sa On Choung and Kamokia, ...	67	30	20	4	17	7	0.12	A⁵	Ditto.
39			9	,,	,,										
						Total, ...	2262	755	1773	4821	557	209	3.74		
						Or per square mile,	605	201	474	1289	148	55			

XI.—Lower Thoungyeen Forests.

No.	Month and Date.	Name of Officer conducting the Survey.	District.	Name of situation of Forest Tract.	Teak trees in girth above				Stumps.	Attacked with Ficus.	Area.	Class of Forests.	REMARKS.
					1st Class. Ft. In. 6 0	2nd Class. Ft. In. 4 6	3rd Class. Ft. In. 1 6	4th Class. Small trees.					
13	March 14,	Dr. Brandis.	Lower Thoungyeen.	Kengay village, ...	38	12	16	0	0	0	0.03	A(1)	Fourth group an isolated patch of Teak on the slope of a hill.
14	" 15,	"	"	Shan side above Kengay village, ...	109	18	35	59	16	8	9.12	A⁹	Fourth group an excellent forest but much worked out.
17	" 21,	"	"	Meikey Choung, ...	27	27	39	49	19	0	0.24	B¹	Fourth group much injured by Toungya cultivation.
18	" "	Shoay Moung Tsauthla.	"	Taekay Choung, ...	42	39	37	88	60	5	0.16	B²	Third group in open dry forest.
19	" "		"	Ditto, ...	31	14	12	12	7	2	0.12	A²	Ditto ditto.
40	April 9,	Dr. Brandis.	"	Thoungyeen river between Kamokla & Mieraway Choung.	37	35	22	0	67	5	0.12	B³	Fourth group; the third group.
41	" 10,	"	"	Mieraway Choung,..	18	13	2	6	37	3	0.04	B⁴	Toungya clearings extensive, and have been very injurious to the Teak in the forest.
42	" "	"	"	South of Tigahore Choung, ...	57	18	2	1	11	17	0.12	A⁴	Ditto ditto.
43	" "	"	"	North ditto, ...	24	22	14	5	84	7	0.06	B⁴	Ditto ditto.
				Total, ...	378	198	179	170	251	47	1.01		
				Or per square mile,	874	196	177	168	248	46			

APPENDIX, No 4.

EXTRACTS FROM CAPTAIN O'BRIEN'S JOURNAL OF A TOUR OF
EXPLORATION INTO THE ATTARAN FORESTS IN 1841.

No. 1.

THINGANNEENNOUNG FOREST.

January 13*th.*—Beyond this boundary, and on the bank of the latter
stream, are found many of the finest possible trees.

Mr. Bently gave a native " Kuo-moo" (the same before mentioned, and who
now accompanied me as a guide), an advance of one hundred Rupees to cut
trees for him, he found this forest about a year ago, and has killed about 500
of the most splendid trees on this spot, and on a rising ground within the bifurcation of the rivers. I measured two of 16 feet in circumference, they were
estimated by " Moungleng" at 60 feet in the clear perpendicular trunk,
there were about twenty such cut ; but several from their extreme size, had
not yet died. These trees if sent entire to Moulmain would value at least
one hundred Rupees each ; they appear to have been killed without any
authority whatever, and, if allowed to be felled, will be destroyed by cutting
into pieces to enable them to be moved to the river, though growing close to
the banks. " Kuo-moo" stated that he had searched for trees higher up the
stream, but that none were found. I think this very doubtful ; but had not
time to prosecute the search myself.

No. 2.

MEGWA FOREST.

January 14*th.*—About two miles from the Winyeo over the undulating
slopes of high hills approaching on both sides, came to a Teak forest and
struck the southern stream of the Megwa. This forest I am told is also the
property of Mr. Wales ; but that it has for two or three years, not been
worked, in consequence of the difficulty of getting the trees down this branch
of the stream. The hills I have passed over, would seem to form the natural
boundary between the forests on the Winyeo, and those on the Megwa. I
traced the stream up till too shallow to admit of trees being floated down by
it even at the height of the monsoon. There are many fine trees on both
banks particularly on the southern, but throughout its course, till meeting the
northern branch, its bed is narrow and much obstructed by rocks, and im-
pediments caused by trees getting across it, a sufficient number of persons
not having been employed to direct them or assist them in their progress.

27

Twelve hundred trees, are said to have been killed on the northern banks by order of Mr. Wales (from my own observation I should say about half that number) 300 converted into bend planks on the spot, and about 200 crooks are said to have been realized previously to the forest having been given up, owing, as above stated, to the loss of timber in its transits, much having been burnt on the bank to clear the stream, and much still forming obstructions.

Were some expense incurred to clear the stream, and an efficient number of elephants and people employed, there is no doubt this forest might be worked with great advantage, producing many hundreds of valuable trees.

No. 3.

Green trees felled in Mr. Darwood's Forest.

February 3rd.—Prosecuted my journey by the right bank of the stream, through high wooded hills, and reached a forest, the property of Messrs. Darwood and Co. at present working under the superintendence of Mr. Napiere (I believe) one of the partners. Much fine timber is standing on this forest, but the principal part of the straight timber has been felled; that which remains being chiefly valuable for crooks of the largest size and for ship-building planks. Fifteen saws are at present at work, with five elephants. There is little or no timber standing which has been regularly killed; but I saw three trees of the finest description in the act of being felled without an attempt or pretence of killing them. I was at the time accompanied by Mr. Napiere and pointed out the circumstance; but the depredation was allowed to proceed. Several, indeed *apparently* all the trees on the saw-pits being converted into planks, were perfectly green, upwards of 200 planks (3 × 12 and 6 × 12 inches) were lying on the bank of the river exposed to the sun to dry. I observed that each of those drawn through the water in my presence instantly sunk. I desired Moung-leng and the headman of the forests (who had just arrived from Moulmain) to examine the timber particularly, and both these persons reported to me that the whole of it then converted, and that being converted was cut (felled) perfectly green.

No. 4.

Kyoon Choung Forest.

February 6th.—Examined the forest as to its extent in land, which I found to be about a mile and a half; and having heard of timber on the high ground under the hills, I passed quite through the range but found no appearance of such.

The timber on this estate is of the finest description, and there is a very unusual abundance of young trees which promise to be of a much straighter and better growth than the old ones now standing. Many trees have been felled and removed without apparent diminution of the value of the forest. It is quite impossible, without great expenditure of time, to make a probable estimate of the number of trees standing; but having passed carefully through this forest in various directions, I would hazard an opinion that there are *from ten to twelve thousand trees* fit to cut (probably much more), but I observed no seedlings or young plants.

No. 5.

GREEN TIMBER FELLED IN MR. PASCAL'S FOREST (KYOUKPJA.)

February 7th.—Crossed the Koongown to what is called the "Mew-hown," forest, having been informed that green timber was being cut and converted by people sent by a Mr. Pascal to this locality.

At one mile distance in a N. N. W. direction, came to a dry ditch, which I was informed was that of the fort or town of "old Mew-hown." I here found several instances of trees just felled without an attempt at being killed, others which had been girdled, but so far from dry as in some cases to have, leaves still upon them, and in every case the bark still containing sap. These latter Mr. Edmunds told me, he is prepared to swear were girdled for the estate of Cockerell & Co. under his superintendence in February last year. There were two saw-pits in active operation, converting this green timber into planks. Mr. Pascal's party of thirty men with fifteen saws employed since the 22nd ultimo.

No. 6.

TREES CUT GREEN AT TALOOPTSIC BETWEEN MEGWA AND MITTIGATE CHG.

February 9th.—Three and a half miles from the Megwa is a nullah within one mile below which found trees being cut, perfectly green, without an attempt at being killed. I saw not less than 20 trees of the finest description (8 to 10 feet in girth and upwards) on the ground and in the act of being felled, and others on the saw-pits, being converted in this state. A person who gave his name as Henry Smith stated, that he was expressly ordered by a Captain Clarke to fell these trees, that he had had sixty (60) men at work for five days. I ascertained there were thirty saws with them, and they had four elephants employed in drawing the timber to the saw-pits.

No. 7.

DESCRIPTION OF UNEXPLORED FOREST MITTIGATE CODOGWAY.

February 15th.—Moved 7½ miles up the Mittigate Codogway. About a mile and a half up the river on the right bank, came to a Teak forest in which about one hundred trees were killed five years ago by Kuo-moo (my guide), who states that he first found this forest, having been sent to look for timber by a person who was drowned in the river a fortnight afterwards (I believe a Captain Barber), and that its existence is not known to any other person but himself. Certainly none have ever been cut, they are all of large size and tall growth. It is very remarkable that there are on this spot a great number of dead Teak trees for which it is not easy to assign a reason, they bear no marks of fire, nor are they shattered as if by lightning, they have never been girdled, and from their size (about 8 and 9 feet circumference) and apparently soundness, it is not likely they have died from age.

The natives tell you that they have been killed by a Nât. They are found on rising knolls, the bed of a small stream winding around them. An old Shan who was with me and is an experienced forest head-man pointed out the roots of the dead trees being exposed along the surface of the ground, and said the soil had been washed away from them, and as the roots of Teak are invariably near the surface, this had been the cause of their death. They have apparently been dead many years.

February 16th.—Sent away two parties in the morning to look for forests. The one party returning with intelligence that they had found an unexplored forest to the eastward, and the other party having returned unsuccessful, I started to examine the former and sent the forest head-man (Moung Careen-bee) to search for Messrs. Cockerell and Co.'s forest, which I supposed to be to the Northward.

About two miles eastward came to some fine young Teak trees which continued uninterrupted for two miles further, in which space are, I should think, several thousand : there are very few large trees amongst them, being from 3 to 6 feet in circumference, the people with me judged them at not more than 10 or 12 years old. They are for the most part perfectly straight, with already from 25 to 40 feet of stem. There is no appearance of this forest ever having been visited, with the exception of perhaps a dozen large trees having been killed many years ago in " the old Burmah time," but none have been felled. If it is preserved for a few years and then judiciously thinned, it will certainly be of great value. Though on the immediate neighbourhood of the Mittigate Codogway, the stream is here too serpentine to admit of trees being sent down its course, but with a considerable command of elephants, the timber may, without much difficulty, be drawn to the northward and put into the broader part of the stream.

Passing along the foot of the hills for somewhat more than a mile, we find a branch stream of the Codogway on which is a most valuable forest, as it contains not only an abundance of young trees, but many of large size, several of which I measured of from nine to twelve feet girth of tall and straight growth and apparently sound, as they have not the swelling at the base which is almost invariably the sign of an old and hollow tree. The old Shan pronounced them to be all young trees which, if permitted, would grow to the largest size. No tree has ever been felled in this forest but my guide Kuo-moo killed 80 of the finest, five years ago, for the person before mentioned (Captain Barber). There at least a thousand trees on this locality, and Kuo-moo estimates 300 of the largest size. Here also occur several dead trees, for which the same explanation was given as yesterday.

This forest extends along the northern bank of the stream to its junction with the Codogway, and in this lower part Kuo-moo has killed other twenty-five trees.

No. 8.

Green trees girdled below the mouth of the Mittigate.

February 17th.—Returned to the mouth of the Mittigate creek, and thence down the left bank of the Zimmay six furlongs to a small forest, the property of a native named To-gown-Oo-geit. There have been large trees on this locality, but they have all been felled, there are, however, a good many fine young trees, but the owner who is here with a party of ten men has lately been cutting these, without a pretence of previously being killed. I saw several instances producing only a log of 18 feet in length with five feet circumference at the thickest part.

February 18th.—Three and half miles further down, made an official report of the above, and the proceedings in the Kyoukpyah forest to the Assistant Commissioner.

February 19th.—Examined a forest the property of Kobân a native. It is perfectly exhausted and very few young trees left. About a mile lower down the river is another forest of Kobân's. On the bank, found a raft of 55 beams, the greater *part green timber, with just enough of seasoned wood to float them.* In this forest almost all the full grown trees have been felled and what remain are of short growth. There are a great number of fine young trees, which if preserved will restore it, but the proprietor who has lately been at work with 16 men, has felled and converted green, a number of these scarcely of the prescribed girth of 4 feet, from which the beams on the bank of the river have been produced.

No. 9.

Mittigate Kyouktaga Forest.

February 25th.—The forest on this side is not extensive, being confined to the space between the small streams, but produces most splendid trees, the ground is also strewed with Teak trees of the largest size that have fallen from age.

Went through another forest two miles lower down within a bend of the river. I have not, during my progress through the forests, seen anything like the quantity of timber on the same space. It is all of the largest size and perfectly straight to an unusual height, the ground is also strewed as above with fallen trees, the *Karens say, to the number of two thousand.* I consider there are several hundred trees on the ground, and those standing are only equalled by the few I have before described on the junction of the Thinganneennoung with the Winyeo, and on the Mittigate below the falls.

No. 10.

GREEN TIMBER FELLED IN THE GUANGEE FOREST.

March 3rd.—Halted and went through the forest. Almost all the full grown trees of straight growth have been felled. There are abundance of young trees to restore this forest, if it is allowed a few years rest, but the wanton depredation of felling green timber, has lately been carried to a considerable extent. We found twenty trees so felled in a walk of one mile along the road.

A true extract.
D. BRANDIS,
Superintendent of Forests, Pegu, Tenasserim and Martaban Provinces.

APPENDIX, No. 5.

No. 14.

To D. G. NICOLSON, ESQUIRE.
Assist. Commissioner, Tenas. and Martaban Provinces.

SIR,

Agreeably to your Court order, No. 2, dated 28th July, 1854, directing me, together with the G. Gyouk of Attaran, to proceed to the forest, and in pursuance of the decree of Commissioner's Court, No. 27, dated 23rd April last, to make delivery of the Teak timber therein referred to on the upper waters of the Megwa. I now beg to report that in the execution of your instructions, I have delivered over to Mr. Dragon, the authorized agent of Mrs. Darwood, the holder of the decree of the Commissioner's Court above noted, 70 logs of Teak timber, under the circumstances fully detailed in my journal of the 11th and 12th instant, copy of which is annexed, and I hope that my proceedings as there shown, will meet with the approval of your Court as well as that of the Commissioner T. and M. P.

2. The Power of Attorney granted by Mrs. Darwood to Mr. Dragon, as her agent and to receive the timber in question, and Mr. Dragon's receipt in duplicate, for the 70 logs delivered to him are appended for record.

I have, &c.

MAULMAIN,
The 14th August, 1854.

(Sd.) W. S. SMITH,
Head Assist. F. D. T. Prov.

———

COPY OF THE JOURNAL KEPT BY THE LATE MR. W. S. SMITH, HEAD ASSTT. F. D. T. PROVINCES.

July 30th, 1854, *Sunday.*—Left Maulmain, but detained exchanging boat at Nyoungbenzeik.

July 31st, Monday.—Pulled up the river all day, but made slow progress.

August 1st, Tuesday.—Continued going forward only reached Needong.

2nd, Wednesday.—Reached Nga Bzeaymah village, and called the Goung Gyouk Mg. Youk.

3rd, Thursday.—Went forward to near the bifurcation of the Attaran.

4th, Friday.—Pulled up the Zimmay to Than Bya village, current very rapid.

5th, Saturday.—Went up to Kzaren, incessant rain hitherto.

6th, Sunday.—Pulled up to Natchoung, Messrs. Rushbrook, Warwick, Wales and Dragon here.

7th, Monday.—Started at 7 A. M. and reached Danoong Choung at 5 P. M., passed some houses which had been destroyed by the flood, which in every place covers the banks. The Karens say the water has not risen so high for 8 preceding years.

8th, Tuesday.—Pulled up to Salahzay choung passing the Wazjee, but the water was not more disturbed or rapid there than at upper part of the Attaran, in fact the large quantity of water at present in the stream has completely covered over the many difficult little passages which delay progress in the dry or N. E. Monsoon.

9th, Wednesday.—Arrived at Kyougzeik at 4 P. M. the current very rapid in confined channels many patches of plantain grounds destroyed by the floods.

10th, Thursday.—Started 7-45′ and reached the Megwa at 10-45′. Here is a Toungya on the right bank in which numbers of fine grown trees have been destroyed, there are about 4 acres in this patch, which will give 6 Rs. per annum for 2 or 3 years, or about 18 Rs. in all as revenue to Government which amount would be obtained for any three of the trees here destroyed. The Toungya will be abandoned in three years' time, but the trees now cut down cannot be replaced under 30 years. There does not appear to be any Teak, but among such a number of trees, there must be some good timber trees, and these forests, are thus ruined by the wandering Karens, whilst the already-cleared plains of the Gyne, the old grain floor of the Taline princes, await hands to cultivate its smooth levels. Mr. Dragon arrived at 0·30′ and Mr. Rushbrook came in at 3·30 P. M.

11th, *Friday*.—Started at 7·30′ A. M. with Messrs. Rushbrook and Dragon, agent for Mrs. Darwood, and Moung Youk G. G. of Attaran, and proceeding along by the Megwa, first passed the Kallnee range of hills, and on reaching the bifurcation of the stream, followed the course of the southern branch, called Meganan, through the Megwa hill by the passage called Joom Joom Jah; here Mr. Rushbrook asserted that we had arrived at the west side of the main range of hills delineated on the map, as separating the Winyeo from the Zimmay, but Mr. Dragon maintained that the hill through which we had just passed was not the main range, but that a range further west was the main range. We accordingly proceeded in a south-westerly direction and arrived at the hills mentioned, and ascended to the summit; here both parties continued their previous assertions, upon which I questioned a Karen who had accompanied the G. G., and who, I consider, could have no bias in favor of either of the contending parties, and this man distinctly stated that, the hills upon whose summits we then were, was the range which divided the two districts, stating that all to the westward was in the Winyeo, and all to the eastward Zimmay. Still Mr. Rushbrook adhered to his former statement, and said that, as I had taken the trouble to ascend that hill for Mr. Dragon's satisfaction, it was but fair play that I should do as much for him by ascending the hill which he maintained to be the main range. This I at once consented; and climbed about two-thirds the side of the hill, which is much more elevated than the range Mr. Dragon and others said was the main range; but when standing on the hill which we had ascended at the request of Mr. Rushbrook, and looking westward, towards the Winyeo, there was unquestionably another range, as stated by Mr. Dragon, and which we had just quitted, intervening between the spot where we stood, and the Winyeo; this Mr. Rushbrook acknowledged, but said that, as the range to the west of us was inferior in height, that it could not be the main range, and was not the dividing range, shown on the map. I again questioned the Karen Nga kaw kai, who is Tsokay of Kyke Maraw village on the Attaran, but who formerly dwelt on the Winyeo, and knows this part of the country, and he said that, the westernmost hills continued on for a great distance to the southward, but that the hill we were then upon, extended but a short distance in that direction. We then descended the hill, I observed that the flow of all the small streams, fall from the rains of this season, was into the Megwa, and thereby into the Zimmay, not in any instance did I observe water flowing towards the Winyeo. I therefore deemed this fact, about which there could be no dispute, a sufficient warrantry for me to deliver the timber lying in that locality to Mrs. Darwood's agent, Mr. Dragon, in this the G. G. Mg. Youk concurred, but Mr. Rushbrook still objected to sanction the delivery of the timber, and desired me to enter his protest against it, which I now record. Mr. Rushbrook then returned to the boat, and we marked with the Government Stamp 20 logs lying near, but as it was now getting late in the day, no more logs were found here, we concluded, and did not reach the boat until 10 o'clock at night.

12th, Saturday.—Marked 50 other logs lying in the Megwa main stream, and upon Mr. Dragon's giving his power of attorney from Mrs. Darwood, dated 29th July, 1854, authorizing him to receive the timber, the subject of Commissioner's decree No. 125-27 dated 10-23nd April and of Assistant Commissioner's Court order No. 2 of 28th July, 1854, made formal delivery of the total 70 logs, taking Mr. Dragon's receipts for the same, and had it certified to, in Burmese by the G. G. Mg. Youk, so that he can bear the witness to the whole transaction. This business being all settled thus far, left this spot on return to town at 10 A. M. and stopped for the night at Moo Choung.

13th, Sunday.—Started at day-break and reached Nat Choung village at 6.30′ Mr. Rushbrook and party here, but left for Maulmain at 7 A. M. Started again at 8 A. M. and rowing all night, on the next day,

14th, Monday.—Arrived at Maulmain at 6 P. M.

(True Copy)

JAMES BARKER,

Head Asst. F. D. T. and M. Prov.

(True Copy)

D. BRANDIS,

Supdt. of Forests P. T. and M. Provinces.

APPENDIX, No. 6.

MEMORANDUM OF GRANT OF A LEASE FOR NINETY-NINE YEARS OF THE FORESTS CALLED THE "MITTIGATE PROPER" AND "MITTIGATE CODOGWAY" ON THE "ZIMMAY" BRANCH OF THE "ATTARAN" RIVER, IN PROVINCE "AMHERST," TENASSERIM PROVINCES.

A Government grant for 99 years will be given to Mr. Donald Campbell Mackey, with the power of transferring the tenure, or any defined or specified portion of it, to be held upon the same terms as are here indicated, but not of sub-letting it, or any part of it, without the sanction of the Commissioner, Tenasserim Provinces, for the forest tracts known by the names of the "Mittigate Proper" (below the rocky pass called Kyouktaga, and lying to the west of the range of hills called the Taungwine,) and of the "Mittigate Codogway" forests, that is, for all the forests yielding Teak, of which the drainage is into the "Mittigate Proper" and "Mittigate Codogway" streams respectively, according to limits to be determined hereafter by survey.

2. No payments will be required on Teak timber brought from the "Mittigate Proper" forest, other than the general rate of duty established by Government. But Teak timber from the "Mittigate Codogway" will pay, in all, in the proportion of 25 to 15 upon such general rate of duty.

The condition of the tenure to be that, at the end of each successive term of 10 years, the Government is to be at liberty absolutely to resume the forests, if Mr. Donald Campbell Mackey cannot show Teak seedlings under 10 years of age growing up within them, to the extent of one-third of the whole number of Teak trees taken from the forests during the previous 10 years.

4. The grant to include all other trees as well as Teak; but the Government to have the power of imposing a duty, should it think fit, not exceeding 10 per cent. of the value of such other trees.

5. No land within the grant to be cleared for cultivation.

6. A moderate portion of wet or paddy land, in reference to the whole area of the said forest tracts, and immediately contiguous to them, will be granted on application, at the discretion of the Principal Assistant Commissioner, on a lease terminable when the forest grant may itself expire or become void, and subject to the payment of the ordinary land-tax of the locality, with a

view of enabling the grantees to settle some resident population near their forests.

MAULMAIN,   (Sd.) J. R. COLVIN,
The 22d January, 1849,   *Commissioner Tm. and M. Ps.*
Registered No. 1.

(A True Copy)
D. BRANDIS,
Supdt. of Forests P. T. and M. Prov.

APPENDIX, No. 7.

EXTRACT FROM THE PARAGRAPH 154 OF THE REPORT ON THE TEAK FORESTS OF PEGU FOR 1856.

In the Prome district on dry hills near the northern Nawing, the burning of the trees and shrubs for Toungya cultivation, does not create a mass of low dense jungle as in the other parts of this country. There, on the contrary, the fertilizing influence of the ashes has another effect, an unusual abundance of young trees are found on deserted Toungyas among which there is generally a due proportion of Teak. Hence a deserted Toungya in those places may with some care be converted into a very valuable nursery for Teak, and an attempt has been made to give practical effect to this idea, by encouraging the cultivators of Toungyas in that district to sow Teak in regular rows with their rice and cotton. The Teak, as it generally germinates after several months, will not impede the growth of their crops and will greatly profit both by the fertilizing effect of the ashes and also by the clear grounds during the first year after the harvest has been removed, which may permit it to make such progress as to enable it to compete successfully with other trees and bushes. This system, if it should succeed, may perhaps even be extended to Toungyas in other districts, where, however, a clearing of the dense jungle on both sides of the rows of young Teak will be necessary.

(A True Extract)
D. BRANDIS,
Supdt. of Forests P. T. and M. Prov.

CPSIA information can be obtained
at www.ICGtesting.com
Printed in the USA
BVOW04s0940120617

486667BV00007B/153/P